PEDALING RESISTANCE

FOOD AND FOODWAYS

SERIES EDITORS:
JENNIFER JENSEN WALLACH
AND MICHAEL WISE

OTHER TITLES IN THIS SERIES

Native Foods: Agriculture, Indigeneity, and Settler Colonialism in American History

Beer Places: The Microgeographies of Craft Beer

Race and Repast: Foodscapes in Twentieth-Century Southern Literature

Food Studies in Latin America Literature: Perspectives on the Gastronarrative

The Provisions of War: Expanding the Boundaries of Food and Conflict, 1840–1990

Rooted Resistance: Agrarian Myth in Modern America

A Rich and Tantalizing Brew: A History of How Coffee Connected the World

To Feast on Us as Their Prey: Cannibalism and the Early Modern Atlantic

Forging Communities: Food and Representation in Medieval and Early Modern Southwestern Europe

Inventing Authenticity: How Cookbook Writers Redefine Southern Identity

Chop Suey and Sushi from Sea to Shining Sea: Chinese and Japanese Restaurants in the United States

Aunt Sammy's Radio Recipes: The Original 1927 Cookbook and Housekeeper's Chat

Mexican-Origin Foods, Foodways, and Social Movements: Decolonial Perspectives

Meanings of Maple: An Ethnography of Sugaring

The Taste of Art: Food, Cooking, and Counterculture in Contemporary Practices

Devouring Cultures: Perspectives on Food, Power, and Identity from the Zombie Apocalypse to Downton Abbey

Latin@s' Presence in the Food Industry: Changing How We Think about Food

Dethroning the Deceitful Pork Chop: Rethinking African American Foodways from Slavery to Obama

American Appetites: A Documentary Reader

Pedaling Resistance

SYMPATHY, SUBVERSION, AND
VEGAN CYCLING

EDITED BY CAROL J. ADAMS
AND MICHAEL D. WISE

FOREWORD BY MARC BEKOFF

The University of Arkansas Press
Fayetteville
2024

ISBN: 978-1-68226-254-2
eISBN: 978-1-61075-824-6

28 27 26 25 24 5 4 3 2 1

Manufactured in the United States of America

Designed by William Clift

♾ The paper used in this publication meets the minimum requirements of the American National Standard for Permanence of Paper for Printed Library Materials Z39.48–1984.

LIBRARY OF CONGRESS CATALOGING-IN-PUBLICATION DATA
Names: Adams, Carol J., editor. | Wise, Michael D., editor.
Title: Pedaling resistance : sympathy, subversion, and vegan cycling / edited by
    Carol J. Adams and Michael D. Wise.
Description: Fayetteville : The University of Arkansas Press, 2024. | Series: Food
    and foodways | Includes bibliographical references and index. | Summary:
    "Pedaling Resistance examines the relationship between veganism and cycling
    through a blend of memoir-style recollections and critical engagements with
    works of cultural and social analysis. Focusing on the intersections among
    cycling, veganism, animal suffering, environmentalism, class, race, and gender,
    this essay collection sheds light on themes of everyday resistance and boundary
    crossing to uncover some of the larger social and political issues at stake in these
    activities"— Provided by publisher.
Identifiers: LCCN 2023055119 (print) | LCCN 2023055120 (ebook) |
    ISBN 9781682262542 (paperback : acid-free paper) | ISBN 9781610758246 (ebook)
Subjects: LCSH: Cycling—Social aspects. | Cyclists—Conduct of life. | Veganism—
    Environmental aspects. | Environmentalism. | Quality of life.
Classification: LCC GV1043.7 .P425 2024 (print) | LCC GV1043.7 (ebook) |
    DDC 388.3/47—dc23/eng/20240309
LC record available at https://lccn.loc.gov/2023055119
LC ebook record available at https://lccn.loc.gov/2023055120

CONTENTS

Foreword: "Vegan Lunch Is on Me" *vii*
Marc Bekoff

Acknowledgments *xiii*

Introduction: Bikolage 3
Carol J. Adams and Michael D. Wise

1. The Politics of Inconvenience: Disruption, Power,
   and Imagination in Cycling and Veganism 17
   Janet O'Shea

2. Stay in Your Lane: The Interconnectedness
   of Being a Vegan Bike Messenger 41
   Lawson "Frogi" Pruett

3. Caring for the Human Horse: Reflections
   on Cycling and the Animal Senses 49
   Michael D. Wise

4. How Cycling Led Me to Veganism, Which
   Changed My Cycling 65
   Amy Rundio

5. Changing Direction 79
   Matthew Calarco

6. Cycling, Noticing, Caring: On Being a
   Vegan Cyclist in Denmark 91
   Sune Borkfelt

7. Three Wheels, Two Arms, and One Planet: Disabled
   Vegan Cycling and Eco-ability Consciousness 99
   Kay Inckle

8. "Christ on a Bike, You're a Dumb Dog"   117
   Naomi Stekelenburg

9. We Live and Ride in Tandem   135
   Geertrui Cazaux

10. Dispelling Myths and Shattering Stereotypes
    as a Vegan Cyclist in Kansas   149
    Sheri E. Barnes

11. Vegan Black Mama Scholar Cyclist   163
    A. Breeze Harper

12. Start Where You Are and Keep Going   171
    Carol J. Adams

    Contributors   195
    Index   199

"Vegan Lunch Is on Me"

MARC BEKOFF

I'm a Boulder, Colorado–based cyclist. Boulder is a popular city for vegans, and it's also a hotspot for cycling for riders from all over the world. On any given day you can see and likely ride with world-champion cyclists and other riders who have come here to enjoy both mountainous and flat rides.

In the mid- and late 1980s I raced a lot. When I competed in the United States and Europe, I'd often have huge bacon cheeseburgers with extra fries after long races and to refuel between stages in multiday races. One night I decided, "I don't need to eat who I'm eating." For a decade or so, my only violation of veganism was a rare slice of cheese. One day, someone nicely asked, "Do you really need that sliver of cheese, three times a month?" And I didn't . . . and I went what I call "cold tofu"—I instantaneously became a vegan from then on.

It never dawned on me that if I were vegetarian or vegan, it would affect my racing. I won some big races after becoming a vegan. And I discovered vegan cyclists in unexpected places and racing at the highest levels.

But the world of cycling/racing can be conservative when it comes to meal plans, both incredulous and suspicious of winners who were vegan. To explain these wins, it was assumed we vegans must really be "sneak carnivores." And so, vegans would often get grief from other cyclists who claimed—without any data—"If you ate meat, you would be much faster and stronger" or "If you ate meat, you'd ride better." They just didn't understand veganism, assuming that we aren't getting protein, because for them protein was synonymous with meat, especially of the red variety.

They couldn't understand we were getting the protein and the calories we need. I would remind them there are a lot of overweight vegans—vegan food is not necessarily low calorie.

Part of their response can be explained by defensiveness, as they held to their beliefs that "if you ate that burger, you'd be faster and stronger." When you think about the term *strong* in biking culture, it means a rider who can keep up with the group, take their pulls, and also take a lot of physical and sometimes verbal abuse. There is some psychological specificity to that term *strong*, in the way it can be both gendered (although then and now there are many women who were and are extremely strong riders who can ditch many men) and insulting (because of the absurd belief that a vegan simply can't be a strong rider).

I know that veganism has made me a better cyclist in terms of stamina and strength. In addition, because of the hours I've spent training, my cycling became good for organizing the rest of the day. I've heard from a lot of riders that cycling is a discipline that begets discipline in many other areas of life. And even today, the more pressed I feel while working, the more likely it is I'll head out to ride, to refresh myself and step away from my brain. My motto for staying physically and mentally healthy is to work hard, play hard, rest hard, and eat well.

Cycling is essentially a lifestyle. I like to be out in nature, which is easy to do around Boulder. I ride alone a lot because I have a flexible schedule and need to be disciplined about exercise, reading, and writing, and I cherish the freedom of being outside—feeling the wind in my face and the sight, sound, and smell of various nonhuman animals and flowers and trees.

The smoothness of cycling generates smoothness—cerebral flow—in my brain. Together, the speed, the wind, the flow, and the smoothness restore and enrich me. Often new ideas pop up and I work on them as I ride; when I get home, I can't wait to scribble often illegible notes. Some seem really good at first and turn out to be good, whereas some aren't all that good when I think about them some more. No big deal—the main point is that cycling gets blood flowing in my body and brain, and ideas flow in and out that otherwise might have been filtered if I'd been sitting at my desk.

Has cycling made me a better vegan? In some ways it has. When I'm riding a lot, I eat healthier. I'm much more attentive to listening to what my body tells me to eat. I haven't laid out meal plans since becoming vegan, and I don't think a lot about calories. Rather, I think about what my body desires. Vegan blue cheese? Miso jalapeño dressing? Bean and rice burritos? All sorts of pasta and sauces? French fries and onion rings cooked in an air fryer? A big bagel with peanut butter? A big bowl of fruit? These are some of my favorites. And for extra calories I go to my favorite potato chips and all sorts of nuts. Cycling and vegan eating feed one another.

Professionally, I've long been interested in the emotional lives of animals—what they're thinking and feeling—and in studying animal behavior in general. I've focused on the social behavior of wild coyotes and wild birds. My book *Minding Animals* is about animal emotions, as is *The Emotional Lives of Animals* and many others I've written over the years. My book with Jane Goodall, *The Ten Trusts*, explains why we need to respect and take care of other animals rather than exploit and harm them.

When I'm cycling, I'm always "minding animals." When biking with others, I always make connections with the animals we see. I will say "a cow *who*," not "*that*," to point out that cows and other nonhumans aren't things, they're sentient animal beings. I'll alert others to look at the horses, the cows, or the birds or fishes. Or I'll ask, "Did you know cows feel emotions?" or "Do you know chickens, turkeys, and other birds are really smart and deeply emotional?" I'll also ask, when we see animals who have been branded, "How would you like it if someone put a hot iron on your arm or if they did it to your dog?" And watching goats play "king of the mountain/hay bale" always gets people's attention and some are incredulous that they engage in that sort of frivolity.

Knowing I'm an ethologist who has written about all sorts of mammals—including companion dogs, coyotes, wolves, and prairie dogs—and various birds, when other riders notice coyotes, eagles, hawks, or other animals, they'll ask me to describe what their behaviors mean. I also use those instances to educate them about veganism in a gentle manner. If we see pigs, I'll talk about how smart and emotional they are. And sometimes I remind them that a bacon, lettuce, and tomato sandwich is really a *Babe*, lettuce, and tomato sandwich, recalling the wonderful movie. On a number of rides my cycling friends and I have rescued animals in need, including a baby bunny who couldn't jump a curb to remain with their mom, and a snapping turtle who was ambling slowly across a road as a large truck barreled down on them. We had to stop traffic in both instances, and not a single person yelled at us—some gave us a thumbs-up.

Here I am with my friend, Winston. We see him on numerous rides, and everyone wants to stop and say hello to him. He also is a wonderful poster pig for veganism. *Photograph courtesy of Marc Bekoff.*

I'm always looking at what animals are doing. Once I saw a prairie dog trying to pull another prairie dog's corpse off the road. Another cyclist asked, "Did you see that prairie dog trying to drag the carcass off the road?" I did indeed, and later wrote an essay for my *Psychology Today* site about how the mother was grieving for the loss of her child who had been hit by a car.

Sometimes when we're riding, we'll see geese flying above us, and someone will put their hand up like they're holding a gun. I'll ask, "Why would you do that? They are sentient beings." And I'll also explain how when geese and other birds fly in a "V" formation, it's like riders riding in a peloton and drafting one another—the geese save energy when they "suck" a wing as we do when we suck someone else's wheel.

I don't miss a chance to talk about the animals we see and explain what they're doing and why. Most people are really interested in this information and ask countless questions I'm more than happy to answer. I'll describe the antipredatory behavior of prairie dogs, who have to avoid both aerial and ground-based predators, and why horses and cows are looking for possible predators when they stand in a particular formation.

As we pass prairie dogs, cows, sheep, goats, pigs, or birds, I'll call out, "Hello, it's Marc here, you don't have to worry." Or if my friends are also present, I'll call out, "It's Marc, Bill, and Christy, you don't have to worry, we aren't going to eat you." I don't miss a beat.

And when we've been out for a long ride, toward the end I'll call out, "Vegan lunch is on me." Or, more specifically, "I'll take you out for lunch, but no Babe, lettuce, and tomato sandwiches." I will always buy lunch if they choose to eat vegan. I know the nonvegans aren't "bad people"—they are wonderful people, and they always take me up on my offer! I do this because they are close friends and it's another thing I can do to educate them about why veganism works, even for these high-end athletes.

All in all, over many years, I have realized that the relationship between veganism and cycling has pretty deep roots. I am thrilled that this collection of essays will go a long way toward showing that "being vegan" is 100 percent compatible with being a "strong" cyclist. And my offer will always stand—"Vegan lunch is on me"—anytime and anyplace.

ACKNOWLEDGMENTS

We wish to thank all the contributors to this volume for being a part of this exciting project as we try to explore multiple kinds of vegan cycling subjectivities.

Having Marc Bekoff's Foreword is extremely meaningful for us; not only because of his entire oeuvre of writing on the subject of animals, but also because of the way he models vegan cycling.

We want to express our gratitude to David Scott Cunningham of the University of Arkansas Press, who recognized the value of this collection; his colleagues at the press, including David Cajías Calvet, Janet Foxman, and Charlie Shields for help with our book as it made its way through the process of publication; our cover designer, William Clift; our copy editor, James Fraleigh; and our indexer, Devon Thomas. Thanks also to Tara Mastrelli for her assistance in preparing the manuscript for submission.

We also should acknowledge how much fun it was to work together on this collection. It may be that Mike gets Carol off the paths and back on the road again, but even if not, we have experienced the joy of recognizing something special is going on with vegan cycling no matter where it happens.

Last, to John Coetzee, who kindly answered Carol's questions about his experiences riding in Austin, Texas, and whose "Meat Culture" essay—and our discussion of it—first got us rolling.

PEDALING RESISTANCE

Bikolage

CAROL J. ADAMS AND MICHAEL D. WISE

We are vegans who cycle. One of us became vegan through a postmillennial journey as a bike racer; the other is a premillennial vegan who returned to the sport of cycling in the current century. We both know that when we cycle, something valuable and exciting happens to us that also is connected to our vegan practices, so we decided to collaborate on this volume of essays after noticing that connections between veganism and cycling kept coming up in our conversations.

As we discussed our idea for the project with friends and colleagues, we quickly sensed there were two predictable categories of response to the phrase "vegan cyclist." The initial (and more superficial) reading referred to a narcissistic milieu of fitness, health, and privilege shared on social media[1] and in other forms of popular culture. For those predisposed to roll their eyes at the neoliberal forces of lifestyle branding, let alone anyone unwilling to ride a bike or to give up eating animals, these associations make "vegan cycling" easy to caricature and dismiss as a self-absorbed lifestyle choice.

A second, more sophisticated reaction often followed our measured rejoinder that we wanted to take vegan cycling seriously as something other than simply a caricature that failed to consider how individuals enacted their political and ethical decisions. Vaguely Bordieuan and temptingly easy, the reaction this time would be something like, "Oh yes, bicycles and veganism—symbols of environmentalism forming the habitus of a twenty-first century professional class seeking to generate cultural capital through performances of ecological virtue." Okay, fair enough. That thesis in general has been argued effectively by a handful of critics in the environmental humanities over the last several decades (including both of us).[2] We already knew how the conventional analyses would appear from the bird's-eye perspectives of critical theory and the social sciences. What we wanted to explore instead were the less obvious experiences, thoughts, and connections generated by diverse individuals whose daily lives encompassed both cycling and vegan practices. In short, instead of analyzing from the top down, we wanted to consider the emergence of "vegan–cycling subjectivities" from the bottom up.

We thought that overall, people too often approached our phrase "vegan cycling" as a kind of punchline to a joke; it reminded Carol of reactions in the 1980s to her suggestion that feminism and vegetarianism should be examined in relation each to the other. As mentioned, we wanted to take the practices of vegan cycling seriously—as something that had actual intellectual heft, rather than a mere set of "lifestyle" choices— and gather essays from a diverse group of contributors to investigate them. Rather than focusing on cycling and veganism as modes of individual self-expression within cultural structures of neoliberal lifestyle politics, we decided to pursue answers to other questions: What happens when a vegan bikes? What sorts of "vegan subjectivities" emerge as one bikes? What is revealed when we think about cycling and veganism as interconnected practices that engage both body and mind? Does cycling open possibilities for people to become vegans? Rather than simply recapitulating inequalities of class, race, gender, and species, does the experience of vegan cycling provide new opportunities for identifying and responding to them?

■   ■   ■

Our goal with this collection was to explore the idea of a vegan–cycling subjectivity through essays that interspersed memoir-style recollections alongside critical engagements with works in cultural and social analysis. From the outset, though, it was difficult for us to provide contributors with a model or a more concrete articulation of the form of writing that we desired to evoke and then capture. We all essentially learned by doing. Only by writing our essays did we come to find ways to express insights into the vegan–cycling subjectivities that emerged when we rode, enabling us to discuss how cycling compelled us to become vegans (or vice versa). We asked our essayists to begin with their lived experiences as vegan cyclists, and to explore themes of everyday resistance and boundary

CAROL J. ADAMS AND MICHAEL D. WISE

crossing to reveal some of the larger social and political issues at stake in these activities.

The catalyzed vegan–cycling subjectivities that resulted are not easy to categorize. As editors, we chose to preserve the heterogeneity of our contributors' experimental outcomes rather than seek to impose a more conventional style upon the essays (as often occurs with edited collections).

As we reflected on all of these works of writing, it seemed that the best way to express their commonality was through the metaphor of a bike ride. As the photographs that accompany the essays indicate, each of us approaches the activity of cycling with a different constitution of parts, and these components determine the varying aesthetics, forms, and functions of our experiences while we ride.

The fluidity of a bike ride puts into motion a concert of these pieces that provokes meanings that aren't possible when the bike and its rider stay motionless. The fleeting nature of the embodied thoughts that occur when one rides are often difficult to relate after the fact, almost like the effort of narrating a dream a day or two later. Vegan–cycling subjectivities are best understood as always being in motion. Just so, the diversity of approaches in this collection mirrors and expresses the situated nature of each rider, and we wanted to preserve that sensation as editors by allowing diverse writing styles that range from experimental approaches (such as fictocriticism), through memoir-like writing, to more traditionally recognizable academic examinations. For some readers, these juxtapositions of style may seem unexpected on first reading, but the signpost we offer is that each approach represents a conscious process of reckoning with vegan–cycling subjectivities, which, like our own bikes and bodies, are unique.

■ ■ ■

Throughout much of the world today, vegans and cyclists both live in automobile- and meat-centered worlds that were not designed for us. These systems of public and private infrastructure were developed over the last two centuries to rely on fossil fuels for transportation and on animals for human sustenance. It was no accident that the industrialization of animal agriculture occurred at the same moment that combustion engines replaced muscle power, a transformation that has repeated itself several times from the early nineteenth century to the present. Inbound railroad cars fueled by coal, for instance, first enabled the large-scale concentration of pigs and cattle in centralized urban stockyards, where they would be held until disassembly in industrial slaughterhouses, their deaths concealed from public view, their packaged remains distributed on the outbound journey (Cronon 1991, 209–12). A century later, diesel trucks and decentralized networks of asphalt highways relocated the stockyards and slaughterhouses back to the countryside, where open spaces and the absence of urban congestion enabled the production of meat and dairy on a more expansive scale (Hamilton 2008, 135–62).

The interstate highway system allowed the new meatpacking industries that first appeared in 1960 to settle in rural Colorado, Iowa, Kansas, and Nebraska, nearer to feedlots and away from urban union strongholds (Schlosser 2003, 154). As the interstate highways were built, the fast-food industry followed along, offering hamburgers at off ramps. Josh Ozersky (2008) suggests that accommodating car culture contributed to the rise of McDonald's and proposes that "one reason the hamburger so far outstripped its rivals in the fast-food era was because it was so easy to eat a burger while driving" (53).

The intensification in our own lifetimes of rural meat and dairy production through the use of concentrated animal feeding operations, or CAFOs, has relied predominantly on gas and diesel power to lift and move enormous tonnages of fodder, flesh, and waste, thus marking animal agriculture with a carbon burden larger than any other sector of global agriculture. (That both the meat industry and the highway system benefit from strong federal support and subsidies is not lost on us.) The industrial enslavement of animals for food coincided with the rise of a transportation regimen based on fossil fuels, and our dependencies on meat, milk, and oil share the same historical trajectories, a reality that can be difficult to ignore when cycling across the world's industrialized farmscapes.

Because the world has been built in response to these dependencies on animals for food and engines for transportation, vegans and cyclists are often dispossessed from public spaces, our presence sensed as a nuisance. Both while cycling and while "veganing," vegan cyclists are usually outsiders, negotiating a built environment designed for a meat-eating and vehicle-driving subject. These maneuvers also force vegan cyclists to confront other oppressive, overlapping structures of class, race, and heteropatriarchy, giving up (if perhaps only temporarily) myriad social

CAROL J. ADAMS AND MICHAEL D. WISE

privileges that the car-driving, meat-eating subject can take for granted. In doing so, vegan cyclists develop opportunities to arrange empathetic frameworks for identifying and understanding other structural barriers to social justice and equity.

Both vegans and cyclists face public assumptions that cast us as feminized and immature, two cultural imaginations that serve to justify our marginalization as our own fault—as a result of "choices" we made to challenge the patriarchal authority of cars and steaks. In such circumstances, when people ride bikes or choose not to eat animals, they marginalize themselves. Opting out of these social dependencies—if only temporarily—often invites aggression and suspicion. On a bike or at a barbecue chain, men who are vegan cyclists are effeminized. Adults are infantilized and perhaps sometimes comprehended as not fully human. Most cyclists have been buzzed by cars more than once, and many of them have heard some rendition of "Get a car!" screamed through a rolled-down window. As Richard Twine has remarked, "the association of cycling with children" positions the activity as "an infantilized form of mobility."[3] Not only do many drivers resent cyclists' right to use the road, but they also interact with cyclists as if they were children in need of a scolding.

Likewise, vegans often suffer the vitriol and mockery of those who consider carnivorism to represent a kind of adult state of human development, whether in terms of the social body at large or within the realm of individual personhood. A T-shirt advertising a popular North Texas barbecue chain reads, "I didn't claw my way to the top of the food chain to eat vegetables," an axiom signaling the consumption of a soppy, shredded corpse served in a Styrofoam carton as some form of evolutionary ascendance. Dominant attitudes about eating animals and driving cars find expression through a sexual politics of overlapping meanings that position meat and cars "with the hegemonic performance of masculinity," as Twine has argued (2017, 249). This insight also has been captured by Peter Baker in his 2022 *New York Times Magazine* essay, where he asserts, "Cars come to us in advertisements, in films, in song lyrics; they're powerful, they're sexy, they're fun. Bicycles, by contrast—the everyday, getting-from-A-to-B type—are offered as the vegetables to cars' steak. Prudent and responsible, maybe. Powerful and sexy, definitely not."

Glancing at certain car advertisements helps confirm these associations. A famous Hummer commercial promised a vegan could best "restore his manhood" (supposedly in crisis after buying tofu at the local grocery store) by immediately buying a Hummer (Rogers 2008). The hegemonic domination of meat and fossil fuels operates in many other cultural arenas as well (see, e.g., Daggett 2018).

To be a vegan cyclist in these conditions, then, is to dwell in a world of routine alienation where one temporarily sets aside certain social privileges to greater and lesser extents, depending on one's own specific configuration of identity and environment. Vegan cyclists experience the ways the built environment has assumed a dominant subject characterized by whiteness, heteronormativity, and omnivorousness. Inevitably, vegan cycling calls into question typical social boundaries and identity categories, both for vegan cyclists and those with whom they interact. What biking allows you to do is liberating: to give up your human masking, offering a moment when you can exist within society and be separate from it. Vegan cycling thus represents commitments that resituate the subject in an environment built for the heteronormative subject, offering opportunities to sense and imagine the world in new ways.

■   ■   ■

Urban cyclists, suburban cyclists, rural cyclists, bike-racing cyclists—vegans can be found wherever cycling happens. They can be found on rural rides that transport them not through bucolic forest scenes but instead past factory farms, painfully aware of all they are seeing, smelling, and hearing. They can be found trying to protect their lane in a hostile urban environment. We all inherited an automobile-centric worldview, one that obscures lived environments that automobiles simply pass over or by. We were also inducted into a meat-and-dairy-centric one. Decentering those world views, we find ourselves situated as critics and essayists, memoirists and theorists, philosophers and urban bike messengers. We can also speak from personal experience of the unfriendly nature of car culture and omnivorous obstinacy to cyclists and vegans creating a continual need to negotiate hostile public spaces.

Janet O'Shea captures this situation in chapter 1, "The Politics of Inconvenience." This first essay starts us off with something akin to a "state of vegan cycling" report. We learn how "utility cycling and veganism appear as and are often represented as unnecessary impositions on public space and attention." And when she describes how automobile drivers fail to respect bike lanes, and recounts the insults hurled at cyclists, she anticipates Lawson "Frogi" Pruett's personal narrative that follows in chapter 2, "Stay in Your Lane." His experience as a vegan urban bike messenger has convinced him that cyclists should "take your lane" and "stick to it, and be ready to break rules when you have to, because most drivers don't realize that these lanes are our lanes too."

As for hostile public spaces, in chapter 7, "Three Wheels, Two Arms, and One Planet: Disabled Vegan Cycling and Eco-ability Consciousness," Kay Inckle describes their impact on vegans and cyclists with disabilities, resulting in their exclusion from both communities. Inckle argues that disability, animal, and environmental rights are all integral to veganism and cycling. Michael Wise's "Caring for the Human Horse: Reflections on Cycling and the Animal Senses" (chapter 3) further reflects on the issues of our own bodies and how biking prompts us to question normative divisions between human and animal. Then, Matthew Calarco's "Changing Direction" (chapter 5) prompts reflection on the violent structures and practices of anthropocentrism and hyperautomobility. Literary animal studies scholar Sune Borkfelt's "Cycling, Noticing, Caring: On Being a Vegan Cyclist in Denmark" (chapter 6) touches on issues of animal agriculture, hunting, categorization of wild and domesticated animals, and loss of insects. He emphasizes the importance of both real and imaginary animal encounters, to which he finds cycling to be conducive.

Cycling can steer us into the process of becoming vegan, as Amy Rundio describes in chapter 4, "How Cycling Led Me to Veganism, Which Changed My Cycling." Personal narratives like hers and Geertrui Cazaux's "We Live and Ride in Tandem" (chapter 9) continue Pruett's reflective engagement, interweaving specific experiences with larger issues. Naomi Stekelenburg's fictocritical essay, " 'Christ on a Bike, You're a Dumb Dog' " (chapter 8, based on a month-long cycling tour of Tasmania, Australia), raises questions about modes of transport and how they enable closer recognition of our own animality. Meanwhile, in chapter 10, Sheri Barnes is "Dispelling Myths and Shattering Stereotypes as a Vegan Cyclist in Kansas," as the vegan consultant to towns hosting meals for the annual Bike across Kansas event, an experience juxtaposed with the awareness of all the factory-farmed animals she bicycles past. In Berkeley, A. Breeze Harper is a "Vegan Black Mama Scholar Cyclist" in chapter 11, describing the scrutiny leveled at her as a Black pregnant vegan cyclist, and how concerns about "safety" are often used by the

conventional medical establishment to dissuade people from either riding bikes or adopting a vegan diet. Last, in chapter 12, "Start Where You
Are and Keep Going," Carol takes us on her regular bike ride through
the Dallas suburb of Richardson, Texas, recapitulating the themes and
movements of the book in a concluding, self-contained piece.

■ ■ ■

The activities of vegan cycling rely on an art of "making do," or *bricolage*,
as Michel de Certeau (1984) once put it; a tactical cobbling together of
parts and processes to achieve results that those tools were never intended
to produce (29). From de Certeau's point of view, *bricolage* represented
the tactics of those forced to navigate and "make do" in everyday life
using pieces, systems, and places intended for others. Given its aptness
in describing the daily activities of cycling vegans, we thought the port-
manteau *bikolage* offered us an appropriate conceptual point of departure.

Carol's bike, a 1970s steel Raleigh updated with a Campy groupset
from the 1990s and a pair of Mavic Aksium wheels from 2015, could
be used as a literal example of *bikolage* as it assembles the old with the
new. Jill Lepore suggests, perhaps with a wink, that with the history of
the bicycle, ontogeny recapitulates philology (2022), but we find its history illustrates the concept of *bikolage*: from the 1817 invention of the
Laufmaschine, or running machine (with its frame, saddle, and wheels),
to the addition of pedals (probably in 1855), wire spokes (late 1860s–early
1870s), drivetrain transmission (late 1870s), and the pneumatic rubber tire
(1888), to the e-bikes of the twenty-first century, we find a history of adap-
tation, improvement, and annexation. As Jody Rosen observes in *Two
Wheels Good: The History and Mystery of the Bicycle* (2022), "A defining
quality of the bicycle's form is its openness to hacks and interventions, to
rejiggering and retrofitting" (61).

Although the literal associations of contemporary bikes with a history of *bikolage* are interesting, in this volume we are thinking more specifically of how that term captures the way vegan cycling breaks down
boundaries and encourages moments of intense reflection that lead to
seeing the world in new ways. Cycling is a way of connecting spaces
through movement; it becomes a way of dwelling in the world that generates new ways of thinking about interconnections among different parts
of one's life. The compartmentalization of one's social identities begins

Seatstay shot of Carol's bike circa 2022, reflecting *bikolage. Photograph courtesy Michael Wise.*

to break down alongside the activities of vegan cycling. In a sense, this experience becomes a grounded way of reconstituting an understanding of one's own body, particularly as vegan cyclists come to understand the animality of their own bodies as a constellation of parts that can take on lives of their own, not always behaving according to expectations. The notion of *bikolage* offers an opening concept from which to describe the experiences of vegan cycling, and the following twelve authors thread their own lines in attempting to add precision to the subjectivities that emerge from these grounded experiences.

In this sense, from a philosophical perspective, *bikolage* leads us toward a phenomenological vegan–cycling subject, whose specific shapes and identities flow from its constant, embedded problem solving within its surrounding worlds. For all the postmodern critiques of the Cartesian subject's divisions of mind from body, what we find notable is the relative absence of generative alternatives, of open space, to take seriously the rich interplay of thoughts and sensations that vegan cyclists improvise as they move, breathe, digest, labor and play, rest and reflect, thrive and struggle.[4] The acts of cycling and eating subvert normative distinctions of where one's body begins and ends. Ingestion and digestion are visceral phenomena that reveal our bodies' continuities with the earth around us. Likewise, our movements astride the wheels of a cycle harness our muscle power to a technical device that alters our perceptions of our embodied capabilities for travel.[5] Both activities compel sensations alike in their capacity to challenge our bodies as mere instruments of our minds, coterminous with our skins.

In another sense, *bikolage* also offers a deepening of efforts to theorize hybrid subjectivities in the wake of the post-Cartesian turn. Whether oriented along the lines of the "cyborg," or of companion-animal relationships, or of Lacanian performances of mimesis and alterity, the discrete hybrid subjectivities of such concepts tend to emphasize ties that endure, not the ones that are fleeting.[6] By contrast, the experiences of cycling and eating find their definition most substantially in the small moments—swerving to dodge a pothole, chewing a piece of bread. Vegan cycling finds its hybridity in these constant negotiations of space, safety, and sustenance. Riding a bike does not transform one into a cyborg any more than eating a zebra transforms one into a lion. There is no "becoming with." The vegan cyclist's accommodations and ameliorations are themselves the becoming.

In other words, rather than simply offering another critique of how normative forces constrain the production of knowledge in relation to assumptions of animal–human difference, and of racialized and gendered performances of power, our goal in this book is instead to bring *bikolage* onto the page; to identify new articulations of the shared concerns that emerge from the embodied experiences of vegan cycling. What happens when "critique runs out of steam," as Bruno Latour once asked? On the metaphorical plane, the project turns toward an articulation of matters of shared concern, rather than the simple matters of fact, as Latour put it (2004, 231–32). On the plane of literality, what happens is that humans rely once more on muscle power; on our own capacity to metabolize the foods we consume into fuel. And just as "running out of steam" harkens to the Industrial Revolution's reliance on fossil fuels to power mechanized labor, individual cyclists also must decide how to generate their own metabolic power. Will our choices arise from and perpetuate the death-oriented practices of animal agriculture, or help liberate us from the mythology that athletic strength comes from eating animals? These constant decisions that frame the vegan's day-to-day experience are also omnipresent in the activities of cyclists who come to understand the animality of their own bodies.

The result of *bikolage*, then, is a dissolution of human–animal boundaries, one that emerges through generative experiences of living in the world as a kind of subject for which the contemporary world was not designed, both in terms of the landscapes of animal agriculture that structure industrialized diets and the global dependencies on hypermobility that often obscure the true costs of movement.

"Movement" in the realm of philosophy is frequently taken for granted as metaphor. This book, however, focuses instead on the physicality of boundary crossings, including those between "metaphor" and "lived experience" in ways that help define the practical worlds of vegan cyclists.[7] They pedal not just against the gear-inched resistance of their wheels and chainrings, but also against structures of automobility and animal agriculture that are so invasively perverse. The authors in *Pedaling Resistance* have worked hard to identify how their thoughts and experiences as cycling vegans help identify "vegan cycling" as a set of subject positions from which to sense, understand, and change the world.[8]

Notes

1. Such social media personalities are exemplified by the self-proclaimed Vegan Cyclist, with 105,000 followers on Instagram (@the_vegan_cyclist) in 2023, whose humble-brags ("Well, I am just an ordinary dude that strives to be the best version of myself") along with his frequent counsel to "be dope bruh" appeal only to a certain subset of cycling vegans.
2. One of Mike's favorite renditions of this thesis is Robert Fletcher's *Romancing the Wild: Cultural Dimensions of Ecotourism* (2014).
3. Richard Twine, email correspondence with Carol, February 1, 2022. Used with permission.
4. For an introduction to these critiques, see Tim Ingold, *The Perception of the Environment: Essays in Livelihood, Dwelling and Skill* (New York: Routledge, 2000).
5. See Sunaura Taylor, *Beasts of Burden: Animal and Disability Liberation* (New York: New Press, 2017).
6. Some classic references in this literature include Gilles Deleuze and Felix Guattari, *A Thousand Plateaus: Capitalism and Schizophrenia*, trans. Brian Massumi (Minneapolis: University of Minnesota Press, 1987); Donna Haraway, "A Cyborg Manifesto [1985]," in *Simians, Cyborgs and Women: The Reinvention of Nature* (New York: Routledge, 1991): 149–81; Haraway, *When Species Meet* (Minneapolis: University of Minnesota Press, 2008); and Michael Taussig, *Mimesis and Alterity: A Particular History of the Senses* (New York: Routledge, 1993).

7. The colloquial language of cycling itself consists of metaphors that ring true only in ways that confuse the metaphor. The bicycle, in all its various forms, is a misnomer, since a bike consists not only of two wheels, but really a series of wheels within wheels. Pushing the pedals spins the chainring around the bearings of the bottom bracket, rotating the cassette; pawls and bearings engage the hub body, spokes (cross-laced or radial) transmitting force to the nipples, driving forward the rim, tires smoothing the ride as they alternately form and deform over cracks and bumps in the road or trail. When ruts and rocks and curbs exceed the tire's capabilities, the cyclist's hips, ankles, patellas, wrists, and elbows become the suspension system, aided sometimes by a properly sagged fork and rear pivot, but always dependent on the rider's sprung body position. Ineluctably, cyclists become their cycle—not only would it not start without them, but it wouldn't continue without them, either. So, when bike racers "drop the hammer," as the judicial metaphor goes, they actually are pushing the pedals with the full force of their whole bodies. The phrase does not actually make much sense as a cycling metaphor. Although there is downward force applied, the pedals revolve in a circle—and the more force applied, the faster that circle spins. The hammer feels real, though, and not at all like a gavel, and most cyclists who have pushed their pedals as hard as they could—a sensation that is otherwise challenging to describe—know what it means.

8. We assume many readers will share our concerns but not that all are vegans or cyclists. The chapters mention some of the foods that we and our contributors like to eat, but you won't find any meal plans or recipes in this book. "Start Where You Are and Keep Going," the title of this collection's last essay, is an appropriate mantra for anyone who is not vegan but wishes to adopt a vegan ethic and diet. We also recommend Carol's co-authored book with Virginia Messina, *Protest Kitchen* (2018), as a starting point with recipes, guidance, and a thirty-day plan.

References

Adams, Carol J., and Virginia Messina. 2018. *Protest Kitchen: Fight Injustice, Save the Planet, and Fuel Your Resistance One Meal at a Time.* Newburyport, MA: Red Wheel.

Baker, Peter C. 2022. "Can a Reality TV Show Sell You on a $2,298 E-Bike?" *New York Times Magazine*, February 23, 2022. https://www.nytimes.com/2022/02/23/magazine/bike-hunters-vanmoof-ebike.html.

Cronon, William. 1991. *Nature's Metropolis: Chicago and the Great West.* New York: W. W. Norton.

Daggett, Cara. 2018. "Petro-masculinity: Fossil Fuels and Authoritarian Desire." *Millennium: Journal of International Studies* 47 (1): 25–44.

de Certeau, Michel. 1984. *The Practice of Everyday Life.* Translated by Steven Rendall. Berkeley: University of California Press.

Fletcher, Robert. 2014. *Romancing the Wild: Cultural Dimensions of Ecotourism.* Durham, NC: Duke University Press.

Hamilton, Shane. 2008. *Trucking Country: The Road to America's Wal-Mart Economy.* Princeton, NJ: Princeton University Press.

Ingold, Tim. 2000. *The Perception of the Environment: Essays in Livelihood, Dwelling and Skill*. New York: Routledge.

Latour, Bruno. 2004. "Why Has Critique Run out of Steam? From Matters of Fact to Matters of Concern." *Critical Inquiry* 30 (2): 225–48.

Lepore, Jill. 2022. "Bicycles Have Evolved. Have We?" *New Yorker*, May 23, 2022. https://www.newyorker.com/magazine/2022/05/30/bicycles-have-evolved-have-we-jody-rosen-two-wheels-good.

Ozersky, Josh. 2008. *The Hamburger*. New Haven, CT: Yale University Press.

Rogers, Richard. 2008. "Beasts, Burgers, and Hummers: Meat and the Crisis of Masculinity in Contemporary Television Advertisements." *Environmental Communication* 2 (3): 281–301. https://doi.org/10.1080/17524030802390250.

Rosen, Jody. 2022. *Two Wheels Good: The History and Mystery of the Bicycle*. New York: Crown.

Schlosser, Eric. 2003. *Fast Food Nation: The Dark Side of the All-American Meal*. New York: Perennial.

Twine, Richard. 2016. "Negotiating Social Relationships in the Transition to Vegan Eating Practices." In *Meat Culture*, edited by Annie Potts, 243–63. Leiden, The Netherlands: Brill.

Janet O'Shea cycling in San Francisco. *Photograph by David Bruce.*

CHAPTER ONE

The Politics of Inconvenience
*Disruption, Power, and Imagination
in Cycling and Veganism*

JANET O'SHEA

Introduction: The Politics of Being in the Way

*Riding on a side street in Los Angeles's Westwood neighborhood, I made
my way toward the yellow line in preparation for a left turn. A silver Prius
sat on a diagonal in a drugstore driveway to my right. Slowly, but with no
turn indication or other hint of her plans, the driver drifted into oncoming
traffic. Then, just as unpredictably, she stopped. Nimble and swift on my
bike, I swerved out of her way. When I was directly in front of her, she
advanced. This time, she struck my shin. She paused again and for one
almost blissful moment, I thought the worst was over. But she moved forward again, knocking me to the pavement. As I retreated, on the ground,
from the wheels of her car, she completed her left turn, driving over my
wrist and breaking it. She finally stopped a block away. She got out of the
car and approached me, looking over my injuries. "You should have gotten
out of my way," she said.*

*I was a participant at an intensive self-defense-instructor training. It
was a two-day event, and we were told food would be provided, including
a range of options. When the morning's training ended, the lead instructor
announced, "Lunch is ready. Serve yourself and be ready to resume training
in half an hour. There are sandwiches for the vegetarians. I didn't get anything vegan. I can't be bothered with all that."*

These two incidents are not, of course, comparable. One incident
was violent, the other thoughtless. One person's actions were illegal and

injurious, the other's merely rude. Choosing between picking up lunch and missing part of a training or skipping a meal while others eat is not equivalent to being seriously injured and spending months recovering. Indeed, had they not both happened to me, considering these events side by side would be inappropriate, perhaps even offensive.

And yet, they share an attribute that has nothing to do with the magnitude of each experience. In both instances, someone's actions and speech indicated that I was taking up space that didn't belong to me. How I approached the roadway in one instance, and the food system in the other, framed me as an obstacle to normal living. In that sense, both encounters seemed profoundly unfair: I was attempting to lighten my burden on the earth and on other beings, yet was twice met with the accusation that I was in the way, an imposition, simply by being where I was, how I was. Both times, the "aberrant" behavior was perceived as an undesired interference into attention and therefore into consciousness. This unwelcome impingement provoked hostility on the one hand and dismissiveness on the other, suggesting that discomfort accompanied these ostensible intrusions.

Queer theorist Sara Ahmed (2006) argues that because consciousness is intentional, in the sense of being directed toward an object, where our attention places itself reveals histories of labor. It takes work—physical, cultural, and intellectual—to encourage attention in one way over another. The intentional nature of consciousness, in turn, facilitates how we exist as selves in the world and who and what we interact with. Ahmed also indicates that this process is corporeal: it operates through how we move in space and how we interact with others. It reinforces itself through spatial imagery that is simultaneously metaphorical and literal. When our behavior is erratic, for instance, we are "out of line" (2006, *passim*). By contrast, when we act in an orderly fashion, we fall *in* line. We agree by lining up behind ideas. We show our fidelity to dominant symbols, such as the nation's flag, by turning toward them. Moreover, some objects—and some bodies—come easily to hand. Habits are formed by what is (literally and metaphorically) within reach and, thus, normative behaviors, such as gender conformity or heterosexuality, emerge from what is easily available and produces social ease. Other possibilities, by virtue of being out of line or out of reach, are effortful. Moreover, from without, they appear disruptive. Ahmed thus argues that political struggle demands a readiness to cause discomfort, a "willingness to be willful" (2010a, 5).[1]

Following Ahmed, I argue that some actions, such as driving and meat eating, are, in contemporary US society, within reach. To partake of them means to go with the crowd (2010a, 5); turning toward them means lining up with expectations. Despite their adverse effects, ranging from ill health to environmental degradation, they produce a sense of social ease.[2] Building upon Richard Twine's application of how Ahmed articulates the relationship between "affect and social norms" (2014, 624) to veganism, I suggest that refusing meat eating and avoiding driving can create a sense of discomfort that is political in nature.[3] There is, in other words, political potential to acts that are in the way: such inconvenient actions potentially disrupt the existing order and reveal rifts in its ostensible seamlessness. Inconvenient actions show the limits of the normal, revealing an outside that, at first glance, seems not to exist or impossible to reach. Moreover, as both Ahmed and Twine suggest, those who turn from "dominant affective communities" (Twine 2014, 624) participate in the making of alternative worlds; these worlds move from the realm of pure imagination to the realm of possibility through physical action.

And yet, opposing the crowd is not equally available to all. To go against the flow is to occupy a marginal space, but social, political, and economic status inform access to and desire for the margins. Some people are pushed to the edges; some can't seem to reach them no matter how much they want to. To choose the margins voluntarily, rather than being forced to them, can appear to indicate (and often does) access to the "residual benefits" (Ko 2019, 84) of a damaging system.[4] "Histories of arrival" (Ahmed 2006, 41–43) enable or discourage the possibility of willful action. They influence what is, and is thought of, as possible, and for which subjects (Ahmed 2006, 132–35).

The association of cycling (specifically transport or utility cycling) and veganism with disruption operates through several histories of arrival: the US (and, to some extent international) subsidy systems, which privilege investment in fossil fuels and highways to the exclusion of active and public transit, and which disproportionately fund animal over plant agriculture, as well as the social movements that challenge them. What follows, then, is an exploration of why neither veganism nor cycling is easily accessible in most of the United States, and what we risk when we assume they are. I conclude by considering the relationship of inconvenience to imagination, especially physicalized imagination, and its ability to invoke alternative political possibilities. I suggest that physicalized imagination, in its immediacy and the relationship it draws between experience and selfhood, offers more radical possibilities for change than other means of envisioning alternative social relationships, structures, and institutions. This chapter is therefore both a critique of the ways in which transport cycling and vegan activism repeat dominant power structures and a celebration of their resistant potential.

A Lighter Load, a Bigger Imposition?

By any empirical measure, cycling and veganism take up less space than their alternatives. Multiple bicycles can inhabit the space occupied by one moving car. With parking, this difference is even more pronounced, as bicycles can be stored in racks or lockers, on sidewalks, and under rail platforms, whereas cars require their own designated spaces, lots, or structures. Similarly, it takes one-fourth the amount of land to feed a person eating a vegan diet than an omnivorous eater (Ritchie 2021). Cycling and veganism also demand fewer resources. Cycling produces no exhaust and no noise pollution (Furness 2010, 61–62), and bicyclists pose less of a threat to other road users than drivers. The feed conversion ratio of animal foods renders them inherently inefficient; veganism entails consuming fewer net foodstuffs, and thus requires less fresh water and fewer inputs, chemical or organic, than meat eating. Further, veganism does not contribute to the animal waste accumulating in manure lagoons, dumped onto communities adjacent to factory farms, and spilled into rivers and, eventually, the ocean. And, of course, removing demand for animal products reduces the need to kill the animals in the first place. Although cycling and veganism can be motivated by self-interest (e.g., a dedication to fitness and personal health), those who chose them also reduce their impact on others.

In contexts where they are not the norm, however, utility cycling and veganism appear as, and are often represented as, unnecessary impositions on public space and attention. American cyclists, for instance, contend with drivers who fail to respect bike lanes and hurl insults and threats as they pass, including the ubiquitous command to get off the road. Cyclists in Australia report drivers throwing objects at them and finding bike paths deliberately sabotaged (Delbosc et al. 2018). Much of this harassment is sexual in nature, with drivers objectifying women and commenting on men's supposed sexual orientation (Foster 2010; Furness

2010, 4). Hostile drivers are known to publicly fantasize about hitting, running over, or killing cyclists (Delbosc et al. 2018). Drivers assault cyclists (Foster 2010), swerve toward them, and even intentionally hit them with their vehicles (Bella 2021; Furness 2010, 4; Tinoco 2018). In the United States, cyclists of color are criminalized (Andersen 2017) and spontaneous cycling events such as Critical Mass have been classified as terrorism under the Patriot Act (Furness 2010, 1–3).

Similarly, animal activism is sometimes met with violence (jones 2006) and even homicide (Eccelston 2021; Revkin 1990; Rosella 2020), whereas efforts to document the abuses associated with factory farms are, like some cycling interventions, subject to criminalization and treatment in the legal system as terrorism (Potter 2011). The rising popularity of veganism in the United Kingdom has been met with high-profile threats of aggression, such as a food editor's emailed suggestion that his publication should feature a series on killing vegans (Waterson 2018), the bank employee who told a customer that vegans should be "punched in the face" (Reynolds 2019), and a vegan café's being subject to arson threats (Gilliver 2021). Overall, however, it remains rare for practitioners of veganism in its dietary form to encounter physical violence. Instead, they are met with deliberately obtrusive and sometimes spectacularized displays of meat eating, be it the family member who shoves meat in a vegan's face, an online troll who posts images of meat in a vegan social media group, or "protestors" skinning and eating animals at a vegan food stall (Reynolds 2019). Even in its most mild form, resistance to veganism hinges upon the assumption that abstention from meat constitutes an unnecessary demand on a host or other food provider, a disruption to an otherwise peaceful meal.

The hostility that veganism incurs suggests that the problem isn't the animal–industrial complex but the person who calls attention to it—that innocence would be bliss in the absence of critique.[5] Those invested in the dominant order perceive the decision to abstain from meat as challenging the status quo; thus, they see vegans as an inherent threat. Sociologists have found that those committed to normative conventions of behavior holds biases against vegans (MacInnis and Hodson 2015) and cyclists (Delbosc et al. 2018) equivalent to those minoritized along the lines of sexuality, race, ethnicity, religion, immigration status, and mental health, even as they are far less likely to express or act on their anti-vegan and anti-cyclist biases.[6]

The antics of anti-vegans suggest that veganism isn't necessarily perceived as a demand on physical space but rather on mental, emotional, and social space. Indeed, the common accusation that vegans are too vocal ("How can you tell if someone is vegan? Don't worry; they'll tell you") assumes an undeserved demand on attentional space. It also seems to suggest, despite evidence to the contrary, that meat eaters keep the habit of consuming animal products, and its related ideology, to themselves.[7] This stereotype endures despite the existence of vegans who self-silence in response to such a priori accusations (Stanescu 2019).[8] Such received ideas and the anti-vegan stigma that accompanies them (Markowski and Roxburgh 2019) seem designed to police verbal and emotional space and, hence, to monitor how attention operates.

Through a phenomenon that social scientists have labeled "do-gooder derogation" (Minson and Monin 2011), efforts to improve damaging or violent conditions appear to condemn nonparticipants. Sometimes this effect is so strong that the mere sight of a bicycle or the absence of meat on one's plate evinces a defensive response.[9] Because meat eaters and drivers anticipate critique, they tend to resent their counterparts' efforts to address social wrongs. This phenomenon operates as a large-scale version of a guilty conscience responding to its own accusations (Adams 2001), but its ubiquity and force also work to silence those who struggle to align their actions with their values. That is, a major obstacle to the uptake and maintenance of both veganism and cycling is the fear of others' judgment (Markowski and Roxburgh 2019; Pucher et al., in Furness 2010, 113).

Paradoxically, then, efforts to use fewer resources appear as emblems of unearned privilege (Furness 2010, 7; Lugo 2018, 118). Bicycle anthropologist Adonia Lugo (ibid.) notes that efforts to minimize resource consumption are not treated at face value but as a display of virtue that then evokes a defensive reaction.[10] As cultural studies scholar Zack Furness points out, this constitutes a peculiar rhetorical move, whereby elitism pertains less to material privilege than to a "moral or behavioral disposition" (2010, 135). Common aspersions, such as "smug vegan" and "entitled cyclist," operate as a shorthand through which elitism is evacuated of structural meaning and becomes an attitude that can be deduced from how a person ostensibly demands attentional space.

Although the assertion that utility cyclists and vegans are taking up literal and metaphorical space that doesn't belong to them can be contradicted with data, it nonetheless has a history. On the one hand, the United

States' food, transportation, and governmental policies have normalized meat and cars, entities that would otherwise be luxury items. This system turns the exception into the norm and renders resource-intensive actions artificially cheap. On the other hand, mainstream cycling and vegan activists, in interrogating this normalization while not seriously considering its material effects, have rested heavily on the benefits of their own status as (typically) middle class, white, cisgender, normative-bodied, and often (but not always) male people.

As American as Hot Dogs, Apple Pie, and Chevrolet: A Brief History of the Subsidy System

Americans eat more meat per capita than any other nationality on earth (McCarthy 2020). We also drive more.[11] In much of the world, plant-based diets and human-powered transport are the norm.[12] Likewise, for much of history, humans survived on plant foods, with meat reserved for the affluent, and relied primarily on their own locomotion or on shared transport, with individual vehicle ownership (e.g., chariots and coaches) the domain of the wealthy and horse riding reserved for elites or rural denizens (Furness 2010, 24). By contrast, the United States has managed to democratize the exception while normalizing excess (Harper 2020, xxvi; Paarlberg 2015).

The standard Western diet, built around meat consumption, is an imperialist construct. British colonizers, for instance, stigmatized the plant-predominant diets of those they subjugated through (metropolitan) colonialism, from the potato-eating Irish and the oat-eating Scots to the rice-eating Chinese and Indians (Adams 1990, 30–32). European colonizers—British, French, and Spanish alike—imposed an animal-heavy diet on those they conquered in the context of settler colonialism and slavery (Calvo and Esquibel 2015; Danielle 2020; Fisher 2011, 115; Kuhn and Lewis 2021).[13] Colonizers valorized hunting-based societies (Adams 2007, 29–30) even as they stole their land, destroyed their food sources, and decimated their communities; conversely, by representing Indigenous people as "violent hunters," settlers legitimized their "conquest and subordination" (Wise 2023, 101). Colonial representations of native life strategically ignored the gathering, horticultural, and agricultural techniques that supported a wide range of Indigenous communities. This entailed a re-primitivization of native societies that eschewed their complexity

(Dunbar-Ortiz 2014), including their sophisticated growing techniques.[14] Indeed, colonizers were unable to even recognize noninvasive forms of agriculture *as* agriculture (Wise 2023, 101).

Dietary colonization (Calvo and Esquibel 2015) was—and is—material as well as conceptual. The large herbivores European colonizers imported were invasive species whose grazing habits destroyed local plant life and damaged associated ecosystems (Crosby 1986; Wise 2023). Their cattle, unadapted to foraging in the extreme cold without supplemental hay, consumed 50 percent more calories than bison, destroying grassland habitats in the process (Wise 2023, 103). In addition, settlers cleared forests to make room for cattle and pigs, taking land and food sources from endemic, free-living animals. Colonists also set pigs and cattle loose to graze in forests and grasslands, creating populations of feral animals that still wreak havoc on natural environments (Wise 2023, 102) and, ironically, create a justification for hunting on the part of settlers' descendants. Free-living animals—both herbivores and predators—were, and still are, killed because they interfere with the raising of livestock for food.[15] Indigenous people who gathered, hunted, cultivated, and farmed in these regions lost, and continue to lose, their sources of sustenance along with their sovereignty and their territorial rights. And, of course, the most arable land was often the first to be stolen.

Despite this checkered history, or perhaps because of it, the rancher has emerged as the American cultural symbol par excellence. Blending (apparent) rugged individualism with (ostensible) stewardship of the land, the rancher, as a representative of hard-working American masculinity, seems unassailable. This image operates so persuasively that even the progressive left and the environmental movement are reluctant to critique ranching. Instead, they often celebrate it as a compromise zone where manual labor and land stewardship meet, despite the status of many ranchers as large-scale business owners, their receipt of government incentives and subsidies, and their association with the violent dispossession of Indigenous people (and other settlers).[16] Despite recent efforts to reclaim ranching as regenerative and, hence, sustainable, popular culture reveals its relationship to the same expansionist logic that results in ecocide through, for instance, the bumper sticker that proclaims, "Eat Beef! The West Wasn't Won on Salad"—a clear instantiation of settler triumphalism (Adams 2007, 31) that consolidates nationalist identity through racism and land grabbing as well as via cow meat (Wise 2023, 104). The result is an almost unshakeable image of the taciturn, rugged, weathered rancher embodying the ostensible "best" of American traits such as independence, hardiness, and self-sufficiency, an image that is also unextractable from private transportation, in the form of the horse and, later, the pickup truck.

If meat eating reveals a history of American expansionism, cars and the ostensibly open road literally concretize it. As historian Peter Norton (2011) notes, the preeminence of the car required a redefinition of the street from common space to thoroughfare; the American "love affair with the car" was a manufactured response to protests against this incursion into public space (Badger 2015). The status of the American highway system as a "pre-eminent national icon" emerged, as Zack Furness suggests, out of resolutely material conditions such as the creation of a permanent tax pool to subsidize interstate and regional highways (2011, 51). Efforts to build an organized, connected roadway system date back to the founding of the United States as a nation-state (Williamson 2012). The history of America's roadways blurs militarism, (advanced) capitalism, nationalism, job creation, and expansionism (Furness 2010, 51). Building the highway system destroyed thriving Black neighborhoods in the interest of creating urban centers fully accessible by car and encouraged suburbanization, thereby amplifying racial segregation in practice even as its legality was challenged (Rothstein 2017). Car culture, white flight, and suburbanization historically have been treated as spontaneous and rooted in individual decisions, but historical evidence suggests they were instead driven by economic and political motivations (McClintock 2011; Norton 2011).

The consolidation of the highway system has resulted not only in the more obvious ubiquity of (and dependence on) cars but also in the wide availability of meat and a diminishment of alternatives, especially in underserved communities. Refrigerated railcars launched this process by allowing the "consolidation of meat production in urban centers" and enabling meat companies to ship their product across the country (Wise 2023, 107). The invention of the diesel truck allowed a reverse move, decentralizing slaughter and shifting it to rural areas (Hamilton 2008, 135–62). The highway system and the glorification of the personal vehicle enabled the creation of the drive-in diner, which presaged the fast-food outlet that eventually superseded it (Adams 2018; Schlosser 2001) while rendering cheap meat ubiquitous.

Decades of systemic disinvestment, combined with suburbanization and corporate consolidation, have resulted in a dearth of grocery stores and a surplus of liquor stores and fast-food outlets in poor neighborhoods and Black, Latine, and Indigenous communities (McClintock 2011; Reese 2019). Economic and environmental racism have permitted housing stock to degenerate, exposed disinvested neighborhoods to traffic pollution, and slashed access to public transit while limiting the availability of fresh, affordable food. The highway system facilitated the move of grocery stores to the suburbs and disinvestment in poor communities and communities of color. Systemically disinvested neighborhoods are underserved by the same transit systems whose construction also devastated their neighborhoods—with residents needing to "drive 20 minutes for a fresh tomato" (Finley 2013)—resulting in private vehicle dependence. For those who can't afford cars or gas, restrictions on how many bags can be taken on public transit and routes that involve multiple transfers render grocery shopping arduous, if not nearly impossible (Food Empowerment Project n.d.). Whether traveling by car or bus, residents of underserved neighborhoods are forced to participate in what food justice activist Neelam Sharma refers to as *economic leakage*, which transfers the resources of poor communities to wealthier neighborhoods. Abandoned by grocery outlets, underserved communities are nevertheless well supplied by fast-food outlets, which prioritize affordable meat, fried foods, and the refined grains that are the byproducts of animal feed (Patel 2007, 266). Thus, a "class-based, food apartheid system" (Terry in Hurt 2012)[17] compounds the impact of subsidies, rendering meat, dairy, and processed foods disproportionately available in communities of color and low-income neighborhoods.

Today's political system normalizes meat-centric eating and private vehicle ownership through economic policy as well as historical precedent and cultural symbolism. The US subsidy system, rooted in special interest lobbying and a "revolving door" between industry and politics (Freeman 2013, 1263), continues to regularize excess. These forces render animal foods and private motorized transport artificially cheap and thus normal and accessible.

Animal products receive subsidies that diminish their cost. As David Robinson Simon (2013) points out, farmers receive direct support for raising animals and indirect subsidies in the forms of cheap water, food-crop funding, insurance, and loans (79). The damaging effects of producing and consuming animal products, such as environmental pollution and public health crises, are borne by the general public, not the industry that created them, which externalizes economic costs (Simon 2013, 107–9, 125–26). Most legumes, grains, fruits, and vegetables are categorized as "specialty crops" and are ineligible for subsidy. This system encourages excess production, advertising, and market "innovation" to stimulate consumption (Nestle 2013). Since the 1990s, the cost of meat in real terms has dropped and the cost of produce has risen (Simon 2013, 74). The influx of money into the business of raising animals "disrupts" (Simon 2013, xix) or at least "mutes" (Laura Montoya Reese, interview with the author on Agriculture Fairness Alliance, September 8, 2021) market signals regarding the demand for animal versus vegetable foods. Through these structural interventions, meat, dairy, and the processed remnants of their feedstuffs, such as white bread (Patel 2012, 266) and high-fructose corn syrup, are easily to hand. Disproportionately cheap, they figure prominently in grocery stores and are often the only food items available in the nongrocery retailers, such as liquor stores and gas stations, that are ubiquitous in underserved communities.

Moreover, within a capitalist system, time is an economic resource.[18] A neoliberal system extends this monetization of time as it financializes nearly all aspects of daily life (Martin 2002). Therefore, when someone says veganism is expensive, what we might be hearing is that the speaker, who works long hours and contends with an arduous commute, must decide between boiling beans and grains and chopping vegetables or picking up a meal up at the drive-through or in the prepared food section of the grocery store. She may well be confronting time poverty as well as cash poverty (Ornelas 2010). Among convenience foods, the plant-based option is invariably more expensive because of the extensive subsidies allotted to animal industries. This is the case even as humble foods such as potatoes, oats, and dried beans remain less expensive than meat or dairy items.

Government subsidy likewise normalizes the "system of automobility" (Urry 2004). As Zack Furness (2010) points out, the US government's investment in a national highway system to the neglect of public transit[19] produced the ostensible American fascination with the car. Furness notes that the flooding of the public sector with highway funds and the suburbanization that accompanied it took place "almost immediately following a period when public transportation and walking were on the rise" and when bicycle purchases were also increasing (52). The roadway system currently receives about $75 billion per year in subsidies for construction and maintenance (Gross 2008)—a sum that doesn't include imbedded subsidies such as tax breaks—whereas public transit receives about one-sixth that amount (Bergal 2021).

Unlike in the case of meat eating, no one persuasively argues that owning a car is cheaper than riding a bike. However, the artificially low cost of all components of driving, and a thriving used-car market, make cars relatively easy to buy for all except the most impoverished in the United States. The car remains within reach even as other markers of middle-class status, such as homeownership, have become increasingly inaccessible. Although paved roads were initially introduced at the insistence of cyclists (Reid 2015), these same roads now cater to cars, often to the exclusion of their two-wheeled counterparts. Contemporary road design factors in the sight lines of drivers but not cyclists or pedestrians (Ryerson 2021). Most highways prohibit mixed use and are only accessible for and by cars.[20] An absence of bike lanes and other forms of bicycle infrastructure on roads with lanes sized for cars renders driving the most obvious choice. Cycling, then, operates as an option for those who lack the resources to buy a car, ride for recreation, or make the conscious and often politicized choice to forgo a car. Cycling is for those who are willing to stand out (Furness 2010, 113) or are forced by circumstances to do so (Lugo 2018, 42–43). The car, furthermore, remains aspirational for many of those who lack it (28).

A reluctance to embrace cycling also may be tied to material concerns beyond dollars and cents. Cycling lengthens most commutes, especially when compared with the private car, an important consideration given the financialization of time and the realities of time poverty.[21] Although most workplaces offer parking, few provide showers or changing rooms to accommodate those who power their own journey (Furness 2010, 4). Cycling in the United States is far more dangerous than in other industrialized nations; US cycling fatalities per kilometer are four to seven times higher than in the United Kingdom, Germany, the Netherlands, and Denmark (Buehler and Puchner 2020). Given that the United States also lacks universal healthcare, the risks of cycling extend beyond personal safety toward questions of economic security. When balancing the cost of the car, and its perceived safety, against the affordable bicycle and its potential catastrophic risk, the decision may favor the short-term cash outlay for a motor vehicle. Although the long-term health (and financial) benefits of cycling outweigh the risk of collision injury (Furness 2010, 4), concerns over the risk of injury itself and associated cash and time costs remain significant. Cyclists of color report additional fears of property crime; assault; and harassment, arrest, and violence at the hands of the police (Andersen 2017).

If veganism and cycling are inconvenient, it is because decades of political policy have rendered them such. Likewise, if their material costs appear great, it is because of enduring economic convention. Far too many cycling and vegan groups critique the priorities of the subsidy system but ignore its material, quotidian effects on individuals and communities who struggle to get by in an increasingly unequal society. Such oversights inform the associations of veganism and cycling with privilege.

Core Riders and Core Vegans: Rethinking Power and Privilege in Justice Efforts

Cycling advocacy has typically divided into vehicular and infrastructure interventions, both of which can replicate class, race, and gender privilege. Vehicular cycling, as Zack Furness (2010, 73) and Adonia Lugo (2018, 156) note, maintains conventional power differentials by assuming that it is the cyclist's responsibility to "take the lane," thereby treating as paradigmatic those who are accustomed to claiming space and having their demands respected—that is, middle- and upper-class, white, cisgender, normative-bodied men. Vehicular-cycling advocates tend to ignore the different risks of violence and threat experienced by riders depending on their race, gender, gender conformity, and apparent class status (Lugo 2018, 156). Infrastructure advocates, by contrast, acknowledge that road access is unequal and accept that cycling should be available to all, not just the most confident and skilled riders, which necessitates the physical accommodation of cycling. However, they nonetheless often replicate hierarchical and discriminatory assumptions as to whose cycling experience matters. Cycling-infrastructure efforts, as Melanie Hoffman (2016) and Adonia Lugo (2018, 138–50) point out, frequently operate as part of gentrification and city-planning efforts to court the "creative class." Bike lanes, for instance, often anticipate gentrification. Cycling advocacy has tended to focus on the needs and desires of its white, middle-class, voluntary adherents to the neglect of what Lugo (2018, 98n30), following Stephanie Pollack, calls *core riders* (those who use a bicycle for economic reasons rather than as a lifestyle choice) and *captive riders* (those for whom cycling is a necessity).[22]

To encourage the boycott of animal products, mainstream animal rights activists often claim that anyone can go vegan. While this may be technically true, choosing plant-based options is much harder in some circumstances than in others. Claims as to the ease of plant-based eating ignore the effects of food insecurity, systemic disinvestment (McClintock 2011), and discriminatory urban planning on consumption habits,[23] thereby repeating white, middle-class privilege.

In addition, mainstream vegan activists who represent their agenda as a single-issue movement replicate conventional power differentials. When insisting that a focus on animal rights excludes other concerns, such activists court potential vegans who haven't experienced (or possibly even witnessed) racism, sexism, economic deprivation, homophobia, transphobia, ableism, or anti-immigrant discrimination. This neglect of other social justice issues is particularly troubling given that oppressive systems do not operate in isolation but rather compound and reinforce one another; indeed, they are "composed of one another" (Ko 2019, 17). People of color, women, working-class people, immigrants, and disabled people have been historically animalized (Adams 1990, 1994; Jenkins, Struthers Montford, and Taylor 2020; Ko 2019; Ko and Ko 2017; Taylor 2017), signaling the extent to which these oppressive systems operate through one other. Those activists who foreground single-issue politics compound their insensitivity by referencing the same histories of animalization for which they claim there is no place in their movement— drawing comparisons, for instance, to slavery and other forms of violence against African Americans without committing to Black liberation struggles.[24] Those who insist that health-motivated plant-based eating "doesn't count" as veganism conversely rely upon white and middle-class privilege. That is, plant-based eating for health in systemically disinvested neighborhoods can be a survival strategy that is not limited to biomedical individualism and healthism (Freeman 2013) but also can extend outward as an act of community care through interventions such as community gardens and local, low-cost produce markets.

Much as mainstream cycling activists ignore the needs of core riders, mainstream animal rights advocates neglect the demographic we might think of as core vegans: those who embrace plant-based eating and compassion toward nonhumans out of respect for tradition, not as a rejection of the status quo. Some animal rights activists highlight the animal protection efforts of Victorian England and North America and the invention of the term *vegan* in the 1940s as the origins of their movement, without accounting for religious traditions, such as those of Jains, Hindus, Buddhists, Rastafarians, Ethiopia's Orthodox Christians, Seventh-day Adventists, Nation of Islam adherents, and Taoists, that prescribe or encourage plant-based eating. Even if some of these religious practices recommend plant-based eating for reasons of ritual purity or health and are not exclusively vegan, they nonetheless frame up diverse origins for abstaining from animal flesh and secretions. Mainstream veganism, like cycling advocacy, celebrates new adopters, who are often white and middle class, to the neglect of core constituents, many of whom are people of color, working class, or both. Both cycling advocacy and veganism, then, have tended to valorize their relatively privileged intentional adopters while sidelining the needs and contributions of their core adherents.

Because of this complex historical situation, it is imperative that cycling and veganism face their histories of implicit (and sometimes explicit) racism, sexism, class bias, and ableism. The potential of cycling and veganism to seriously derail societal injustice hinges upon an awareness of whose right to disrupt is respected and whose is dismissed, ignored, or criminalized. Likewise, more-just movements would attend to who has the means to choose inconvenience rather than having it thrust upon them. Attending to these considerations would deepen cycling and vegan advocacy, refining their connection to other justice movements by fighting for the needs of all cyclists and vegans, not just those most used to taking up space. This, in turn, would assist in a process of normalization that could enable a shift to plant-based and active transit economies.

Conclusion: Inconvenience and Imagination

Adonia Lugo (2018) suggests that no amount of vehicular cycling training or infrastructure investment can alter a "culture of street contempt" (149). Only by changing the culture and building human infrastructure, Lugo argues, can we alter how we interact with one another on the road; only such a shift, in turn, will make cycling safer. Lugo's insights extend beyond the transportation system, as our current economic and political systems are built on violence, subjugation, and disrespect.

Aspirational veganism and utility cycling—that is, efforts that reach beyond the individual and toward a vision of a more just world through restructured transportation and food politics—have the potential, if approached with reflection and care, to intervene into such violent systems. They can extend beyond individual consumption habits toward relationship building and acts of community support. Accordingly, they are acts of desire that allow the imagination of a more just world. Like Ahmed's feminist subjects, cycling and veganism activists "want the wrong things" and "build life worlds around those wants" (2010b, 593), world-building longings that have political capacity. Although, as we've seen, this advocacy frequently fails to realize its liberatory possibilities, it is this potential with which I want to conclude.

Cycling and vegan activism physicalize imagination. By posing questions such as whether euphoria could characterize the daily commute rather than anger and frustration, cycling activism envisions alternative relationships in public space. By asking what the food system could look like in the absence of animal exploitation, veganism likewise gestures toward alternative human–animal relationships versus those built on the inefficiencies, violence, and destruction of animal agriculture. Here, participants conjure alternatives not only through envisioning a future and discussing how to bring it about but also through lived, enacted, corporeal actions in the present. As such, these actions operate as what Susan Foster (2003) has identified as reflexive activism: efforts that protest unjust conditions while also living out their alternative.[25] They also align with both Anurima Banerji's (2010) understanding of paratopic practices, in which alternative ways of being exist alongside the hegemonic, and Ruth Levinas's (2013) argument that utopia operates in existing elements of society as well as in both concrete aims and imaginative desires for the future.

Physical practices, in their immediacy, allow us to live out other ways of living beyond what we see in front of us (O'Shea 2019). When we enact something corporeally, it becomes part of our life experience; it becomes real in a way that renders imagination more plausible. Practices such as aspirational veganism and activist utility cycling, particularly when engaged politically, allow the possibility of replacing a culture of contempt with one of wonder, awe, and empathy.[26]

Acts of imagination don't appear automatically or incidentally. They are crafted through practice. They come to bear when we have the opportunity to exercise them. This includes acts of political imagination.

Transportation cycling and veganism as justice interventions, then, need to create opportunities for practices of imagination. This includes moving beyond single-issue politics to reflect on what a more just world would truly look like, not just along lines of transportation, the environment, and the food system but also those of antiracism, decoloniality, gender inclusion, and economic equality.[27] Cycling and veganism advocates must work together to invite and protect the right to imagine on the part of all who wish to do so.

Notes

1. "To be willing to go against a social order . . . is to be willing to cause unhappiness, even if unhappiness is not your cause" (Ahmed 2010a, 2).
2. Examples include the unprotected bicycle route with its faded sharrow (a road marking consisting of two inverted "V" shapes above a bicycle that designates cyclists' part of the road when it is shared with motor vehiclists), which suggests that roads are made for cars and that cyclists are an afterthought; and the bike lane that runs for several blocks before disappearing, implying that cyclists are, literally and metaphorically, interlopers. The meat-free option that appears at the celebratory event after the other entrées are served signals its status as an exception; the vegan option at the institutional event relegated to a separate, hard-to-find table suggests that the meat avoider is, literally and metaphorically, out of line.
3. A 2014 Faunalytics study indicates that two-thirds of former vegetarians/vegans stated that they disliked that their diet "made them stand out from the crowd." Markowski and Roxburgh (2019) identify anti-vegan stigma as a primary obstacle to the uptake of plant-based eating. Similarly, researchers point to "the perception of cycling as lying outside the mainstream of American life discouraging bicycle use" (Pucher et al., in Furness 2010, 113).
4. "There is privilege in being able to choose risk instead of having no option but to take the risk" (Hoffman 2016, 24).
5. In this regard, veganism operates as a clear example of what Ahmed (2010 a, 2010b) labels "killjoy" behavior.
6. Of course, as I discuss in detail later in this chapter, vegans and cyclists are not distinct categories from those who experience discrimination on the basis of their race, ethnicity, immigration status, gender, sexuality, socioeconomic class, and ability.
7. Here, I am paraphrasing Melanie Joy's (2011) argument that meat consumption is not the absence of a belief system but is an ideology in itself.
8. Vasile Stanescu's (2019) meta-analysis of polls, which aimed to determine the percentage of vegetarians and vegans, found that several of these surveys revealed a large number of respondents who ate plant-based but did not identify as vegan or even vegetarian, thus raising the number of vegans-in-practice from the oft-reported 2–3.3 percent to 5 percent.

9. "Proximity gets in the way of other people's enjoyment of the right things, functioning as an unwanted reminder to histories that are disturbing" (Ahmed 2010b, 584).

10. "If you try to consume less, people sometimes react as though you're a privileged jerk. [. . .] Once I mentioned riding a bike, or when they saw my bike or some related accessory, strangers thought it was okay to unload their contempt for bicycling onto me in polite conversation. [. . .] The bike thing evokes a defensive reaction, as though I'd announced my moral superiority (I think vegetarians and vegans probably know what I'm talking about here)" (Lugo 2018, 118).

11. Tabulations that compare US driving to that in other industrialized nations indicate that Americans drive more miles per year than, for instance, their European, Australian, or Japanese counterparts (Federal Highway Administration 2018; "Transportation" 2020). Some calculations indicate that Chinese drivers accumulate more mileage per year than their American equivalents, but these figures are calculated per vehicle, not per capita.

12. Annalena Hope Hassberg (2020) points out that traditional African diets are "plant based and sustainable" as well as being agriculturally rich and diverse (85). Linda Fisher (2011) likewise states that "[t]he conventional Hollywood depiction of the Native American diet and lifestyle is false. The Americas were a rich and fertile land, providing plentiful berries, vegetables, nuts, beans, squash, roots, fruits, corn, and rice. Most tribal people survived comfortably eating meat sparingly while thriving on the cornucopia of the land" (115).

13. The eight highest meat-consuming nations are settler colonies (McCarthy 2020).

14. For example, permaculture techniques built around corn, beans, and squash are shared across the Indigenous Americas, where they are known as the *milpas* or the three sisters (*tres hermanas*). Indigenous Mexico Valley relied upon a system of *chinampas*, or floating gardens.

15. Michael Wise (2023) points out that ranchers, in the late nineteenth and early twentieth centuries, "formed private associations and public coalitions to support the eradication of wolves, coyotes, and other carnivorous wild animals" (103). Killing wildlife seen as competing with ranching continues to this day. This includes the targeted killing of "competitor" species such as bison and of carnivores who prey upon domesticated animals.

16. Ranchers hired assassins to target and kill homesteaders who attempted to raise crops on their land (Wise 2023, 103).

17. Karen Washington, activist and founder of the food justice organization Black Urban Gardeners, coined the term *food apartheid*.

18. As in the adage "time is money."

19. Highway funds were not used for mass transit until 1973 (Furness 2010, 52).

20. Louis Mendoza (2012) narrates an effort to cycle across the United States, which was complicated by traffic arteries that excluded bicycles. Mendoza was often forced to take circuitous routes and bring his bicycle on public transit because direct routes were navigable only by motor vehicle.

21. In cities with major traffic problems like Los Angeles, cycling can sometimes be faster than driving. It is, however, still perceived as slower and less convenient.

22. The neglect of core riders appears even in efforts to speak to their needs. Cycling author Dan Koeppel (2015) put the term *invisible cyclist* into currency

to describe those who ride cheap bicycles to and from work, often in alleys and on sidewalks, without protective gear, drawing a contrast to the lifestyle cyclist, typically a white, middle-class man with an expensive bicycle, designated cycling wear, a helmet, and other safety gear. Although Koeppel intended to (and did), raise awareness of how the experience of the road differs depending on a rider's race and class, his terminology repeats what it critiques by assuming the identity of the person doing the viewing.

23. Some vegan organizations, however, are designed to intervene into these very conditions. The Food Empowerment Project is a nonprofit organization that addresses food insecurity and advocates for the rights of food system laborers. Süprmärkt is a social-enterprise initiative that addresses food insecurity from a vegan perspective. Thrive Baltimore offers support to assist individual community members in transitioning toward healthier eating.

24. I draw this critique from Ko and Ko (2017) and Ko (2019).

25. In the larger project, of which this essay is part, I distinguish between reflexive activism, which includes an active engagement with and struggle against existing institutions, and the anarchist notion of prefiguration, which focuses on changing the individual and the immediate community in the interest of changing society.

26. I draw this list of (cultivated) emotions from Bryant (2006) (awe), Kheel (2007) (wonder), and Gruen (2015) (empathy).

27. My turn toward paradoxically practical utopias that provide imagined alternatives to multiple violent systems at once is inspired, in a general way, by Katja M. Guenther's (2020) reflection on the same in the context of companion animals and the shelter system.

References

Adams, Carol J. 1990. *The Sexual Politics of Meat*. New York: Continuum.

———. 2001. *Living among Meat-Eaters: The Vegetarian's Survival Handbook*. New York: Three Rivers Press.

———. 2007. "The War on Compassion." In *The Feminist Care Tradition in Animal Ethics*, edited by Josephine Donovan and Carol J. Adams, 21–38. New York: Columbia University Press.

———. 2018. *Burger*. New York: Bloomsbury Academic.

Ahmed, Sara. 2006. *Queer Phenomenology: Orientations, Objects, Others*. Durham, NC: Duke University Press.

———. 2010a. "Feminist Killjoys (and Other Willful Subjects)." *S & F Online* 8, no. 3 (Summer). http://sfonline.barnard.edu/polyphonic/ahmed_01.htm.

———. 2010b. "Killing Joy: Feminism and the History of Happiness." *Signs* 35 (3): 571–94.

Andersen, Michael. 2017. "For People of Color, Barriers to Biking Go Far beyond Infrastructure." *Streetsblog USA*, April 18, 2017. https://usa.streetsblog.org/2017/04/18/for-people-of-color-barriers-to-biking-go-far-beyond-infrastructure-study-shows/.

Badger, Emily. 2015. "The Myth of the American Love Affair with Cars." *Washington Post*, January 27, 2015. https://www.washingtonpost.com/news/wonk/wp/2015/01/27/debunking-the-myth-of-the-american-love-affair-with-cars/.

Banerji, Anurima. 2010. "Paratopias of Performance: The Choreographic Practices of Chandralekha." In *Planes of Composition: Dance and the Global*, edited by Andre Lepecki and Jenn Joy, 346–71. Kolkata, India: Seagull Press.

Bella, Timothy. 2021. "Teen Who Hit 6 Bicyclists with Truck While Allegedly Harassing Them Faces Criminal Charges, Authorities Say." *Washington Post*, November 9, 2021. https://www.washingtonpost.com/nation/2021/11/09/texas-teen-driver-bicyclists-truck-charges/.

Bergal, Jenni. 2021. "Biden Plan to Boost Public Transit Funding: Visionary or Wasteful?" *Pew Stateline*. April 28, 2021. https://www.pewtrusts.org/en/research-and-analysis/blogs/stateline/2021/04/28/biden-plan-to-boost-public-transit-funding-visionary-or-wasteful.

Bryant, Taimie L. 2006. "Animals Unmodified: Defining Animals/Defining Human Obligations to Animals." *University of Chicago Legal Forum* 1 (6): 137–94. https://chicagounbound.uchicago.edu/cgi/viewcontent.cgi?article=1390&context=uclf.

Buehler, Ralph, and John Puchner. 2020. "The Growing Gap in Pedestrian and Cyclist Fatality Rates between the United States and the United Kingdom, Germany, Denmark, and the Netherlands." *Transport Reviews* 41 (1): 48–72. https://www.tandfonline.com/doi/full/10.1080/01441647.2020.1823521.

Calvo, Luz, and Catriona Rueda Esquibel. 2015. *Decolonize Your Diet: Plant-Based Mexican-American Recipes for Health and Healing*. Vancouver: Arsenal Pulp Press.

Crosby, Alfred W. 1986. *Ecological Imperialism: The Biological Expansion of Europe 900–1900*. Cambridgeshire, NY: Cambridge University Press.

Danielle, Melissa. 2020. "Nutrition Liberation: Plant-Based Diets as a Tool for Healing, Resistance, and Self-Reliance." In *Sistah Vegan: Black Women Speak Out on Identity, Health, and Society*, edited by Harper, A. Breeze, 47–52. New York: Lantern Press.

Delbosc, Alexa, Farhana Naznin, Nick Haslam, and Narelle Haworth. 2018. "Dehumanization of Cyclists Predicts Self-Reported Aggressive Behaviour toward Them: A Pilot Study." *Transportation Research Part F* 62:681–89.

Dunbar-Ortiz, Roxanne. 2014. *An Indigenous People's History of the United States*. Boston: Beacon Press.

Eccleston, Ben. "Jill Phipps: 26 Years Since Campaigner Died at Coventry Airport." *Coventry News*, February 1, 2021. https://www.coventrytelegraph.net/news/coventry-news/jill-phipps-26-years-campaigner-19741341.

Faunalytics. 2014. "How Many Former Vegetarians and Vegans Are There?" December 2, 2014. https://faunalytics.org/how-many-former-vegetarians-and-vegans-are-there/.

Federal Highway Administration. 2018. "Annual Automobile Vehicle Miles of Travel (VMT) per Capita and Number of Automobiles per Capita 1997." Last modified May 31, 2022. US Department of Transportation. https://www.fhwa.dot.gov/ohim/onh00/bar4.htm.

Finley, Ron. 2013. "A Guerilla Gardener in South Central LA." Filmed February 2013. TED video, 10:30. https://www.ted.com/talks/ron_finley_a_guerrilla_gardener_in_south_central_la?language=en.

Fisher, Linda. 2011. "Freeing Feathered Spirits." In *Sister Species: Women, Animals, and Social Justice*, edited by Lisa Kemmerer, 110–16. Urbana: University of Illinois Press.

Food Empowerment Project. n.d. "Food Deserts." Accessed November 22, 2023. https://foodispower.org/access-health/food-deserts/.

Foster, Dawn. 2010. "Record and Ridicule: Female Cyclists Expose Sexist Idiots Online." *The Guardian*, August 18, 2010. https://www.theguardian.com /environment/green-living-blog/2010/aug/18/cycling-sexist-abuse-female.

Foster, Susan. 2003. "Choreographies of Protest." *Theatre Journal* 55 (3): 395–412.

Freeman, Andrea. 2013. "The Unbearable Whiteness of Milk: Food Oppression and the USDA." *UC Irvine Law Review* 3: 1251–79.

Furness, Zack. 2010. *One Less Car: Bicycling and the Politics of Automobility*. Philadelphia: Temple University Press.

Gilliver, Liam. 2021. "Vegan Café Receives 'Torrent' of Violent Threats over Plant-Based Menu." *Plant Based News*, May 10, 2021. https://plantbasednews.org /news/social-media/vegan-cafe-receives-violent-threats-over-plant-based-menu/.

Gross, Daniel. 2008. "Highways Paved with Gold." *Slate*, July 30, 2008. https://slate .com/business/2008/07/you-think-the-government-is-wasting-a-few-billion-a -year-on-mass-transit-subsidies-but-what-about-the-huge-subsidies-for-cars -and-trucks.html.

Gruen, Lori. *Entangled Empathy: An Alternative Ethic for Our Relationships with Animals*. New York: Lantern Books.

Guenther, Katja M. 2020. *The Lives and Deaths of Shelter Animals*. Stanford, CA: Stanford University Press.

Hamilton, Shane. 2008. *Trucking Country: The Road to America's Wal-Mart Economy*. Princeton, NJ: Princeton University Press.

Harper, A. Breeze. 2020. "Social Justice Beliefs and Addiction to Uncompromising Consumption: Food for Thought." In *Sistah Vegan: Black Women Speak Out on Identity, Health, and Society*, edited by A. Breeze Harper, 20–41. New York: Lantern Press.

Hassberg. Annalena Hope. 2020. "Nurturing the Revolution: The Black Panther Party and the Early Seeds of the Food Justice Movement." In *Black Food Matters: Racial Injustice in the Wake of Food Justice*, edited by Hanna Garth and Ashanté Reese, 82–106. Minneapolis: University of Minnesota Press.

Hoffman, Melanie. 2016. *Bike Lanes Are White Lanes: Bicycle Advocacy and Urban Planning*. Lincoln: University of Nebraska Press.

Hurt, Bryon, dir. 2012. *Soul Food Junkies*. Northampton, MA: Media Education Foundation.

Jenkins, Stephanie, Kelly Struthers Montford, and Chloë Taylor. 2020. *Disability and Animality: Crip Perspectives in Critical Animal Studies*. Milton Park, UK: Taylor and Francis.

jones, pattrice. "I Know Why the Caged Bird Screams." *Satya*, February 2006. https:// web.archive.org/web/20060322212026/http://satyamag.com/feb06/jones.html.

Joy, Melanie. 2011. *Why We Love Dogs, Eat Pigs, and Wear Cows: An Introduction to Carnism, the Belief System that Enables Us to Eat Some Animals and Not Others*. San Francisco: Conari Press.

Kheel, Marti. 2007. "The Liberation of Nature: A Circular Affair." In *The Feminist Care Tradition in Animal Ethics*, edited by Josephine Donovan and Carol J. Adams, 39–57. New York: Columbia University Press.

Ko, Aph. 2019. *Racism as Zoological Witchcraft: A Guide to Getting Out*. New York: Lantern Books.

Ko, Aph, and Syl Ko. 2017. *Aphro-ism: Essays on Pop Culture, Feminism, and Black Veganism from Two Sisters*. New York: Lantern Books.

Koeppel, Dan. "How Low-Income Cyclists Go Unnoticed." *Bicycling*, November 9, 2015. https://www.bicycling.com/news/a20049826/how-low-income-cyclists -go-unnoticed/.

Kuhn, Keegan, and John Lewis, dir. 2020. *They're Trying to Kill Us*. New York: Ohh Dip!!! Productions.

Levinas, Ruth. 2013. *Utopia as Method: The Imaginary Reconstitution of Society*. Basingstoke, UK: Palgrave Macmillan.

Lugo, Adonia E. 2018. *Bicycle/Race: Transportation, Culture, & Resistance*. Portland, OR: Microcosm Publishing.

MacInnis, Cara C., and Gordon Hodson. 2017. "It Ain't Easy Eating Greens: Evidence of Bias toward Vegetarians and Vegans from Both Source and Target." *Group Processes and Intergroup Relations* 20 (6). https://journals.sagepub.com /doi/abs/10.1177/1368430215618253.

Markowski, Kelly, and Susan Roxburgh. 2019. " 'If I Became a Vegan, My Family and Friends Would Hate Me': Anticipating Vegan Stigma as a Barrier to Plant-Based Diets." *Appetite* 135:1–9.

Martin, Randy. 2002. *The Financialization of Daily Life*. Philadelphia: Temple University Press.

McCarthy, Niall. "The Countries That Eat the Most Meat." *Statista*, May 5, 2020. https://www.statista.com/chart/3707/the-countries-that-eat-the-most-meat/.

McClintock, Nathan. 2011. "From Industrial Garden to Food Desert: Demarcated Devaluation in the Flatlands of Oakland, California." In *Cultivating Food Justice: Race, Class, and Sustainability*, edited by Alison Hope Alkon and Julian Agyeman, 89–120. Cambridge, MA: MIT Press.

Mendoza, Luis Gerard. 2012. *A Journey across Our America: A Memoir on Cycling, Immigration, and the Latinoization of the U.S.* Austin: University of Texas Press.

Minson, Julia A., and Benoit, Monin. 2011. "Do-Gooder Derogation: Disparaging Morally Motivated Minorities to Defuse Anticipated Reproach." *Social Psychology and Personality Science* 3 (2). https://journals.sagepub.com/ doi/10.1177/1948550611415695.

Norton, Peter D. 2011. *Fighting Traffic: The Dawn of the Motor Age in the American City*. Cambridge, MA: MIT Press.

Ornelas, lauren. 2010. *Shining a Light on the Valley of Heart's Delight*. San Jose, CA: Food Empowerment Project.

O'Shea, Janet. 2019. *Risk, Failure, Play: What Dance Reveals about Martial Arts Training*. New York: Oxford University Press.

Paarlberg, Robert. 2015. *The United States of Excess: Gluttony and the Dark Side of American Exceptionalism*. New York: Oxford University Press.

Patel, Raj. 2012. *Stuffed and Starved: The Hidden Battle for the World Food System*. New York: Melville House.

Potter, Will. 2011. *Green Is the New Red: An Insider's Account of a Social Movement under Siege*. San Francisco: City Lights Books.

Reese, Ashanté. 2019. *Black Food Geographies: Race, Self-Reliance, and Food Access in Washington, D.C.* Chapel Hill: University of North Carolina Press.

Reid, Carlton. 2015. *Roads Were Not Built for Cars*. Washington, DC: Island Press.

Revkin, Andrew. 1990. *The Murder of Chico Mendes and the Burning of the Amazon Rain Forest*. Washington, DC: Island Press.

Reynolds, George. "Why Do People Hate Vegans?" *The Guardian*, October 25, 2019. https://www.theguardian.com/lifeandstyle/2019/oct/25/why-do-people-hate-vegans.

Ritchie, Hannah. "If the World Adopted a Plant-Based Diet, We Would Reduce Global Agricultural Land Use from 4 to 1 Billion Hectares." *Our World in Data*, March 4, 2021, https://ourworldindata.org/land-use-diets.

Rosella, Louie. 2020. "Truck Driver Charged in Incident at Burlington Slaughterhouse that Left Animal Rights Protestor Dead." *Toronto Star*, July 20, 2020. https://www.thestar.com/news/gta/2020/07/20/truck-driver-charged-in-incident-at-burlington-slaughterhouse-that-left-animal-rights-protester-dead.html.

Rothstein, Richard. 2017. *The Color of Law: A Forgotten History of How Our Government Segregated America*. New York, London: Liveright Publishing Corporation.

Ryerson, Megan. "Episode 351: The Rules Require Death." *Talking Headways: A Streetsblog Podcast*, September 16, 2021. https://streetsblog.libsyn.com/episode-351-the-rules-require-death.

Schlosser, Eric. 2001. *Fast Food Nation: The Dark Side of the All-American Meal*. Boston: Houghton Mifflin.

Simon, David Robinson. 2013. *Meatonomics: How the Rigged Economies of Meat and Dairy Make You Consume Too Much—and How to Eat Better, Live Longer, and Spend Smarter*. San Francisco: Conari Press.

Stanescu, Vasile. "Guest Post: Response to the Claim that Only 2% (or Less) of People in the United States Are Vegetarian." *Critical Animal* (blog), July 1, 2019. http://www.criticalanimal.com/2019/07/guest-post-response-to-claim-that-only.html.

Taylor, Sunaura. 2017. *Beasts of Burden: Animal and Disability Liberation*. New York: New Press.

Tinoco, Matt. "After Two Hit-and-Runs, LA Bike Riders Are Shaken, Plead for Safer Streets." *Los Angeles Curbed*, April 14, 2018. https://la.curbed.com/2018/4/14/17230828/bicyclist-killed-los-angeles-frazier.

Twine, Richard. 2014. "Vegan Killjoys at the Table—Contesting Happiness and Negotiating Relationships with Food Practices." *Societies* 4: 623–29.

Urry, John. 2004. "The 'System' of Automobility." *Theory, culture & society*. 21 (4–5): 25–39.

Waterson, Jim. "Waitrose Magazine Editor Quits after Joke about Killing Vegans." *The Guardian*, October 31, 2018. https://www.theguardian.com/business/2018/oct/31/waitrose-magazine-editor-william-sitwell-steps-down-over-email-mocking-vegans.

Williamson, John. "Federal Aid to Roads and Highways since the 18th Century: A Legislative History." *Congressional Research Service*. January 6, 2012.

Wise, Michael. 2023. *Native Foods*. Fayetteville: University of Arkansas Press.

Lawson "Frogi" Pruett, at work delivering what the customer said was a one-piece, one-pound delivery that was closer to twenty pieces and fifty pounds. *Photograph from the author's collection.*

CHAPTER TWO

Stay in Your Lane

The Interconnectedness of Being a Vegan Bike Messenger

LAWSON "FROGI" PRUETT

Bike couriers move. We bob and weave cleanly and decidedly. We ignore painted lines, signs, and directives intended to direct those traveling in an entirely different way than us; our cycling lives in the streets is completely different. Defiantly free, cyclists have a markedly unique experience in the frustrating and congested urban landscape. Opposed to stagnation and the status quo of traffic jams, parallel parking, and road rage, we bend this system and its landscape to our will and make it our own. Rushing "haphazardly" yet fully aware through the urban sprawl for most of us to make just enough money to get by and retain bragging rights. We narrowly avoid one collision after the next. Splitting lanes, holding on to buses, hopping curbs and swinging wide out of the way of potholes and high-set manhole covers, zipping through empty-ish construction zones, making use of sidewalks and crosswalks as safety and traffic allow, avoiding what to us are well-known grates just wide enough to admit a bicycle tire placed smack dab in the middle of the lane without so much as a second thought by the Department of Transportation (DOT). We are traveling in some cases faster than cars, able to move with more freedom in and out of pockets cars couldn't even open their doors in.

This isn't to say that this is how most of us WANT to navigate the world were things a bit more "friendly" for us . . . but I'm not going to pretend there isn't a decent amount of pride, skill, and excitement involved. I do not say this to self-aggrandize or to celebrate the defiance of "breaking rules"; it is just how we couriers have learned to engage with our environment. Of course, most all of us start out observing "the rules of the road" until we get doored in the gravel-obstructed bike lane left by street sweepers or attacked by an irate driver saying that we were "in their way" when they had another two lanes as they race from one red light to another. Most all of us have been hit, brushed, had things thrown at us, been run off the road, or outright attacked while following the rules to a "T." When that happens you have two options: make it work for you or give up.

After enough of that, with us still having to get around the city—and make a paycheck—most of us begin to realize that, in order to meaningfully and effectively get around, we have to remain aware of the rules but bend and break them, safely and decidedly. In my experience it wasn't until I was comfortable breaking the rules and standing my ground that I felt confident to take the lane effectively and "legally." I've been hit and chased, had guns pulled on me, been taken out by "urban transport scooters" and attacked, and experienced the destruction of my bikes and harassment by police, all while following the rules. With all that experience, I learned that you take your lane, you stick to it, and be ready to break rules when you have to, because most drivers don't realize that these lanes are our lanes too. Maybe it's a rule dictated by fear and size, but so many cyclists feel bullied by drivers and struggle to take the lane they are legally entitled to take. I advocate standing for your rights as a cyclist and taking your lane, but with so many drivers convinced that my following the rules is somehow breaking the rules, I have zero problem showing them exactly what breaking rules means.

As a cyclist and maybe more specifically as a bike courier, I make my way daily operating in and around a series of systems that oppose my efforts. Posted speed limits are routinely ignored in high-traffic areas; bike lanes are often used as additional parking or an easy spot for delivery and rideshare drivers to drop off in with next to no warning; bike lanes offer no safe way or place to turn through or around traffic, or they are littered with rocks and trash except in the touristy areas, which present their own issues, like scooters and dog walkers. Bikes can easily be left and locked to signs with no damage, but if we get seen locking up there, we have to go around the corner and lock to "designated bike parking"—often overcrowded with no way to lock without piling on top of another bike or risking having your bike locked to another.

We develop our own methods of getting around safely and effectively, but we are often met with malice in the face of our opposition. Most negative interactions seem to regard me as a mixture between a wannabe Chris Froome and/or human trash. We have to navigate around what is available, break what rules we have to, and still try our best to interact with this system in a way to not get hurt or risk further aggravating someone wielding what can easily be a several-thousand-pound weapon. It's not just peloton-riding, Spandex-wearing, would-be Power Rangers on Pinarellos out for their morning exercise before a desk job who are impacted by car culture. It's couriers, it's food-delivery drivers, it's folks riding rusted hybrids to the bus to go to work, it's kids who can't drive, it's scooter renters and share-bike riders heading to lunch. It's so much more than frustrating; it's dangerous. It's also incredibly expensive. It's a systematically car-centric culture that makes placation efforts for recreational cyclists while doing very little to steer the cultural discourse regarding alternative transportation. It's like having vegan options at a steakhouse: yes, I can order a salad with oil and vinegar, no croutons and no cheese, and maybe I can convince the waiter to ask if the asparagus is cooked in butter or not . . . but it's very clear the menu isn't for me.

The obnoxious yet somehow calmly aggressive movements we cyclists make are often mistaken as a disregard for our safety. We see three steps and five car lengths ahead at all times, inherently aware of the danger before us. If we do not stick our lines, we are accosted for taking our lives into our hands in the face of those intent on misunderstanding what it is exactly that is truly dangerous. I am more concerned with getting hit by someone texting who missed their light and so decides to gun it last minute, than I am about running that same light when the traffic is clear. It feels more like we are threatening their sense of order and control. People are not usually concerned about our safety, as they so often tout, but more concerned with the rules. We ride defiant, reflecting what I can only assume seems to the uninitiated like a harsh caricature of our modern world.

I encounter a cruel portrait of the absurdity of modern life with drivers no more worried about the corpses on their plate than the existential crisis facing all of us as their world quickly loses its "sterile" and "safe" day-to-day feeling. If these people didn't need a paycheck, they wouldn't be doing this. They wouldn't be able to suffer hour-long commutes into town to do mind-numbing tasks followed by a two-hour commute home, all to be celebrated on the weekend by overindulgence and consumerist narcissism. This isn't everyone, but in my experience this is a vast majority of people in our capital-centric culture. Humans stripped of the experience of living in favor of following rules and feeling safe. If these people needed to eat and they had to hunt, skin, and kill the animals that come prepackaged at the supermarket, most of them couldn't do it. These days being vegan is easier than ever—there are literally options every single place you go—but so many people make excuses or justify continuing as nonvegans based on a claimed "human need" for animal products . . . while ignoring everything else that makes us human. On a planet struggling to maintain balance, where social norms are cultural and generally trivial, where the value of product is valued over the value of the workers, where the value of flesh to consume is worth more than the life lost to produce it . . . of course folks don't like it. Cognitive dissonance is a hell of a drug, y'all.

For me, veganism, cycling, and radical sobriety are all the same thing—I got into them all at around the same time in my life. They filled a void or at the very least helped me notice that there was a void. A sense of personal purpose announced and communicated through my actions whether I say anything or not. Committing full stop as more than just part of my lifestyle but a heartfelt, strongly held set of beliefs that lined up with my personal sense of community, ethics, and morality. Abstaining to the best of my abilities from a culture that I think makes it difficult to stand on your own or be your own person.

Part of why veganism and cycling intersect is that they both require you to be focused, while working around a system that doesn't serve you; you simultaneously pay a higher cost than most folks around you, despite needing fewer resources. Placated with signage and buzzwords, there's nothing like getting buzzed by an SUV with a license plate that sports a "Share the Road" motto or realizing that your new "plant-based" protein shake has grass-fed whey protein from "only the happiest cows." Dodging a new pothole or discovering that the tofu dish at the local restaurant boasting veg options is cooked in chicken or beef stock are frustratingly similar. Whether I am dodging gravel in the "bike lane" from one of the two hundred high-rises going up or eating at a new restaurant and scouring the menu for hidden ingredients—it's easier than it used to be, but still feels harder than it should be.

For me, the most obvious place that these two things cross is when I am ordering lunch while working. Locking my bike (usually to a sign because bike racks are occupied with scooters or not there at all), rushing in between deliveries, considering food prep time, scanning for short lines before even entering the building. Looking at the menu with the "age-old questions" ready to ask at any time: "This doesn't have cheese, right?" "I'll have the #5 as a bowl with no dairy." "Can I get this with no egg?" "If I leave off the meat is it still four dollars more than it should be?" I rarely say the word *vegan*, as I find that word often confuses people or prompts an even longer wait, and time is something I generally don't have a lot of. How I order is getting clearer and clearer, as I use my common sense and ask questions, so after ten years or so abstaining from animal products, I generally know what to ask. Sometimes I get people asking me "Is ranch okay?" or "There's just a little fish sauce, is that all right?" or "We can just cook the chicken without the breading if you're gluten free." I am beside myself that I have the luxury to even have the ability and resources to eat out sometimes. I am even more ecstatic that there are whole menus, grocers, and restaurants dedicated to vegan items. But that doesn't mean I can't be somewhat "put out" by the feeling of having to explain what to me seems very easy.

And don't even get me started on having the unintentional "ethics" conversation with a stranger. Very often these days I have twenty-somethings behind the counter responding with, "I want to be vegan," "I tried veganism for a week and almost died twice," "I was going to be vegan but I lift weights so I can't," all of which are easy enough to parlay into conversation about how to "go" vegan as if it's a switch you flip. . . . Unless I'm asked, though, I generally don't go deep into my reasoning for veganism, as that is a much heavier topic I don't want to have while hungry. I will make short conversation, let them know where to look for information and about any vegan-centric events and places to eat (sometimes I have pamphlets to hand them from my time as a more engaged activist). In those conversations, I often toss in that I have been vegan for around ten years, not to "brag" but because that tends to help subconsciously drive the point home that it's not just a fringe or trendy thing that came around with the advent of the Impossible Whopper or the Beyond Sausage, that this is something that a lot of us commit to for a variety of reasons.

Most people engaging in this discourse are privileged enough to make choices about what it is we eat. There are, of course, people with extenuating circumstances, and that's a whole different conversation. But when it comes down to it, we are all navigating the same system and have the same capacity to make positive choices. When I tell people that I race bikes, work on a bike, weightlift, spar, do yoga, parent my high-energy toddler, take care of house chores, and get active time in with my partner, it kind of defeats the "I need protein," "We're carnivores," "I sometimes ride mountain bikes on the weekends," "I'm top of the food chain" arguments before they have a chance to make them. If I'm out here doing the most as a vegan and I'm not lacking in physicality or life in general, then the only thing you can offer me is excuses. If my life is crafted with courage, virtue, and strength, if my actions are backed by my beliefs and not by fear or excuses or convenience, there is no hole you can poke and nothing you can say that will convince me that a good amount of people are more content not challenging the things around them.

The sad fact is that bike messengers and commuters are tolerated at best and killed more often than I'd like to think about. It's getting better year after year in regard to awareness as more and more people are switching to alternative transport. That said, in the last few years we have lost more members of the messenger community than I know how to enumerate. More specifically for myself, my friend Robyn was hit and killed while on the job in New York. A young person who organized races, worked hard for equality, overcame obstacles most people can never even imagine, and did so with an infectious smile and a warm heart. They were a bright, wholesome, strong light to the community as a whole and losing Robyn had such a profound impact on me. Over the years I've lost quite a few people, but losing someone so young, so vibrant, someone so seemingly un-fuck-withable just broke me. Robyn once described themselves in passing as my "biggest fan" because we had such similar feelings and circumstances, and we connected like family. They were one of the kindest people I have ever known and losing them was one of my toughest losses. Even though we weren't incredibly close, the parallels of being from the South and working a difficult job, our connection to veganism and being straight edge, and the sense of community we drew from our profession and our passions connected us instantaneously. For several days after they were struck I lost the lionheart I needed to get around safely. I was riding slowly, constantly looking over my shoulder, death-gripping my handlebars, and just generally feeling a little weak and scared, emotionally broken.

The messenger community is small and heavily interconnected. A lot of us are at or around the poverty line or can't find jobs that we "fit" at. Some of us are in college and go on to be internationally recognizable.

LAWSON "FROGI" PRUETT

Spike Lee, Anthony Bourdain, GZA of Wu-Tang Clan, Chuck Palahniuk . . . all of them at one point were just moving packages and grinding out a living. We see a side of life that a lot of people never even know exist. Most of us who have been doing this for a while have suffered some weird and seriously dangerous shit, and it connects us in the ways a lot of communities tend to form, around a weird sense of pride in our collective trauma. We all to some degree know (or at the very least know about) each other. We find camaraderie and family in a way very few jobs could possibly bring about. We are a small, dedicated group and have ties not just nationwide but worldwide. No matter where you're at, you face the same dangers, the same attitudes, and the same stressors. We watch out for each other far and wide and rely heavily on one another to get through our day.

Vegans and cyclists alike have our own language, our own separate experiences, our own heroes, our own beliefs. They are all individualized and shaped by each person's life experience, but we all share these commonalities, or at least all share the awareness of these experiences. In that way we are all connected, as a lot of other communities are, by shared history, shared culture, shared experience. We are all doing things the best we know how for ourselves, and, whether consciously or unconsciously, standing up against a culture that is increasingly unethical and disconnected from nature. I think for me, the purpose of living this way is to get the most out of my natural body and experience like we did centuries ago, living in defiance of a world bent on destruction and distraction.

I generally have a pretty unbalanced diet of protein bars/shakes, fruit (mostly oranges and watermelon recently), burritos/wraps, and any sort of Chinese or Vietnamese noodle/rice bowls if I buy food while working. I generally look for food I can grab and go.

CHAPTER THREE

Caring for the Human Horse
Reflections on Cycling and the Animal Senses

MICHAEL D. WISE

Before I was a vegan, I was a bike racer, and for many years I could never easily explain either facet of my life to friends or family members. The bike racing, though, stood out as especially unusual. The compulsion to "turn myself inside out," as they say, either at the local Tuesday Night Worlds, or at a weekend stage race of middling significance, seemed inscrutable even as I did it week after week. Winning didn't matter to me. Often I sat up toward the end of a race, not bothering to contest the final sprint, not fully exhausted but still satisfied as I rolled across the line mid-pack, letting others jostle for bragging rights. Nevertheless, by my early twenties I had cobbled together enough inadvertent podium finishes to upgrade through the road and mountain bike categories, setting the general expectation I was there to compete. My father, also a cyclist, joked (approvingly) that I was no racer; that I had no killer instinct. Instead, I made friends during races. The seriousness with which others took the task of achieving victory at amateur events—in a sport few people cared about—seemed comical. I gravitated toward the pranksters of the peloton, joining and leading teams of riders who shared a joie de vivre, shirking the stoic, Spartan heroism so common to the Lance Armstrong doping era, affecting instead a "journey is the destination" vibe, partly to indulge my inexplicable love of riding hard for no good reason, and partly to salve my ego at races where the on-form riders dropped me like a bag of hammers—an outcome that occurred more frequently each season as my underrecovered legs endured even more reckless training miles.

What most appealed to me was the heavy, rhythmic work of pedaling the bike. It was a tonic more reliable than expectations of rest-
week supercompensation, let alone any promise of palmarès. My favorite
workout was usually a late pre-season base-miles ride. One year when
Easter fell in March, my friend "Tuba Adam" (a former Texas time trial
champion who also played the tuba) convinced me (it wasn't hard) to
add some more miles to our usual six-hour Sunday loop. The winds were
favorable, increasing in speed as we made our late turn toward home,
and we rolled tempo side by side, covering the extra fifty miles in less
than two hours. By the time we made it back, clicking out of the pedals
whumped my kneecaps like they were empty steel tanks being banged
with a wrench, a network of inflamed tendons reverberating from my
ankles to my wrists. Sour secretions of lactic acid coated the back crev-
ices of my mouth. The sore tension between leg bone and muscle fiber
undulated with each breath, and I craved that skeletal sensation of my
legs aching.

One night, when some noncycling friends of mine roasted a chicken
and pulled the flesh from its bones, I felt a visceral kinship with the bird,
realizing—startlingly—the insecurity of my own meaty body. My vegan
journey accelerated from there. Not out of a concern for eating healthier,
but because the more I rode and raced, I felt less like a human and more
like an animal.

■   ■   ■

Although I couldn't articulate it at the time, these animal experiences
on and off the bike led me down a path of intellectual questioning, first
oriented toward historical understandings of animal–human difference, then toward cultural histories and geographies of the senses that
explored how quotidian, bodily activities—such as eating—served as
powerful expressions of place and identity. Along the way I earned a PhD
and became a vegan and a tenured history professor. At the heart of my
work was always a concern with how the so-called humanities defined
the boundaries of the human, an unease that emanated from my animal
sensations. I wanted to situate ideas about "human subjectivity" within
their appropriate historical contexts, assisting with the broader interdis-
ciplinary project of the animal studies field to expose the problematic

differences between normative subjectivities of human and nonhuman animals, while contributing to then-nascent conversations about the possible emergence of a "posthumanities." I read a steady diet of authors I admired from philosophy, ecocriticism, ethology, and gender studies, including many contributors to this volume. Perhaps ironically, though, it took many years for me to more fully concede the extent to which my own bodily experiences—mostly as a bike racer—drove my research agenda.

Part of that delay came from shame. I knew few academics who shared my taste for bike racing, even among those I knew were cyclists. In the cycling mecca of Portland, Oregon, for instance, I raced for a few years with a chemistry prof from Portland State and a political scientist at Reed, but my own colleagues at Lewis & Clark College looked at me like I was crazy when I emerged from my office at 5 p.m., clad in spandex, rolling out on my 'cross bike for an evening race at Alpenrose. One time as I left campus, the dean, who I'm guessing didn't consider the possibility a bike racer could be one of her faculty, buzzed me aggressively in her BMW.

At my peril, perhaps, I also remained an enthusiastic bike commuter as I entered higher education as a professor, rather than as a student. But I soon found that among our scholarly ranks, the proportion of faculty bikes on the racks was minuscule. On the days I didn't commute to a race after work, I locked up my commuter bike—a family heirloom yet otherwise unremarkable cro-moly Trek 830 (purchased, in 1994, from Landis Cyclery in Phoenix)—alongside bikes belonging to students and the occasional staff member. (On race days, however, I would cheerfully shoulder my 6.8 kilograms of carbon upstairs to my office so it could live in climate-controlled comfort.)

It hit me, at some point, that there must be a connection between the sluggish disruption of the humanities with the scant faculty representation at the bike racks. Of course, in graduate school we all read the critics who interrogated the problematic origins of the modern university in the Cartesian separation of mind from body, an ordering that elevated "thought" above its embodied groundings while producing classroom protocols that alienated our ideas from our experiences and established a campus that, for the last five centuries, has served to replicate social and ecological inequalities. Even so, when I showed up sweaty to class, wearing my bike helmet, my department chair (an environmental historian) gave me a dirty look—the so-called bodily turn in the humanities notwithstanding.

■　■　■

I came from a family of horse traders who (until a century ago) raised, broke, bought, and sold horses. On my dad's side, my grandfather's father died in 1930 after getting kicked in the chest by a horse in the barn. Soon after that, our families' equine relationships shifted from work toward play as tractors overtook horses across the American farmscape. My parents have a horse to this day, a twenty-four-year-old liver chestnut Morgan named Time, whom my sixty-eight-year-old mother jumps in competitions. Although I've always preferred to ride and race bikes instead of horses, caring for the animals has long been a personal point of reference.

I think about my mom grooming Time before and after every ride, comparing the pain she takes to care, clean, and prepare with my own rituals of bike maintenance: pumping the tire pressure correctly, ensuring that the tires are seated on their rims the right way—bent over much as one during a hoof inspection. I have a particular way of lubricating the chain: putting a single drop on each roller, then spinning the cranks backward while wiping down the excess with an old T-shirt (one that won't leave any lint) and using a clean patch of the same fabric to clean off the rear derailleur pulleys, then shifting up and down the rear cassette, tightening barrel adjusters as needed. After a hard 'cross race in the mud, the whole bike needs cleansed: stripped down to the frame, washed, dried, and reassembled; bearings in the hubs, bottom bracket, pedals, and headset either regreased or replaced; each spoke wiped down with microfiber.

"Inanimate" though it may be, a bike nevertheless embodies a life of its own, and it is life that can only last so long. When a bike dies, its rider mourns. It happens often, especially with race bikes engineered for light weight rather than longevity. A single rough ride can ruin them, or at least leave them disfigured. Once, goofing around after a criterium in Saint Paul, I crumpled an aluminum down tube trying to ride a dirt jump from the drops of my road bike. Carbon, of course, is even less robust, as well as expensive enough to set off a mild panic attack even when leaning it up against the plastic start-line porta-potty. Experiencing and accepting

MICHAEL D. WISE

these inevitable losses is one of the things that separate a bike rider from a mere bike collector ("Never trust a bike without scratches," counseled an old teammate), and the occasional race bike that outlives its career tends to become a cherished member of the household.

One of my old favorites is a full-suspension cross-country mountain bike with twenty-six-inch wheels that I now ride daily with my six-year-old son on the hardpacked Texas single track. It makes noises that can't be fixed, since fifteen years ago I raced it in deep mud at a six-hour race in Washington State, where everyone had to pressure-wash their bike in the pit after each lap just to keep the wheels and cranks spinning. I took things a step farther out on the course, winning the race by squirting chain lube out of my water bottle while riding in order to keep the brake calipers, chain, suspension pivots, and other delicate parts moving, but that bike has never been the same. Nevertheless, it's a survivor, and I wouldn't trade it for any of the shiny new rigs we see at the trailhead each day, most destined for a scratch-free career collecting dust in a garage.

■ ■ ■

Bike racers shave their legs for two specific reasons: it's easier to massage legs that aren't hairy after a race or a workout, and it's also easier to clean out road rash if there isn't any hair. On the latter count, I learned the hard way that you need to shave all the way up the outsides of your glutes for this to be effective, not just the skin that shows below the hem of your bike shorts. Shaving the inner parts is also important, but mostly to prevent chafing; chamois cream and bib shorts are also essential.

Raised as a boy in the United States, where shaving your legs is a symbol of effeminacy and a sexist expectation of women, I found a strange power the first time I did it myself. I started with a beard trimmer, then transitioned to Barbasol and a safety razor, amazed at how much easier and more pleasurable the whole experience was than I had expected. Before long I had mastered the art of dragging a pink disposable razor across my legs in the shower to maintain a glossy hairlessness, smothering any razor burn after the fact with body oil and fistfuls of lotion.

Aside from special trips to southern California, for San Dimas or Redlands, the early-season calendar in the Pacific Northwest usually featured a mix of cold rain and wet roads. In the peloton, it was often hard to tell if it was raining or not, since the spray coming off the wheels in front of you splattered your legs, face, and forearms in an incessant wake, the excess water wicking away and leaving a slurry of road grit. Wearing full-length tights to stay warm was therefore never an option, since they would soak up the road like giant sponges, each pant leg weighing about fifteen pounds.

Under such conditions, another advantage of smooth skin was that my hairless pores more easily took up embrocation, a greasy ointment of capsaicin and menthol, activated by water, that provided an effective illusion of warmth down to the freezing mark, transforming cold, naked legs into red-hot tongues. My own concoction stayed strong enough to last well beyond the end of a race, and back home I would have to wipe down with a dry cloth before taking a shower, otherwise the piercing, fiery sensation (difficult to describe) of pressurized water hitting superheated leg skin would be overwhelming. Applying embro also required careful attention. If done too early, and necessity arose to take your skinsuit off and put it on again, the fabric might pull the unctuous paste into places where it wasn't intended.

These were rituals one might call "self-care," but they were also practices—of shaving, smearing, wiping, massaging—that generated feelings of self-alienation. I prepped my legs for a race as I might prep a chicken for the oven, removing plumage and adding oil and seasoning. Mid-race, I'd catch myself salivating with delight at the thought of my après-course recovery, when I'd lay on my back, resting my legs vertically against a wall, gravity pooling the drippings of lactic acid into the cavities of my stomach and spine. My legs were no longer part of me; they were separate, cramping, spasmic beasts of burden, reliant on husbandry. When I shaved my legs, I was a shepherd shearing sheep.

■   ■   ■

Two therapists and a psychiatrist diagnosed me with ADHD shortly before I turned forty, the case overdetermined by a lifetime of fidgeting, restless leg syndrome, bad high school report cards, and—of course—an inexplicable career as a bike racer. The hyperactivity of racing, they told me, along with hundreds of hours I had spent in the saddle each year, had constituted an unintentional coping apparatus, helping me to ward off anxiety and sensory dysregulation. As the tide of middle age crept

MICHAEL D. WISE

Returning from a ride with Augie—and with Darcy and Bingley, the canine members of our household. *Photograph by Jennifer Jensen Wallach.*

upon me, however, new caregiving responsibilities, professional duties, and other obligations—not to mention injuries—had brought me to a point where I had to quit bike racing cold turkey.

Fortunately, my young child had just reached an age where he was ready to ride. Nurturing his precocious ability and interest in cycling meant that we hit the trail after school almost every day, which not only reintegrated some significant saddle time into my weekly routine (at five years old, Augie could easily ride fifteen miles of pavement or ten miles of dirt, which kept us out for an hour or two each day), but also reframed my entire perspective on cycling and sensory input. Diagnosed himself with neurological divergences, including autism and some motor planning issues associated with delays in verbal communication, Augie's general areas of challenge—like many people on the spectrum—also comprised some specific domains of incredible talent. In his case, it was clear from the moment he started crawling that he was an athlete, and as he grew older (and larger), his sense of balance and muscular endurance developed exponentially. For instance, he was the only toddler I had ever seen who would modulate his pace while running. Instead of sprinting for a few seconds and then taking a break, Augie would literally run for miles, lifting and lowering his tempo above and below threshold in order to maximize his speed without blowing up. It really sank in one morning at the Huntington Library gardens, the day after his third birthday, when his mom and dad (on a research trip) ran for four continuous miles while chasing him through the desert garden, the Australian garden, the Japanese garden, and then back uphill through the bamboo to the art galleries. At that point Augie finally sat in his stroller and let us go back to the archives.

At one of Augie's occupational therapy sessions, I learned about the "seven senses," which included vestibular and proprioceptive senses in addition to sight, hearing, smell, taste, and touch. In tandem, these sixth and seventh senses govern body position, movement, and the application of force. Excluded from the fivefold pantheon of the "human senses," discussions of proprioception and vestibulation were uncommon outside of medical or clinical settings, and typically seemed most relevant when patients suffered from an absence of one or more gross motor skills, a presentation sometimes generalized as "low muscle tone" in the ambiguous language of developmental pediatrics.

Empowered by this new knowledge, though, I began wondering if proprioception and vestibulation might represent the "animal senses" in relation to the so-called human ones. It was a crude, categorical dissociation, of course, but perhaps a starting point for theorizing my own vegan–cycling subjectivity. Did it help explain why my legs felt like roasted drumsticks after a hard ride? Why did my son and I both need to spin ourselves out at least a few times each week? Is this why, when I sometimes acquiesced to Augie's demands to trailer our family dogs (a pair of Chihuahua mixes named Darcy and Bingley) on the back of my bike to the dog park, Augie leapt off his bike immediately upon arrival, took off his shoes, and crawled on all fours with his canine friends, barking with them in unison?

■ ■ ■

Charles Darwin asserted that the evolution of man from animal relied on his ability "to stand firmly on his feet," allowing the free use of his hands, "so admirably adapted to act in obedience to his will," without which he "could not have attained his present dominant position in the world" (Zimmer 2007, 88). Darwin was a man of both his era and his affluent class, who over the course of a nineteenth-century lifetime witnessed an energy revolution in transportation from muscle power to fossil fuels. Travel was increasingly conducted from a seated position, the legs at rest and the hands freer than ever to facilitate human ascension, whether by reading the newspaper on the train or smoking a pipe in the gentleman's car. "So it was that the elites of Europe," quipped Tim Ingold (2011), "came to conduct and write about their travels as if they had no legs" (38).

Cycling devolves the human body back toward its earlier animal form—more ape than Darwinian man. On a race bike, legs and feet take priority over arms and hands: head fixed toward the ground, neck straining to follow the wheels ahead, panting for breath, ignorant of all the heavens (and hoping the race promoters didn't put a climb up Mount Olympus on the course). Even with your hands in the drops, you steer with your hips, dipping the one inside as far as possible without clipping the bottom of your pedal as you roll through the corner—your burning calves, quads, hamstrings, and ass dropping hundreds of watts as you exit and rotate up, commanding all the blood and oxygen; your hands simply ready to feather the brakes or shift the gears up an index or two if there's an attack. When I was in race shape, I'd gaze at my naked thighs with blurred vision in the bathroom mirror and see a cartoony *Tyrannosaurus rex*. My fantasies reduced to the realities of inflammation, I'd soak from the waist down in a bathtub of freezing ice water.

■ ■ ■

I made a lot of bike racing friends, among them Tuba, whose own animal sensations, like mine, seemed to be activated while riding. When it was just the two of us on training rides he would howl with me like a wolf, which made sense since we probably would have spent the last sixty miles discussing revisions of a book I was writing about wolves. Tuba was the same age as my younger sister, and I admired his creativity and carefree irreverence—as I did hers. He moved to Oklahoma City for some reasons I don't remember. One afternoon, a week after Augie was born, Tuba rode the two hundred miles back to Denton with some of his Brazilian bike-racing friends, texting me at 4:30 p.m. to ask if I would ride up and meet them in Slidell—thirty miles northwest of town on unlit rural highways—to help pace them into town. It was December and getting dark. Since LED bike lights are never fully charged when you need them to be, I stuffed a backup Maglite into my jersey pocket and hit the road.

It turned out that none of us had good lights that night, so we rolled off the hard-topped FM 1173 and snaked our way home on some gravel roads to avoid getting run over by trucks. As the old man on the ride, I found things getting dicey from my perspective. Riding one-handed, trying to answer concerned phone calls in a 3G dead zone, I sat at the back, trying to ensure whichever guy fanned out in front of me hadn't disappeared into a pothole. I made it safely home that night much sooner than I (though not everyone) had expected, since we all worked together calling out the holes and taking pulls.

Bike racing, of course, is a team phenomenon, despite the perplexity of sports commentators, who often strain to narrate the race as a tortured feat of individual heroism. The sociality of cycling leans far more toward cooperation than competition. Yet its zoomorphic metaphors tend more toward charismatic megafauna than routine pack animals. For his flowing mane and unmatched ego, the sprinter Mario Cipollini was dubbed "Il Re Leone" ("The Lion King") by the media. For his protruding ears—taped to his head by soigneurs to reduce aerodynamic drag—the late great Marco Pantani earned the nickname "Elefantino." After moving to Texas, I joked that my bike-racing avatar was the turtle, both because I would often move them off the river-bottom highways so they wouldn't get smashed, and because I was slow.

■　■　■

In his memoir about doping, the former ProTour superstar Tyler Hamilton referred to himself as a "work pony" rather than a racehorse—an animal that could grunt out the miles but would get shot out the back when the pace lifted. Injections of erythropoietin and secret race-day blood transfusions helped solve that problem.

One of my old racing friends is an equine veterinarian who knows many of the animals out on our rides through the rolling pastures of the North Texas horse country. A narrow band of sandy soils west of US 377 are easy on hooves, and once the Dallas exurbs reached Denton County in the '80s, a convergence of market forces hastened the transformation of its peanut farmers into horse breeders. Unlike the large quarter horses my family worked with during the last century, the ones around here are sleek jumpers, trained for competition and companionship instead of agricultural labor.

Earlier that week, I had agreed to give a talk about the historical context of plant-based meat to an audience of stock growers at a well-known land-grant university's annual "Meat Forum." Concerned that I was a vegan, however, a couple of the conference directors reached out ahead of time to talk things through over the phone. One of them trotted out the tired argument that if society went vegan, then cows, pigs, and chickens would go extinct. "Good point," I replied. "The same thing happened to horses once tractors were invented." They ended the call and rescinded their invitation.

I thought about that meeting a few days later, as my veterinarian friend and I rolled off FM 455 west of Pilot Point, descending a recently paved road that led to my favorite neighborhood: a cool, leafy, ten-mile stretch of wedding venues and million-dollar horse ranches along the Elm Fork river bluffs. It was Labor Day weekend. "See those horses over there?" my friend asked, pointing to a half-dozen of them grazing in the foreground of faux castle with a steel roof. "That guy's going bankrupt. He owes me about $10,000 in unpaid bills, but I'm still taking care of those horses. It's not their fault."

We kept rolling. Eventually we climbed back away from the river, passing a country cemetery on two sides, taking that familiar corner abreast with no brakes. On the outside, craning my neck to glance at the stones, I had a thought that if I were a gravedigger, I'd want to work here—the graveyard with the soft, horse-friendly soils. Spading through that sandy loam would be a lot more pleasurable than hammering holes into the Blackland prairie's hardpacked clay—a soil so heavy it suffocates trees. With your head down on a race bike, staring at the road or trail ahead, feeling the earth's surface through the frictive deformations of

Big snapper on the side of Massey Road, just south of Belew Cemetery, Denton County, Texas. *Photograph by Michael D. Wise.*

your tires, it sometimes starts to feel like your body is melting into the ground—a new deposition of the soil horizon. Or sometimes the gravitational pull has you imagining that you and your bike are a wave of water, lapping up a rise and flowing over the other side. Either way, I'm never surprised when I meet a bike racer with an interest in the earth sciences.

We rolled through another corner and then had to stop so I could advise a turtle to move off the road. It was a huge snapper, and I took a picture to show my students on Tuesday.

■   ■   ■

There is an episode of *Black Mirror* that I like to watch with students in my Animal Histories course (HIST 4276). Titled "Fifteen Million Merits," it stars the actor Daniel Kaluuya as a man in a dystopian future required to ride a stationary bike to help generate electricity for an unseen upper class.[1] Alongside it we read the 1844 essay, "What, Then, Constitutes the Alienation of Labor?" where the young Marx reflects on the tendency of capitalism to produce a world where "man [. . .] no longer feels himself to be freely active in any but his animal functions—eating, drinking, procreating [. . .] what is animal becomes human and what is human becomes animal" (Marx [1844] 1978, 74). This class session always reminds me of a course on Marx that I took in grad school, during a frozen Minnesota winter, when I read volume one of *Capital* in the basement while pedaling out base miles on the trainer.

My residence at the time, a century-old, eight-hundred-square-foot bungalow off East Thirty-Eighth Street in south Minneapolis, was about a four-mile ride from campus, and I built up an aluminum hardtail with a low-maintenance, single-speed chain line as my winter commuter. In Montana I had learned to ride through the winter by studding my tires with machine screws to keep traction on the ice that commonly accompanied the freeze–thaw cycles of the Gallatin Valley. Far removed from the tempestuous Rockies, though, the Twin Cities pretty much stayed below freezing from November to March, so I could easily get by on the snow-packed roads with a pair of eight-hundred-gram mud tires. (This, of course, was back before the ascendence of "fat bikes.") I wore lobster gloves, a ski helmet, a face mask, and goggles, and took a bike trail along West River Parkway most of the way there, climbing up to my perch in the Social Sciences Tower on an access road a few hundred yards downriver from where the I-35W bridge would collapse in 2007.

By the middle of my second winter, I had determined that 6° Fahrenheit was the cutoff mark for leaving my bike at home. Around that temperature, my fingers would go numb before I made it to school, even swaddled with an extra pair of oversized mittens. Sometimes they would hurt so badly that I had to take my hands off the bars entirely, riding no-handed and cramming my fingers into my armpits to try to thaw them out. Something about 6° also meant that the exhalations that condensed through my ski mask and fogged up my goggles also would start to freeze, making it impossible to see. And when I took them off, my breath would freeze to my eyelashes instead, making it hard to keep my eyes open. Those days, the bus was more convenient.

At first, I thought the young Marx had been on to something with his theories of alienation, but he lost me with his insistence that capitalism turned workers into animals, since we were already animals from the start. (And, in any case, it made me wonder what was so underwhelming to Marx and his admirers about feeling "freely active" in their "animal functions." What a turnoff.) Moreover, the general exclusion of nonhuman animals and the excision of their profligate contributions to "value" from any Marxian formulae of surplus labor frustrated me. That winter I wrote a seminar paper about Marx's problems of animal–human difference, first in my head as I rode home from class, and then on my laptop in the basement as I banked some more miles on the trainer.

Around that time, I realized my brain worked best when its legs were moving, and I would routinely rotate back and forth from the trainer to a desk where I would type out a paragraph, then jump back on the trainer to read my notebooks. I dropped an 8000-level philosophy course on the "mind–body" problem after reading the syllabus and realizing the class *ended* with Descartes. On my ride home I stopped for a vegan Reuben at the Hard Times Café in Cedar-Riverside.

■ ■ ■

The more I felt like an animal, the less I wanted to eat them. The proprioceptive and vestibular inputs from riding and racing bikes overwhelmed my "human" sensations of sight, sound, smell, taste, and touch. My hands were reduced to numbed mitts; my skin snuffed with smoldering hairlessness; mouth washed clean by tasteless drool; my nose and esophagus seared with sterile gasps for oxygen; my ears hearing only the sound of pumping blood; my gaze blindered on the ass of the wheel ahead of me, eyes stung by salt.

I chose to feel that way—or did it come naturally? Unlike a horse harnessed to a plow, or a hen roasted for a dinner party, I had the privilege of deciding what to do with my own body. But bodies—even our own—don't always listen to the decisions we make for them. That realization is a constant companion in a bike race, and you only learn to ride faster, farther, and more smoothly by decentering your "human senses," relying instead on a sensory diet of proprioceptive and vestibular inputs. Likewise, I could never fully "be myself" without those animalized sensations. Even growing up in a family of omnivores, none of us ever would have eaten a horse. So how could my diet include other animals once I understood myself as one? More than just encouraging an ethics of care, bike racing also entailed a sensory experience that threw into question the utility of the whole human category, offering a glimpse of the pleasure, life, and freedom possible from its transcendence, both for myself and for other animals.

Notes

1. Black Mirror, series 1, episode 2, "Fifteen Million Merits," directed by Euros Lyn, written by Charlie Brooker and Konnie Huq, aired December 11, 2011, on Channel 4 (UK).

References

Ingold, Tim. 2011. *Being Alive: Essays on Movement, Knowledge and Description*. New York: Routledge.

Marx, Karl. (1844) 1978. "Economic and Philosophic Manuscripts of 1844." In *The Marx-Engels Reader*, 2nd ed., edited by Robert C. Tucker. New York: W. W. Norton.

Zimmer, Carl. 2007. *Charles Darwin, The Descent of Man: The Concise Edition*. New York: Penguin.

Amy Rundio. *Photograph from the author's collection.*

CHAPTER FOUR

How Cycling Led Me to Veganism, Which Changed My Cycling

AMY RUNDIO

When I signed up to ride my bike across the country with Bike the US for MS, I figured it would change my life. It was daunting to think about riding that far (3,785 miles to be exact, from Yorktown, Virginia, to San Francisco, California) and over mountains (at the time I lived in eastern North Carolina, which is flat as a pancake . . . maybe flatter). There's no way that wouldn't have an impact on me, if not psychologically then definitely physically. I also knew from my research (looking at long-distance cycling rides and similar sport experiences and how they affected people) that it could be tremendously transformative (Rundio, Dixon, and Heere 2020). Because a cross-country ride would be a new experience for me, I had only a vague idea of what to expect beyond some difficult challenges and meeting and riding with new people—all of which are characteristics of extraordinary experiences (Arnould and Price 1993). What I didn't know was how this extraordinary experience also would change my life, particularly my relationship with food.

The ride would take sixty-two days across nine states, with six service days on which my fellow riders and I would volunteer for people living with multiple sclerosis (MS). Bike the US for MS has been organizing rides across the country since 2007, coordinating the trips for riders through a small staff and large group of volunteer route leaders. These leaders handle the logistics of the trip, such as arranging overnight hosts and working to ensure rider safety. Riders come from across the globe and represent a wide range of ages and backgrounds; they must raise $1 per mile that they ride for the cause and can have very little to years of cycling experience. The year and route I rode featured about twenty people who would spend their summer riding their bikes and helping others.

Before the ride, I had been "mostly" vegetarian, partly because it was cheaper and partly because it seemed healthier (although upon reflection now, it definitely wasn't). I usually only ate meat at restaurants and social gatherings, but decided that probably wasn't sustainable on a cross-country ride that included a section on the "Loneliest Road in America" (Highway 50 in Nevada); through Kansas, Colorado, and Missouri, which rank as top livestock- and poultry-slaughtering states, according to the North American Meat Institute;[1] and small towns with no grocery stores for miles (such as Haswell, Colorado, and Hite, Utah). And that didn't really bother me, as I wasn't ready to face the challenges I imagined would accompany being vegetarian in remote places with limited food choices: finding food I could and would want to eat, locating fresh fruit and vegetables, ensuring that the produce wouldn't spoil without refrigeration, getting a variety of foods and nutrients, and what I anticipated as awkward social situations in which there weren't vegetarian options. It seemed overwhelming to me, so I decided not to face these challenges. I could always go back to being "mostly" vegetarian when I got back.

So with that in mind, I arrived in Yorktown excited (and nervous) for the summer. And I wasn't the only one both excited and nervous. At orientation that afternoon, when all the riders stood in a circle and introduced themselves, giving both the usual who we were and where we were from along with why we were riding (many people had a connection to MS or gave an "adventure"-related reason), we learned that only one individual had ridden with the organization before. So almost none of us knew what to expect over the summer. That included what to eat—as was evidenced on our trip to the grocery store.

Let me pause here to explain how food on the trip worked. We had to provide our own food (although in some overnight locations, our hosts provided dinner) and were given a small cubby in both the trailer for breakfast/dinner foods and the Rest Stop Van for snack/lunch foods to eat on the bike. The Rest Stop Van would set up every twenty-five to thirty miles to ensure we had food and water throughout our ride for the day. Sometimes this was on the side of the road, sometimes in towns with restaurants, sometimes at gas stations—basically anywhere that didn't mind having us set up some chairs and a table next to the van. In all, our cubbies weren't very big, so you had to restock every couple of days (see the end of this chapter for a description of what I would carry in my cubbies and eat throughout the day).

On that first grocery run, most of us were trying to figure out what to get. About ten of us piled into one of the vans, and on the ride over, we got to know one another—where we're from, what we do, what we were looking forward to. But as we began our shopping, we quickly began asking questions about food: What would we eat for dinner? Breakfast? On the road? How much food should we get? What would fit in our cubbies? What are you going to get? Frankly, it was overwhelming and a tad stressful, not having any experience with eating and cooking on a road trip with unknown access to grocery stores, restaurants, and food in general. This led to a lot of overpurchasing—to be prepared for the what-ifs. What if there aren't grocery stores when we needed them? What if there are no restaurants? What if we run out of food? I'd like to say eventually I learned, but really, I always had too much food in my cubbies.

The one experienced rider went with us to the store, so we asked him some of these questions and then took sly looks into his basket as we wandered the store, mostly in pairs. For me, there was a lot of asking other people what they were getting, picking things up and putting them down, and ultimately hoping that what I got would work (peanut butter, jelly, bread, granola bars, instant rice and canned beans, soup, and tuna pouches). Some of the food I got would be shared with others—for example the bread, peanut butter, and jelly I shared with Izzy so that we could save space in our cubbies. Once we hopped back in the van, we talked about what we had all purchased, trying to share as much information as possible.

After that trip was some frantic last-minute unpacking and repacking before our ride began in the morning. It was so exciting to know we were heading off on an adventure!

Very early the next morning, we took our team photo and then began our ride, leaving Yorktown, riding through historic Williamsburg, and then onto the Capital Trail in Virginia. We mostly rode in small groups, getting to know each other and learning how to eat throughout the long days of riding and while camping overnight. It took a few days to figure out fueling, mostly through trial and error, some through learning from others. What foods would settle well? How much was too much at a rest stop? How much was too little?

On the second day of the ride, the group of four I was riding with decided to skip a rest stop because we thought it was too early for lunch. I was used to riding up to a hundred miles in training with only one rest stop, so skipping one didn't seem like a big deal. I couldn't have been more wrong, and got very cranky because I hit the wall—my legs didn't want to go, my stomach was growling, and I was getting a terrible headache. Ultimately, I took it out on someone else and snapped at them when they made a simple comment about the hills being more than they expected, and clearly, skipping a rest stop qualified as too little. This was certainly an example of emotions running high due to fueling issues.

Regardless of these (and other) challenges, I was having fun and seeing lots of new and amazing things. Our ride took us through the Blue Ridge Mountains in Virginia, through several state parks in Kentucky, the Ozark Mountains in Missouri, the farmland of Kansas, the Rockies in Colorado, the Sierras in California, and don't even get me started on how crazy beautiful Utah is. Seeing these new things allowed me to learn a lot about myself and my cycling.

For example, we rode on the Blue Ridge Parkway. I had been especially nervous because I'd never ridden my bike in the mountains and wasn't sure if I could do it. I made a plan with the two guys I was riding with that day to stop at all the overlooks to catch our breath while appreciating the views. Rather than being an insurmountable challenge, it was a spectacular day of riding. It was tiring but rewarding, both physically and mentally, to reach the top of a climb and learn what my body was capable of. I rode 115 miles in one day in Kansas—the last few miles were beyond what we needed for the day, just so that I could say I'd ridden the farthest I've ever ridden. And while that was challenging because of the distance, and the heat, and the long, straight roads with unchanging views, it was more challenging mentally. I rode most of the day myself, and realized I liked riding alone with nothing but the road in front of me. It was untraditionally beautiful.

Utah, on the other hand, was exceptionally and unexpectedly beautiful. Many of us were disappointed to be leaving the beautiful Rockies, figuring that we were headed for miles of desert and uninteresting views. We were quite surprised to find that it was gorgeous, filled with stunning red canyons and rocks, beautiful white stone formations, and even some mountains. It was like a different planet. Many of us found ourselves asking, "Is this even real?" And we got to see all of these things by bike, which allowed us the time to truly appreciate them.

Ultimately, our ride took us through cities, small towns, state and national parks, and other protected lands, and along rivers and lakes. Many of these areas were sparsely populated and felt very close to nature and far away from human pollution (despite the road going through them). This, in and of itself, was beautiful and new to many of us—in our regular lives we didn't get to experience these things.

But our bikes also took us past chicken and pig farms, ranches with a variety of animals (including horses, goats, llamas, and more), tiger sanctuaries, and cattle feedlots. And while I had seen many of these things before, and even cycled past some on other rides, I usually ignored them or didn't think deeply about them because I was on my way to something else. This ride, however, was free of many of my daily responsibilities and allowed for a lot of time to experience and think deeply about new things.

One of the earliest instances of this was while I was riding along State Road 56 into Sebree, Kentucky. Cycling alone toward the end of the day, I was trying to get to camp first (because then I'd get first choice of place to sleep and first shower—and because I'm a little too competitive) when I rode past a Tyson hatchery: a large building whose sole purpose was to provide an environment to hatch chickens for later use as food. I didn't think much of it as I flew by, but later, as I was the first one to camp, I had lots of time to consider what it meant. How these animals didn't have a choice and how their existence was solely for the benefit of humans. Humans that would eat the chickens or their byproducts, but also humans who worked at the factory. In a conversation with the former pastor of the church we stayed at, I learned that many community members were employed by Tyson, and thus earned their living through the suffering of others. Their livelihoods and sustenance depended on the idea that animals could be controlled for human benefit.

It was a sobering moment, but easy to put at the back of my mind as the ride continued. We rode by cattle in fields or farmhouses, and I had been used to seeing these things—they were normal sights in my training and on this ride. However, about two weeks later, I was again faced with sights, sounds, and smells that I couldn't ignore. This time I was riding into Larned, Kansas (again alone), at the end of a 110-mile day, when I rode past thousands of cattle in a feed yard. The first thing you notice on a bike is the smell—in a car, you can easily ignore the pungent scent of cow dung, but not so much in open air. Then you see the cattle, that on this day were packed into pens with what seemed like barely enough room to move two feet, let alone to turn around or go anywhere. Then you hear them, their moos of distress and discomfort, again easy to ignore in a car but not on a bike.

As I rode by and into town, I couldn't help but think about how my choices to eat hamburgers and cheese and ice cream and chocolate milk (great for recovery, not so great for the cows) had caused this. And while I wasn't the one who chose to put the cattle in these pens to be sent off for slaughter, my money made me complicit by supporting it. Which is quite the sobering thought, especially since we'd ridden past many cattle farms and feedlots so far (although the one in Larned was the biggest I remember seeing). It's one thing to choose to suffer on the bike, it's another to have no say in the matter. Even now, writing this, I get teary-eyed thinking about how scared, distraught, and uncomfortable the cattle must have been. What's "normal" and acceptable to me has changed for the better, I think. The new experience of biking by a feed yard forced me to address my old perspective on where my food came from and connect it to this experience.

At that point, though, I still didn't change my diet. I was struggling with eating on the trip—some days I didn't feel like eating, and on others I wasn't eating enough. Eliminating food choices just seemed like too tough a battle during the day. In the evenings, though, and at breakfast, I started to be more conscious about my choices. I began choosing vegetarian options when eating out (such as getting eggs with my pancakes instead of bacon) and buying food to cook rather than having meat or eggs for dinners and breakfasts.

Some of the people I was riding with made it easier to eliminate meat and dairy from my cooking. At first, I was cooking dinner by myself, but after a couple weeks I started cooking with two other riders, one of whom is vegetarian, which meant many of my dinners were vegetarian. Cooking with others is advantageous in many ways, including saving money, time, and energy, as well as for the fellowship. I was able to learn from these two riders about different food options and how to cook and eat on the road. For example, we often made a dish we called "Quinoa

AMY RUNDIO

'N Stuff," which was just quinoa and a bunch of other stuff we happened to have—diced tomatoes, beans, corn, taco spice, and so on. I'd always cooked with a recipe, but I was learning how to improvise. I was also eating things I didn't normally eat, because in daily life I could choose not to eat something if I didn't like the taste. On the road, and eating with others, I didn't have that option. I could take these lessons back home and try new foods and recipes (which actually has been one of my favorite things about being vegan).

There were also two vegans on our ride, Rachel and Robby, who, as I got to know them, proved to be influential in my journey to being vegan. Early on in the trip, I didn't interact with them very much, but from the beginning their food choices made a big impact on the team, including myself. We all learned from each other in the first few days as we figured out what worked and didn't work. And the vegans (as they were often called) ate a lot of avocados—they had their own "container," were easy to transport, and were perfect in tortillas with chips and salsa. Pretty soon many riders were also making avocado wraps at rest stops—you just had to plan carefully to make sure the avocados didn't get overripe before you could eat them. We were told that we were probably the team that ate the most avocados ever in the organization.

But I also watched from afar as Rachel and Robby struggled. Maybe *struggled* isn't the right word, but they definitely faced many challenges. About a week into the trip, we stayed at a church, and members of the congregation cooked us a potluck dinner. None of the dishes were vegan, though—even the vegetable dishes and salad had meat, dairy, or eggs. The vegans had food they could cook, but all I could think was, "I'm so tired, and so glad I don't have to cook anything right now." I was grateful for the kindness these parishioners (and other individuals along the way) showed us in cooking for us and feeding us, even though they didn't know us and certainly weren't expected to do any of this. But later, I wondered how hard it was to show appreciation for a meal that you can't partake in; even as it had been so kind of these strangers to cook, it was perhaps insensitive to the dietary needs of the vegans, and certainly was unkind to the animals who were consumed. Likewise, as we began riding through food deserts, shopping became a challenge for all of us, but particularly for the vegans. They never complained, though, and made sure both to plan ahead by buying things that would last—fresh fruits and veggies when they could—and to treat themselves when options became available.

At first, it seemed hard to get to know Rachel and Robby, as they were on the ride with their roommate George, and the three spent a lot of time doing things together. So, I wasn't sure if they were looking for new friends or how they would feel about an outsider joining their group. They were very friendly, but I was still intimidated. However, on one particularly difficult day in Kansas, where my legs were just tired and there was a strong headwind, I rode with them for about fifty miles. Or more accurately, I sat on their wheels for fifty miles. Either way, I got to know them a little better; we had lunch and hung out at the rest stops that day together, just chatting and enjoying each other's company. After that, I began to ride with them more regularly, even spending my first day in the Rockies riding with Rachel and George. Rachel and I ended up having a lot of difficulty breathing at that altitude, so at one point we were pulling over to try to catch our breath every half mile or so. It didn't affect George, however, and he did his best to try to encourage us and keep us going—although often he was met with complete silence and some dirty looks as Rachel and I were clearly suffering while he was not. It was probably one of the most challenging days on the bike, although now it's easy to look back with fondness and laugh.

As we went through these challenges together, and I began eating meals with them, it was easy to see how they were able to eat well and not feel like they were missing out on anything. My food choices changed from burgers to veggie burgers whenever possible, from chocolate milk to chocolate soy or almond milk, and from chicken burritos to veggie burritos. During these meals, I learned a lot more about them, including their eating habits—Rachel had been vegetarian for most of her life before going vegan, and Robby switched for health reasons.

Once I felt comfortable with them, and had decided I wanted to change my lifestyle, I asked them about their veganism. We were at a Mexican restaurant in Utah, nearing the end of our ride, and I told Rachel I was thinking about switching. She was so excited and told Robby when he joined us. I asked them what it was like to be vegan, what recommendations they had for switching, what complications did they have, how did they navigate social situations (in which there likely wouldn't be vegan options), and more. They were patient with my questions and answered as best they could, although they lived in a big city on the West Coast, and I lived in a small, rural, southern city, so some things they couldn't answer. I still had questions, but this had been a good starting point, and once I returned home they remained a resource for my questions through my transition.

I'm not sure when I specifically decided I wanted to try switching to a vegan diet, but I do know that as I rode farther and farther west, experienced more and more first-hand encounters with mistreatment of animals, and developed deeper relationships with cyclists on the ride, I began to feel that I needed to make a change and stop being complicit in the oppression of animals.

These new experiences, my strong emotional responses to them, and the friendships I gained through this extraordinary journey led to my personal transformation. Such transformations can be defined as "a dynamic, uniquely individualized process whereby an individual becomes critically aware of old and new self-views and chooses to integrate these views into a new self definition" (Wade 1998, 716). The interactions with my fellow riders and people I met along the way, the challenges and emotions I felt, and the newness of it all allowed me the time to be critical of my old self-view. Why was I eating dairy, eggs, and meat? How were my actions affecting those who could not speak up for themselves? Why didn't I think about those lives as I made my food choices? As the ride continued, I became aware that I had a choice, a new view of myself as a potential vegan. Making that choice to change, though, shifted the transformation from one of being aware of these differing views to integrating them into a new self-definition—one of a vegan.

Yet once I left this extraordinary experience, once I wasn't around these new friends or feeling such highly intense emotions, once I knew what to expect and there was less newness, I was going to have to introduce this new self to my old life and adjust my old life to the new self. Practically, this meant flying home and transitioning to a vegan diet and lifestyle. I started by eliminating meat completely from my diet (not that difficult because I had been mostly vegetarian before my ride), then dairy, and then eggs. I searched for lots of information from books, the internet, and my friends who were vegan or vegetarian (both Rachel and Robby as well as friends from my everyday life). I had to navigate and evaluate the challenges of my old self and the knowledge and habits I had grown up with. I began reading labels, deciding whether or not to keep my leather goods (I remember being so proud of purchasing my first pair of cowboy boots—I was becoming Texan!—yet now my new self shuddered at the thought of wearing them again), investigating where my food and consumer products had come from, and determining what impact my choices were having on those I could not see or hear from.

Another (and what I feel was the biggest) challenge was social in nature: telling close friends and navigating social eating situations. These were people who knew the old me. They hadn't met the new me, and I didn't know how to tell them I wasn't that person anymore. One time, for example, I went out with noncycling friends to our usual place a couple of weeks after I got back. I spent a while browsing the menu. Lots of meat, cheese, and butter—it was the South, after all—severely limited what I could order: a "salad" consisting of iceberg lettuce, tomato, and onion; French fries; or nachos with no cheese or sour cream.

As soon as I ordered the nachos, my friends said, "But the cheese is the whole point of nachos!"

I replied, "Yea, I'm vegan now." And I felt quite uncomfortable—I had changed and they had to adjust to this.

They asked about why I had changed, and I gave my reasons—how I had seen a lot of suffering on the ride, but also how I could live a life that didn't contribute to that suffering. They were pretty understanding, but it just felt awkward and uncomfortable. They had known me for a few years now, and this was a big change. How would this change impact them? I can't answer for them, but I often wonder if my decision to change and not participate in animal suffering has caused them to consider the impact of their own choices.

I also had to integrate my new vegan self with my cycling. This also meant sharing my new views with my cycling friends. They had some of the same questions and more—perhaps because we had known each other through countless hours of training and shared a lot more highs and lows than I had with my noncycling friends. They asked, "So, do you eat honey?" "Did you know there was a study that showed plants feel pain too? Will you stop eating plants?" I didn't have answers right away for them, as I was still asking myself many of the same questions (although perhaps not "Will you stop eating plants?").

Integrating my vegan self with my older, familiar experiences of cycling around eastern North Carolina required adjusting habits and advocating for myself. For example, on Saturdays, we often rode to Yoder's Dutch Pantry, a local bakery known for its French toast and cinnamon rolls. And while the group still did Yoder's rides, I was no longer as excited about them because there was nothing for me to eat. I struggled at first, feeling like I was missing out; my old self loved these trips because the food was delicious and rewarding for a hard and long ride. It made me feel like I was part of the group. Now, however, I wasn't, because I had to change how I took part in this ritual. I was different. And these two views—old and new—didn't seem like they could be blended. Because they couldn't. Ultimately, I did my best to shift my view from missing out to still being part of the group, because we rode our bikes all the way to Yoder's (!) unlike 99 percent of the other visitors, I got to spend some time with some wonderful people, and most importantly, I was no longer contributing to animal suffering when I ate.

My new self also had to be more assertive to stay true to this view. Before, I didn't care what route we took—just as long as we rode our bikes. I usually just went along with whatever Tori (who usually picked routes because she knows all the smoothest roads) chose. Now, however, I frequently asked not to do certain routes. On Lower Field Road, for example, there was a hog farm that you could see and smell as you rode by. And while not riding by it didn't mean the hog farm stopped existing, it did mean that my ride would not be interrupted by the sight of pigs suffering and the associated feelings of sadness, anger, guilt, and shame. On rides when we did go by this farm, Tori would often apologize—"I'm sorry, I know you don't like this road but we need to get back before dark." It meant a lot that she recognized, acknowledged, and respected the new me. To me, it meant that I could voice my opinion and share my thoughts with this group, and that although they might not agree, they would still accept me.

My old experiences took on a sense of newness, and my interactions with others ultimately influenced my transition and transformation to veganism. Most significantly, though, this transition and transformation would not have happened without my extraordinary experience riding across the country. It led me to consider how my choices affected others and the need to be more conscious in everyday decision making. The combination of the sights, sounds, and smells, discussions with other people, and the time and space to think and reflect were so vitally important in coming to the decision to be vegan. To realize the suffering that occurred as a result of my previous decisions to eat animals and their byproducts. To stop being complicit in the suffering of others. This decision in turn has affected my cycling—from where I cycle to how I cycle, but thankfully not who I cycle with.

Cooking and eating on the road is quite different than riding and cooking at home. Bike the US for MS provides riders with a Day Cubby, where riders can store a few things to eat mid-ride, and a Food Cubby in the trailer, for food to eat before and after the day's rides. Given that there was no way to refrigerate things, here's what I had in my cubbies.

My Day Cubby usually had tortillas, peanut butter, jelly, potato chips, a couple of granola bars, Nuun tablets, and a couple of baby food pouches (I can't eat gels as they tear up my stomach, so these pouches are a good substitute).

My Food Cubby in the trailer had oatmeal packets; instant coffee; raisins; a couple of cans of soup; a couple of cans of veggies and beans; Oreos (or some other sweet); a gas can and camping stove; and a pot, pan, and dish for eating.

A typical day started out with oatmeal, raisins, and coffee from my Food Cubby. Then, on the road, we would have one to three rest stops. Tortillas are better than bread because they take up less space, so I usually had a PBJ tortilla at one rest stop and an avocado and potato chip wrap (a specialty the vegans introduced to everyone on the trip) at a later stop. Dinner was usually Quinoa 'N Stuff with two of the other riders. I did also eat out once a day, so sometimes I would eat dinner at a diner or lunch at Subway or other fast-food choice, or my favorite, a diner for breakfast with huge pancakes or waffles—it depended on what was available while traveling!

Notes

1. North American Meat Institute, n.d., "The United States Meat Industry at a Glance," accessed September 18, 2019, https://www.meatinstitute.org/index .php?ht=d/sp/i/47465/pid/47465.

References

Arnould, Eric J., and Linda L. Price. 1993. "River Magic: Extraordinary Experience and the Extended Service Encounter." *Journal of Consumer Research* 20 (1): 24–45.

Rundio, Amy, Marlene A. Dixon, and Bob Heere. 2020. " 'I'm a Completely Different Person Now': Extraordinary Experiences and Personal Transformations in Sport." *Sport Management Review* 23 (4): 704–18.

Wade, Gail Holland. 1998. "A Concept Analysis of Personal Transformation." *Journal of Advanced Nursing* 28 (4): 713–19.

Matthew Calarco. *Photograph by Christina Calarco.*

CHAPTER FIVE

Changing Direction

MATTHEW CALARCO

My aim in this chapter is to suggest that both cycling and veganism can be important components of a philosophical way of life. At first glance, such a claim will no doubt appear odd, for cycling and veganism would seem to have little to do with the discipline of philosophy as now practiced by the vast majority of professional academic philosophers (among whom I count myself). So, my first task here is to present an alternative conception of the practice of philosophy, one rather different from what takes place in most university classrooms. With this variant vision of philosophy explained, I then explore how cycling and veganism can function as important parts of a philosophical life in contemporary societies.

The common notion of philosophy as an arid, abstract, and technical academic discipline fairly accurately represents its dominant form in the United States. To practice philosophy at one of the leading departments, one typically specializes in "M&E" (metaphysics and epistemology) or a subfield that is closely related to the sciences (e.g., one might specialize in philosophy of mind with a focus on neuroscience). The gold standards of the mainstream philosophical guild are conceptual refinement, logical rigor, and making small but distinctive contributions to ongoing debates in the leading specialist journals in one's field. Normative issues are not entirely absent from the discipline but are considered relatively unimportant in comparison to core metaphysical and epistemological research.

Even to insiders, it is often unclear what relevance debates of the sort pursued in advanced academic philosophy have to anyone beyond the handful of specialists who participate in them. In fact, if one frequents any of the large national meetings where such academic philosophers congregate, one will almost certainly encounter several philosophers *bragging* about how their work has no relevance to public or political concerns of any kind.[1] For practitioners of this sort, academic philosophy is akin to puzzle solving and has little or no importance to the way in which one lives one's life outside the academic setting. Indeed, except for most professional philosophers' peculiar intellectual interests, distinguishing their way of life from that of typical citizens in advanced industrialized societies would be impossible.

Things have not always been so with philosophy. Particularly in ancient Greece and India, philosophy was associated with a thoroughgoing existential commitment to thinking and living differently from the dominant culture. Consider, for example, the life of Socrates, perhaps the most influential figure in the Western philosophical tradition. Socrates explicitly rejected the idea that philosophy's goal was to engage in abstract speculations about the scope of knowledge and the physical nature of the world; instead, he argued that what was at stake in doing philosophy was *epimeleia tes psyches*, or care for the soul. As philosopher Sandra Peterson (2011) notes, for Socrates "soul" refers not to some immortal essence but rather to the source of one's actions: "Care for the soul is thus care about how best to conduct your life. . . . [It] is a very practical matter of figuring out how you will conduct your life day to day. It is care for your dispositions and beliefs, your mental and emotional equipment out of which you act every day" (40).

For Socrates, having one's soul properly disposed meant turning away from the dominant culture's empty obsession with pursuing wealth, vanity, and power and instead toward a genuinely worthwhile way of life. The task of philosophy, as Socrates conceived it, was to articulate a vision of what it looks like to live such a life and to develop spiritual (or soul-shaping) exercises and practices for making this transition.[2]

Although wealth, vanity, and power continue to fascinate and capture the souls of many people in contemporary culture much as they did in ancient times, the particular systems of power and methods of control through which we become subjects of the established order differ across time and place. In other words, power is always on the move, and common forms of selfhood are always undergoing concomitant transformations. If philosophy hopes to respond to the era in which it is being practiced, it also must respond to these changes in power and subjectivity and be attentive to the various ways in which people are formed by the dominant culture of that age.

Contemporary philosophers have described our age as dominated by power in the form of governmentality (Michel Foucault), control (Gilles Deleuze), phallocentrism (Luce Irigaray), the spectacle (Guy Debord), and exposition (Bernard Harcourt), among others. All of these frameworks seek to discern *the* overarching mode of power characteristic of the age; and while such overarching accounts can serve as useful heuristics, I will avoid any grand claims about the nature of contemporary power and simply focus on two undeniably powerful systems relevant to the concerns of this volume. I refer to these systems of power as *hyperautomobility* and *anthropocentrism*. Here I explain briefly how these systems function, then explore how certain philosophical practices—in particular, cycling and veganism—can work to disrupt our being captured by such systems.

■　■　■

I was born in the United States in 1972, just as the era of hyperautomobility was getting underway. While the concepts of *mass motorization* and *automobility* are often used to name the transformations in transportation that marked the twentieth century, beginning in the mid-1970s these systems underwent important intensifications and modifications. From 1900 to the mid-1970s, individual car ownership went from being the privilege of a handful of individuals to becoming customary for the vast majority of the population. After this time, the number of individuals *owning* cars became relatively stable while the *usage* of cars started to accelerate. From 1975 to the present, the number of trips people took with their cars increased by more than 50 percent, the length of those trips increased significantly, and the number of occupants per car on each trip noticeably dropped. These changes in automobile use are tracked and explained with keen insight by sociologists Peter Freund and George Martin (2009). They argue that these and related changes in individual automobile use are so significant that the period from 1975 to the present requires us to move beyond the standard theories concerning mobility and think in terms of hyperautomobility. For Freund and Martin, hyperautomobility is best understood as "a deepening and broadening of personal car use to new levels" (478). As individual car use and the systems that support it grew rapidly from the mid-1970s onward, the automobile became increasingly central in the lives of individual drivers, and systems of automobile transport came to affect more individual lives. In short, in an era of hyperautomobility, "more people drive more miles in more complex vehicles" (481).

Freund and Martin rightly emphasize that these intensifications of automobility are not simply reducible to consumer preference; they are driven and supported by government policy, local forms of urban architecture, and a wide variety of industries involved in automobile transportation. As such, systems of hyperautomobility and their supporting infrastructure can be remarkably resistant to change, even when they have obvious negative effects. The astonishing mortality rates, pervasive harmful health consequences, and catastrophic ecological effects associated with current transportation systems are well known; yet these systems are still expanding and intensifying amid widespread public support and government investment. The hard truth here is not just that systemic and infrastructural transformation is a difficult and lengthy process, with powerful economic forces allied against it; that is all quite true. The more vexing issue is that there is very little *desire* on the part of most individual car owners to make the required changes.

We find ourselves in this seemingly paradoxical situation because hyperautomobility is not something simply "out there," a system and set of structures that exist in a social world from which we as individuals are distinct. Rather, this system and set of power relations are now fully inside many of us; they have captured our souls. Literally hundreds of millions of people in the United States (and, increasingly, abroad) *desire* to drive their cars and strongly *identify* with this way of being-in- and moving-through-the-world. To radically transform these practices would thus be tantamount to radically transforming many people's subjectivity. For people who have little familiarity with other systems of mobility or visions for being-in-the-world, such prospects of radical change pose a profound existential challenge.

As a young person, I was swept up in and captured by systems of hyperautomobility. Daily life with my family in my childhood hometown of Escondido, California, was characterized by constant and extensive automobile use. I was shuttled around to school and social events, as little alternative transportation infrastructure was available and urban sprawl made it necessary to travel ever longer distances. Like many American teenagers of my generation, I longed to have a driver's license and my own car, and I began working at an early age to help pay for my car loan, gas, and maintenance. Once I turned sixteen, I drove myself everywhere and (because of low gas prices) thought nothing of regularly driving thirty to forty miles round trip to visit friends across town or go to the beach. Using a car for most of my daily tasks and activities became an entirely normal and nearly invisible part of my life.

During my youth, though, I was also being introduced to other modes of mobility. When I was around ten, my family took up cycling for health and recreation. We started on a small scale, with short rides on clunky, old bikes. Before long, though, we were befriended by more serious cyclists and took up the sport with a passion. My parents purchased a tandem and became avid long-distance cyclists. Some our favorite family legends revolve around epic rides—upwards of a hundred miles in length—on which my parents dragged me along when I was ten and eleven years old. At age twelve, I went with my parents on an extended, six-hundred-mile biking and camping trip along the coast from Northern to Southern California. Despite my regular whining during these difficult rides (also part of family legend), these experiences instilled in me a deep love of and passion for cycling. I participated in competitive cycling from ages twelve to eighteen and have continued to ride semicompetitively throughout most of my adult life.

Thus, even as my sense of self was being formed in the context of an increasingly hyperautomobile society, I was simultaneously developing a taste for other ways of being-in and moving-through-the-world. In effect, cycling was also capturing part of my soul. Over time, I came in no small part to relate and identify with people and other beings who didn't drive everywhere. While out on my bicycle, I had a tendency to talk more frequently with folks who were not in cars: other cyclists, walkers, people at bus stops, people in the neighborhood standing out in front of their homes, and so on. I also tended to take fuller notice of the more-than-human world when on a bicycle than I did while in my car. I developed a strong sense of relationship with the animals and local ecology, learning bit by bit to take in the richness of the more-than-human sights, sounds, and smells I encountered on various rides. Over time, a part of me was becoming unstuck from the world of hyperautomobility into which I had been thrown, and that same part of my self eventually came to redirect my life toward a new end.

■   ■   ■

The other set of power relations into which I was thrust from birth onward I refer to as *anthropocentrism*. Although many of my fellow colleagues and activists prefer the term *speciesism* to describe the phenomena at issue here, I prefer the term *anthropocentrism* for reasons that I shall specify. Speciesism is typically described as an intellectual and illogical prejudice that denies moral consideration to animals on the premise that they do not belong to the human species; stated in reverse, the speciesist believes that all and only members of the biological species *Homo sapiens* deserve full moral standing and consideration. What makes speciesism a prejudice, according to its critics, is its dogmatic character and its inability to withstand critical intellectual scrutiny. Pro-animal critics of speciesism charge that the species boundary is not a relevant or defensible moral marker, and that the traditional markers of full moral standing found in human beings (such as sentience or subjectivity) are found in many animal species as well. Consequently, if the speciesist is to be logically consistent and avoid prejudice, then moral standing must be extended to all beings—whether human or animal—who bear the relevant moral traits.

Although the logic of this pro-animal position might be compelling, I think it fails to explain why many animals are often granted little or no moral standing by the dominant social order; it also fails accurately to describe the situation of many marginalized human beings. The world into which I was born was characterized not by a simple speciesism and corresponding notion of the supremacy of the human species as a whole, but by a complex series of power relations that cut across the human and more-than-human worlds in various ways. What I was consistently taught—both explicitly and implicitly—by the dominant culture was that *full* human beings (what in ancient Greece were referred to as ἄνθρωποι [anthrōpoi]) were those who deserved full consideration, and that many human beings (women, people of color, immigrants, the poor, and so on), as well as the vast majority of more-than-human beings, failed to achieve this subject position. And what I was also being taught here was much more than a series of intellectual beliefs; I was being inducted into an entire way of life, a set of embodied habits, logics, rhythms, economies, and practices reinforcing the notion that full human beings carried more worth than other beings, that only full human beings had lives worth living and deaths worth grieving. It is this more complex, interrelated system of habits, practices and structures that I refer to as anthropocentrism.

As pro-animal writers have demonstrated in great detail, the vast majority of nonhuman animals suffer immensely when captured within the orbit of anthropocentric structures, subjected as they are to the violent machinations of the animal–industrial complex and its associated commercial enterprises of factory farming, experimentation, entertainment, labor, and so on. Throughout my childhood years, my daily life was entirely and uncritically immersed within this set of structures. I ate meat, used animal byproducts, and participated in countless social and economic activities that were predicated on the displacement, violation, and death of animal lives. Although I was extraordinarily fond of animals during these years, I had no understanding of how my way of life was destroying innumerable individual animals as well as the biophysical systems on which whole species depend for sustenance and well-being.

Just before my teen years, my parents decided to adopt a vegetarian diet for health reasons. As they began to remove meat from our family meals, I recall insisting that I still wanted to eat "my hamburgers" (one of my favorite meals at the time). Already at that tender age, I was a committed meat eater and had at least a passing awareness that giving up meat meant losing an important part of myself. My parents were understanding and didn't force me to eat strictly vegetarian food, but shortly thereafter, I voluntarily joined them in that way of eating. I had begun reading some of the vegetarian diet books my parents kept around the house, some of which contained descriptions of contemporary factory farming practices, replete with pictures and a detailed litany of horrors to which farm animals were subjected. I can still recall the visceral response I had to those books and the realities toward which they pointed. The pictures opened a pit in my stomach and made my whole body burn violently hot with shame. I became a committed vegetarian from that point forward for both ethical and political reasons, although I had only the vaguest sense of what those emerging sensibilities would entail.

As with the practice of cycling, being a vegetarian set me on the path of a series of changes in my everyday life. Alongside my family, who were also gradually coming to grips with the ethical and political dimensions of vegetarianism, I began to rethink not just the food I ate but the products I used daily, many of which I learned either incorporated animal byproducts or harmed animals through such means as testing or destroying their habitats. With further research and consciousness raising from fellow pro-animal advocates, I came to understand that the egg and dairy industries treated animals in a cruel and entirely instrumental manner, which in turn led me to become a vegan in my teenage years.

Thus, even as I found myself ever more immersed in an anthropocentric culture that violates animal lives at every turn, through a vegan diet I was being introduced to another set of practices, routines, and habits that produced in me a taste for other ways of thinking about and interacting with animals. I didn't know it at the time, but I was undergoing a process of what theorist Michel Foucault refers to as *desubjectification*. In other words, veganism was partially unraveling my previous form of subjectivity, my previous sense of self. I was slowly learning how to occupy a subject position that was at odds with the one handed to me by the dominant culture. As I studied such thinkers as Carol Adams and Jacques Derrida, among others, I began to recognize that as a young male meat eater, I had been indoctrinated into the "sexual politics of meat" and had absorbed the rhythms and logic of "carnophallogocentrism"—terms that refer to the ways in which masculinity is linked (at least in the dominant culture of the West) with the exploitation of both animals and women. In adopting a vegan diet, I realized my deep immersion in these systems of power and began to gain a sense of how important but challenging it would be for me and others like me to twist free of their hold.

■ ■ ■

Those early experiences with cycling and vegetarianism/veganism were, in effect, placing me on the path toward a philosophical way of life. By partially pulling me out of the common routines and practices of the dominant culture, I was able to somewhat readjust my vision and sensibilities and see more clearly the violent institutions and relations in which I was immersed. Once I became more habituated to the new perspectives that cycling and veganism offered me, though, I had to make an intentional decision about how to respond to the structural and subjective violence I had glimpsed. Would cycling remain primarily a form of exercise and veganism remain chiefly a dietary choice, allowing the dominant culture to maintain its hold on my subjectivity? Or would I intensify and expand the critical practices I had begun and convert to an entirely different way of life?

As I entered my late teens and early twenties, I opted for the latter path. I then started to view cycling and veganism as crucial practices for altering one's disposition toward the world and participating in needed structural reforms. As cycling shifted from being a stand-alone practice separate from the rest of my life to being central to who I was as a person, I began to think and live more intentionally in relation to systems of transportation. I sold my car and started commuting, doing errands, and shopping entirely by bike. If I needed to get somewhere I couldn't navigate by bicycle, I rode the bus. Upon learning of the massive social impact and carbon dioxide output of airplane travel, I stopped flying. I became involved in local politics surrounding transportation systems. Although I have access to a car when I need one, I have come to prefer riding whenever possible. The habit of and taste for riding I picked up in my teen years has now settled into an established disposition, and I now see the world through a cyclist's eyes, a perspective that allows for a sideways glance at innumerable phenomena that driver-based subjectivity tends to conceal.[3]

Similarly, I have come to see that adopting a vegan diet is just the tip of the iceberg when it comes to resisting violence directed at animals. With time and research, I learned that a pro-animal disposition demanded much more of me than a change in my dietary choices. I realized the variety of ways in which animals are subjected to instrumental and violent use by the pharmaceutical, fashion, and entertainment industries and newly appreciated the fact that I needed to supplement changes in my individual actions with participation in large-scale political movements aimed at structural and systemic changes for both animals and marginalized human beings. As a result, for the past twenty-five years I have been active in animal defense and social justice circles, and have dedicated much of my energy to ongoing efforts of various sorts to better the lives of animals and bring justice for them into conversation with struggles for social justice.

■   ■   ■

As with any practice and way of life, the longer one inhabits it, the more one is able to see from within its orbit. Along these lines, philosopher Gilles Deleuze advocates adopting formative practices and subjectivities that help us become increasingly "worthy" of the events that happen to us. For unless we have been shaped and constituted in a particular way that somewhat attunes us to what comes our way, certain events might pass us by and have little transformative effect.

Consider roadkill, for example. Many of my earliest and most vivid memories relate to seeing animals struck by cars and lying either injured or dead in the roadway. Like most readers, I have witnessed many horrific roadkill incidents, including seeing my companion cats and dogs being struck and killed, and hitting animals of various sorts while driving my own car. These roadkill events certainly remained in my consciousness and even provoked profound sympathy. But throughout my teens and early twenties, they failed to inspire any deeper or sustained reflections on my part and no observable changes in my day-to-day life. In fact, I continued to drive heavily for most of this time and rarely reflected on the effects my driving had on animals and other beings.

Sometime in my twenties, though, I began to feel tremendous, almost paralyzing grief when I saw roadkill while out riding. I became expert at spotting it in the roadway ahead, and would often slow down and say a word or two of condolence as I passed. Eventually, I started removing dead animals from the road while out riding (when it was safe to do so), for several reasons: first, out of concern for the well-being of scavengers who eat roadkill; second, out of respect for the dead animal itself; third, as a reminder to myself to slow down and be attentive to how I move through the world.

It was after engaging in this roadkill-removal practice for many years that I finally convinced myself to sell my car and try to get around by bicycle as much as possible. It was as if I needed to do all of these things—be a vegan for many years, regularly ride a bike, and spend time attending carefully to the material carnage that driving caused—before I was ready to see, *truly to see*, roadkill and change my behavior. Using Deleuze's terms, it was not until that point that I became worthy of the event of roadkill. I needed those spiritual exercises, those soul-shaping practices, to reorient me in such a way that I could offer a more just and respectful response to the roadkill events I encountered.

It is in view of these ongoing changes in my subjectivity that I believe it is fitting to say that both cycling and veganism are important components of a philosophical way of life. I never could have simply *thought* my way to the form of life I now inhabit. I desperately needed those transformative practices to assist me in becoming unstuck from my old habits and to provide me with the space necessary for constituting new relations and new practices. In intentionally adopting and maintaining the practices of cycling and veganism, and opening myself to the transformations they continue to bring my way, I am trying my best to live in the world philosophically. Following the lead of Socrates and many other philosophers throughout the ages and across cultures, I am trying to ensure that my soul is properly oriented and that I am as worthy as possible of the events that grace my daily life.

> My go-to fuel while on long rides are Clif Bars, although I prefer to bring food from home with me (fruit, sandwiches, etc.) when possible to avoid using throwaway packaging. One of my favorite things to do while riding is to take detours through out-of-the-way neighborhoods near breakfast and dinner time and linger in the smells of homemade cooking coming from the houses.

Notes

1. For further reflections on the apolitical nature of much of mainstream philosophy, see McCumber (2001) and Wilshire (2002).
2. See Hadot (2002) for an influential account of how this conception of philosophy gets developed in Socratic and post-Socratic philosophy. Although I do not have the space here to offer a comparative analysis of Western and non-Western philosophical traditions, related but distinct models of philosophy as a process of subjective conversion to a meaningful way of life can be found across ancient traditions, especially in Buddhism. For a helpful discussion of these themes, see Gowans (2018) and Kapstein (2013).
3. I should emphasize that I am not suggesting the specific choices discussed here can or should be universalized. Many people cannot travel by bicycle for any number of reasons; others may be unable to avoid flying and other carbon-intensive forms of transportation due to various constraints. The point here is not to universalize a given alternative mode of transportation but to seek out what I would call *altermobilities*, a variety of ways of moving and being in the world that challenge hyperautomobility. Cycling is but one such practice among many.

References

Freund, Peter, and George Martin. 2009. "The Social and Material Culture of Hyperautomobility: 'Hyperauto.' " *Bulletin of Science, Technology & Society* 29 (6): 476–82.

Gowans, Christopher W. 2018. "Buddhist Philosophy as a Way of Life: The Spiritual Exercises of Tsongkhapa." In *Buddhist Philosophy: A Comparative Approach*, edited by Steven M. Emmanuel, 11–28. Malden, MA: Wiley-Blackwell.

Hadot, Pierre. 2002. *What Is Ancient Philosophy?* Translated by Michael Chase. Cambridge, MA: Harvard University Press.

Kapstein, Matthew T. 2013. "Stoics and Bodhisattvas: Spiritual Exercise and Faith in Two Philosophical Traditions." In *Philosophy as a Way of Life: Ancients and Moderns—Essays in Honor of Pierre Hadot*, edited by Michael Chase, Stephen R. L. Clark, and Michael McGhee. Malden, MA: Wiley-Blackwell: 99–115.

McCumber, John. 2001. *Time in the Ditch: American Philosophy and the McCarthy Era*. Evanston, IL: Northwestern University Press.

Peterson, Sandra. 2011. *Socrates and Philosophy in the Dialogues of Plato*. New York: Cambridge University Press.

Wilshire, Bruce. 2002. *Fashionable Nihilism: A Critique of Analytic Philosophy*. Albany: State University of New York Press.

Sune Borkfelt. *Photograph by Deva Borkfelt.*

CHAPTER SIX

Cycling, Noticing, Caring
On Being a Vegan Cyclist in Denmark

SUNE BORKFELT

In an essay called "Meat Country" (1995), Nobel Prize–winning novelist J. M. Coetzee explores the subject of vegetarianism from a personal perspective. More specifically, he takes his starting point in how he "obstinately" tries "to hold to a regimen" that includes "a dislike for cars, a deep affection for the bicycle and a diet without flesh" during extended stays in the United States, in Texas to be precise (43). As he observes, "It is eccentric not to drive a car in the United States, doubly so in Texas. It is eccentric not to eat meat in the United States, doubly so in Texas," and hence he tries to be discreet, aware as he is of the "comic potential" of his preferences (43–44).

To the degree that Coetzee's description of Texan mentality with regard to cycling is accurate, Denmark is certainly quite different from Texas. We are known for cycling to the extent that the number of bikes here is used as a selling point in advertising the country as a tourist destination. It may not be that everyone cycles—there are plenty of cars as well—but at least in the cities, almost everyone owns a bicycle, and riding one is not in any way eccentric or comical in itself. Hence biking, for me, is simply the main mode of transportation I grew up with. It was how my friends and I would get to and from school, how I would get around as a kid, and how I still get to most places these days if they are within a reasonable distance from where I live and the weather permits.

Nevertheless, since the first time I read it, I have always found something about Coetzee's essay on cycling and abstaining from meat in Texas very relatable. In terms of meat eating, it is not difficult to see why.

Growing up in Denmark, my vegetarianism (later to become veganism) was eccentric to say the least. My friends and I may have shared riding bikes to school, but the packed lunch I brought with me looked very different from any of theirs, and many people did not really know what a vegetarian even was. In several ways, my not eating meat stood out as much as anything possibly could, and the intuitive ethical stance behind it surely must have been unfathomable to most people, if I even dared try to explain it. After all, Denmark is famous for its supposedly excellent "bacon," "ham," and other "pork" products, and animal agriculture is often credited with having provided the economic building blocks of the Danish welfare state. Hence, not eating its products can seem, to some, positively un-Danish—hardly anything could be weirder or more eccentric.

And yet, commonplace as cycling was among my childhood friends, it also eventually turned out that my particular love for the bicycle was, like my vegetarianism, somewhat unusual. While most of my friends eventually got driver's licenses, I never developed a desire for one, not even later when I started a family. Instead, I now own a cargo bike with a box in front, for when I need to get more groceries than my usual bike bags can hold, or need supplies for gardening and home improvement. As it turned out, even though it did not always seem so, my dislike for cars and love of the bicycle are eccentric, too.

For me, cycling has turned out to be more than a mode of transportation or a favored form of exercise. It is a way of experiencing and being in the world, as well as an implicit expression of values I hold dear—what might indeed be termed my vegan sensibility or worldview. I feel a direct confrontation with the world on my bike that I do not have when I am occasionally in the passenger seat of a car. When cycling, I have more time to contemplate what I see. I hear more of the sounds of birds and other animals, and I smell more of the various odors on offer—pleasant ones as well as the stink of manure that seasonally envelops Danish countryside landscapes. This, to me, is also part of what veganism is about: noticing the world around you. Noticing is, I think, the precondition for caring, and the fact that I care strikes at the root of why I live a vegan life.

I am on my way to an area where rewilding experiments are carried out, about two and a half hours from where I live. It is a sunny autumn day, and as I cycle along the coast, I see seals lying on sandbanks in the distance, as well as the occasional head that pops out of the water

SUNE BORKFELT

a bit closer. As I approach the rewilded area, where horses have been allowed to roam and the landscape is otherwise minimally managed, I encounter snakes on my path and even catch a glimpse of a fox. I leave my bike and walk into the area itself. It takes a while before I encounter the horses, and I keep a respectful distance. I take my time, sit, and let myself notice their behavior and social interactions as they graze, nuzzle each other, and occasionally gallop around. Then I go back to my bike and cycle home as the sun begins to set.

While cycling, noticing becomes effortless. The signs of other lives are everywhere. Though of course, the more you already know, the more you are likely to notice. For instance, cycling in the Danish countryside means seeing almost endless fields of feed crops, which remind you (if you know) that at any given time in this country, pigs reared for the meat industry outnumber people by at least two to one (Danish Agriculture & Food Council 2019). The pigs themselves are rarely seen by anyone who does not work in the industry. When cycling, I am more likely to pass or even stop and interact with cows in fields, although industry statistics actually show less than 30 percent of the cows in Danish milk production ever get to go outside (Borkfelt et al. 2015, 1058; Danmarks Statistik 2021). There are other animals, too, who I may catch a glimpse of or get the chance to stroke: horses and ponies, mostly, and the occasional donkey, sheep, or goat. These are the animals who seemingly belong behind fences in the Danish countryside.

We create and naturalize categorizations of other animals by placing them behind fences as part of the domesticated, as opposed to the supposedly wild animals the cyclist may encounter in Denmark: deer, foxes, hares, pheasants. I still remember the pure excitement of seeing these kinds of animals when I was growing up, the feeling of rare privilege to have them cross my path as I was (most likely) cycling at the edge of the city where we lived. I still get excited, but what I see now is not exactly the same as back then. Rather, the animals I now see are also reminders of not just why I am vegan, but also why I do what I do in my professional life as a critical animal studies scholar, where other animals are constantly present in the abstract, but actual contact with them is often missing.

It is a spring morning, around 7:30 a.m., and I am cycling to work. The path leads me through a wooded area that is actually part of a park, but near the edge of the city. As I cycle through, I notice four roe deer close to the path. I stop. They have, of course, noticed me before I noticed them, so they are looking at me. We have seen each other a number of times before in the past month or so. One morning, I stopped and waited, as I could see they were crossing the path up ahead, and I wanted to disturb them as little as possible. Now, I stand still, trying simply to enjoy the encounter. After a while, they go back to eating, looking up at me only occasionally, perhaps taking turns to watch out. Aware that I should cycle on and get to work, I nonetheless try to just stay and enjoy this meeting. Eventually, another cyclist comes up behind me, disturbing the peace, and the deer trot farther away.

Like many things in life, our relations with other species are messy, and the more you learn, the more the easy categorizations of "wild" and "domesticated" break down. Wild animals are not always that wild. I remember, for instance, the sense of bewilderment the first time I cycled past a deer farm; but even those deer that are outside fences, it turns out, are fed with the aim of keeping them on particular grounds for the selling of hunting rights. Pheasants, ducks, and partridges, I have learned, are reared in captivity and released once a year to be shot (Gjerris et al. 2016, 22). Thus, these animals are just as much part of an industry as the ones I see behind fences. Whether to a greater or lesser degree, they are production units in systems of capital, where people profit from their deaths.

Yet this is not my primary experience when I encounter them while cycling. At the moment of encounter, they are wild, singular individuals that I can notice as such, just as the cow I stroke when I stretch my arm over a fence will stand out to me in that specific interspecies encounter. Ultimately, these are the kinds of encounters that occupy me the most, and they happen just as much—if not more—in my mind as in reality. Certainly, before I see a deer or a calf, I have more than likely already imagined the encounter as I was cycling, especially if I am in an area where I have had such encounters in the past. Cycling, I think, is in this way just as much about the inner journey as the one that stretches along country roads and paths, about going places in my mind while I am going places in the countryside.

I have cycled together with my children and other family members, which lends itself to different kinds of experiences, but I cover more ground, in both geographical and imaginary terms, while cycling alone.

When the Vegetarian Cycling Club was founded in the United Kingdom in 1888, the meat-eschewing cyclists of the time had ideas about the joys of cycling as a collective vegetarian endeavor. As the club's founder wrote enthusiastically in *The Vegetarian Messenger*, "We will have exercise, fresh air, the beauties of nature, ideal picnics, and merry returns to London afterwards, with vocal harmony to shorten the way!" (Large 1888, 18). I find this idea neat, if a bit eccentric (one sees the "comic potential" of which Coetzee writes more than a hundred years later), but ultimately unappealing. The idea of a group of singing vegetarians cycling along a British country road clashes too starkly with the space I prefer to give my mind to travel when I cycle.

It would be disingenuous of me to claim that my mind is always especially focused on vegan or animal-related issues whenever I cycle, but it is certainly often the case. In many instances, I get my best ideas and insights while cycling, as if this outdoor bodily exercise frees the mind to cruise down paths that work life does not always uncover. As a literary animal studies scholar, my mind is often preoccupied with animal encounters, whether real ones or the imaginary ones in the pages of books. This is directly tied to my veganism insofar as the latter is continually informed by the ways in which I consider animal minds and feelings in my work, and—probably—vice versa. I tend to believe our imagination, and what we feed it with, is more important for our ability to care and our recognition of other beings than we give it credit for.

At the best of times, this can make cycling trips with nonhuman animal encounters seem almost magical; here, while my mind may wonder about animal-related research interests, I may also imagine future animal encounters and have such encounters. There is an entanglement between imagination and reality there that somehow heightens my senses to the world around me, fine-tunes my caring, and connects my daily work life to the real animals I see, touch, or hear—but also, perhaps increasingly, to the animals I don't see or hear, simply because they are no longer there.

Noticing their absence is yet another way of observing what happens to animals. In 2017, a German study concluded that more than 75 percent of flying insects had disappeared within the previous twenty-seven years, and there is certainly no reason to think that the situation is any different in my own slightly more northern country, intensely cultivated as it is (Hallmann et al. 2017). Fewer insects obviously means fewer of the birds that feed on them, which can mean fewer of the larger birds and mammals that feed on the smaller birds. All in all, this would suggest that I am likely to encounter fewer wild animals when I cycle now than when I cycled as a kid. It may not always be my experience, but it seems clear to me that this should worry everyone, and cycling is good for processing my worries, too.

> *I am cycling rather leisurely along a gravelly forest path in a part of the country where I do not often go. In a clearing, a snake is crossing the path and I quickly stop before disturbing her. A viper, gray with black markings, the only venomous species of snake in this country. She must be at least as long as one of my arms. I stand there and watch as she finishes crossing, slithers into the tall grass at the side of the path, and is out of my sight.*

It is not that I no longer find myself cycling through swarms of insects—trying desperately to remember to keep my mouth closed—but there definitely are fewer insects than there used to be. There can be little doubt that intensive animal agriculture has played a significant role in this loss, both by turning what was formerly habitat for many species into monocultural fields of fodder for the few and by using pesticides for these crops. I suspect drivers of cars may notice this difference more easily than cyclists, if they compare the number of bugs on their windshields after a countryside drive to what would have been the experience twenty or thirty years ago.

I remember hearing my dad joke a few times that he was not really a vegetarian because cycling with his mouth open means he has occasionally been forced to swallow an insect that flew too far down his throat. With a dark sense of humor, one might add that it is thus easier to be a veggie cyclist these days. Taken seriously, of course, the joke makes no sense. Are you supposed to be more vegetarian or vegan when driving a car where hundreds, even thousands, of insects die as your windshield smashes into them? But as a joke it is not meant to be taken seriously. And yet, this bit of tongue-in-cheek veggie humor does point to issues that seem to me to matter—about ideas of vegans versus the ideals (and practice) of veganism, and about caring. This joke, in its own little way, does reveal that noticing and caring about even the lives of small individual insects can be a part of your self-perception as a vegan. At least it is for me, and it always has been; I remember semi-desperately trying to avoid running over earthworms with my bike trailer as I delivered papers on rainy days in my late teens. Being a vegan cyclist can make me contemplate such things.

Further, there can be little doubt that if one calculates the numbers, they will show that cars kill more animals than cycling. Not just insects, but larger animals, too—including humans, of course (having the time to notice animals reduced to "roadkill" by the roadside is yet another way of noticing animals, which may be more likely for the cyclist). Not to mention the more indirect effects of cars' contribution to the emissions causing the current climate crisis. Dare one then say that cycling is "more" vegan for this reason than driving a car? Or is that going too far?

Growing up, vegetarianism for me was first and foremost an intuitive relation to animals and a wish not to harm them. I suspect my current veganism is ultimately the same, underneath all the philosophical and scientific arguments that, as a critical animal studies scholar, I now know so very well. Cycling reconnects me with that intuitive relation to other animals. It allows me to see animals in the countryside who remind me of their individualities and of my feelings about them, should I have forgotten amidst the constant intellectualization one experiences in academic life. They even remind me to always put a little bit of the intuitive approach of my less educated yet somehow more immediate child self—the wish to do no harm and to help animals—into my academic work, so it becomes more than the semi-eccentric, nerdy interest it probably also is.

It is worth remembering that cycling can also highlight my vegan approach to life in other, more practical ways. In his essay, Coetzee (1995) writes briefly about "making the mistake of stranding myself on a bicycle on a country road near Bastrop, thirty miles east of Austin," and at least two hours away from home, having "fantasies of food" (44). I can relate; although the availability of vegan food has increased significantly in recent years, there are still parts of Denmark that will present vegans in search of a meal with a challenge, at least if it needs to be more elaborate than a few pieces of fruit or bread without much to put on it—which, in turn, leaves plenty of room for fantasizing about the vegan feast one might by comparison prepare at home or enjoy in the city. As a vegan cycling in the Danish countryside, one thus often needs to have a plan—or a packed lunch. With just a bit of luck in the right season I might even top this off with what could be both the most basic and most blissful of vegan meals: wild fruits or berries, picked as I take a short break from cycling through the woods.

I do not always give much thought to what I eat before I go cycling, but I also definitely do not cycle on an empty stomach. If I think about it, I am likely to go for a meal that I know will last me a while. Perhaps baked beans and toast for breakfast, with a couple of vegan sausages or some fried mushrooms and tomatoes on the side, depending on what I have available.

A long bike trip demands a good packed lunch to be enjoyed on a hilltop, on a bench in the woods, or by the seaside, but also one I can make quickly when I spontaneously decide to go biking. Perhaps Danish rye bread with homemade hummus or other vegan spreads, along with some raw veggies and fruit . . . and a bit of chocolate for those instances on the way back when an extra boost of energy is needed.

It is easy to fantasize about food as I bike. Oh, if only every town offered a place with exciting vegan meals! An Indian chickpea curry, perhaps; or Ethiopian flatbread (injera) with various toppings; or tacos and burritos; or perhaps just a vegan pizza—with artichokes, always. The possibilities are endless.

References

Borkfelt, Sune, Sara Kondrup, Helena Röcklinsberg, Kristian Bjørkdahl, and Mickey Gjerris. 2015. "Closer to Nature: A Critical Discussion of the Marketing of 'Ethical' Animal Products." *Journal of Agricultural and Environmental Ethics* 28, no. 6 (December): 1053–73. https://doi.org/10.1007/s10806-015-9577-4.

Coetzee, J. M. 1995. "Meat Country." *Granta* 52 (December): 41–52.

Danish Agriculture & Food Council. 2019. *Statistics 2018: Pigmeat.* Copenhagen: Danish Agriculture & Food Council. https://lf.dk/~/media/lf/tal-og-analyser /aarsstatistikker/statistik-svin/2018/2018-a5-statistik-svin-en-v2.pdf.

Danmarks Statistik. 2021. "Næsten halvdelen af Danmarks kvægbestand kommer på græs en del af året." Press release, July 20, 2021. https://www.dst.dk/da/Statistik /nyheder-analyser-publ/bagtal/2021/2021-07-20-Naesten-halvdelen-af-danmarks -kvaegbestand-kommer-paa-graes.

Gjerris, Mickey, Sune Borkfelt, Christian Gamborg, Jes Harfeld, and Sara Kondrup. 2016. *Jagt: Natur, mennesker, dyr og drab.* Aarhus, Denmark: Klim.

Hallmann, Caspar A., Martin Sorg, Eelke Jongejans, Henk Siepel, Nick Hofland, Heinz Schwan, Werner Stenmans, Andreas Müller, Hubert Sumser, Thomas Hörren, Dave Goulson, and Hans de Kroon. 2017. "More Than 75 Percent Decline over 27 Years in Total Flying Insect Biomass in Protected Areas." *PLoS One* 12, no. 10: e0185809. https://doi.org/10.1371/journal.pone.0185809.

Large, Leslie. 1888. "The Vegetarian Cycling Club." *The Vegetarian Messenger* 2 (New Series), no. 1: 17–18.

CHAPTER SEVEN

Three Wheels, Two Arms, and One Planet

Disabled Vegan Cycling and Eco-ability Consciousness

KAY INCKLE

Introduction: A Morning in Spring

It's just after seven in the morning, and the rain clouds have made the sky darker than it would normally be at this time of year. Heavy drops of water descend rhythmically from the trees, but the clouds have finished shedding their load, for now at least. The path is wet, and water sprays up my legs, muddy droplets shocking the bare skin between my leggings and my sneakers and reminding me why I bought Wellington boots last winter. I weave an uncertain path; the earthworms have taken this opportunity to emigrate from one grassland to the other, and my cycle route is littered with their soft pink bodies moving earnestly to their new location. Cycling on three wheels rather than two makes the task of avoiding the worms more challenging.

When I have finally arrived at the swimming pool, detached my handcycle, and am getting changed, I am horrified to find a mangled but still moving worm crushed against the brake of my wheelchair. I have no idea what to do. Shock and distress course through my body, and I am overtaken with indecision. It is almost as if the worm's pain is mine, I identify so much with that hurt body, injured by something utterly incomprehensible to it. But I know I have caused it. Full of guilt, I muster my resolve, gather the worm in toilet paper, and flush it down the toilet. I don't know if worms can drown, but I don't know if that was the right thing to do, and I am utterly decentered by the whole experience.

Kay Inckle. *Photograph courtesy of Kay Inckle.*

■ ■ ■

For me, both veganism and cycling are integral to my relationship with the planet we inhabit and the life forms and beings we share it with. They are part of an anti-oppressive consciousness based on living without harm and respecting the equality of all life. Thus, moments like this one, when my actions result in the opposite of my intentions, are profoundly traumatic for me.

This trauma is inseparable from my disability experience and the expanded dimensions of perception and empathy it engenders. My experience of disability, both as an embodied reality and as a source of violence and oppression, has sensitized me in ways that I cannot (and have no desire to) repress. I know what it is to be denied personhood, to endure medical experimentation, to be objectified, to have cries of pain forcefully silenced. I know what it is to be harmed in systems that deny my capacities, my rights, and my sentience. For me, then, the ethics and politics of disability are foundational and inseparable from veganism and environmentalism. And yet I exist mostly in isolation: there is no place, no community, no movement or ideology where all of these dimensions of my being belong. There are cycling groups that exclude disabled people, and disabled groups that do not accommodate vegans,[1] and there is much vegan ideology and infrastructure that is hostile to disabled people.

In this chapter I reflect on my experiences as a disabled vegan cyclist. I explore the politics and practices that have propelled me onwards, and the barriers in my path. I highlight the connections between disability, veganism, and cycling, and the exclusions within the vegan and cycling movements, in the hope of a more diverse, sustainable, and beautiful future for all.

"Do You Need Any Help?" Cycling as Mobility

I exit the swimming center with my hair still wet and my gym bag secured on the back of my chair, and wheel over to the bike stands where I have locked my handcycle. There are two men and a woman standing adjacent to it, clearly trying to figure out what it is and how it works. It does look a little strange: a single wheel with a long, rigid stem and chain leading to hand pedals, all resting on two silver legs—a little bit like some kind of unicycle with no saddle.

They step back a little as I approach, still trying to make sense of my handcycle. I smile and begin my usual explanation to the curious: it's called a handcycle; it attaches to my wheelchair and turns it into a hand-powered tricycle; yes, it does also have power assist on it—very important for getting up the hills of Liverpool! The trio decide to stay and watch as I unlock my cycle and attach it to my wheelchair.

It's a very simple process and takes around forty seconds to complete. I wheel my chair up the handcycle and make sure the clamps are aligned with the front bars of the chair. I then slide the chair into place and tighten the clamps around it. Next, I push two metal holding clips in place and then lift the cycle so that the clips lock and the supporting legs of the cycle and the front casters of my wheelchair are raised from the ground. I am now on three wheels and ready to roll.

Well, I would be, but halfway through my tightening the clamps, one of the men has decided that I must need his help. Before he has even finished asking if this is the case, he is already grabbing at the clamps and pushing my hands out of the way.

"I'm fine. I don't need help, thank you," I say, and then again, a little louder.

He does not even know what he is doing, but—typical of the confidence of an able-bodied man—he assumes that he must know more about a piece of mobility equipment he has never seen before than a disabled woman who uses it every day. When I have finally shaken him loose, I cycle away, leaving the annoyance behind me, this kind of occurrence far too frequent to let it ruffle my day.

■   ■   ■

Cycling has been my primary means of mobility ever since I left home. Although my parents insisted that I learn to ride a bike as a child, it was not something that they wanted me to do independently or to achieve autonomy through as I reached adulthood. However, I soon realized that cycling was the easiest and most pain-free way for me to get around—and it also made my disability invisible. As a young woman, still recovering from the trauma of medical abuse, and living in a familial and social context in which disability was utterly shameful, being free of the ableist gaze felt like a liberation. Moreover, being able to move freely and quickly through the power of my own body was new and exhilarating (I later discovered swimming).

Cycling therefore provided me with a pain-free form of mobility through which I could also hide my disability. However, while this was in many ways liberating, it was also very confusing: I wondered if I was entitled to use the lift, sit down on a bus, or avoid stairs, even when I desperately needed to. I felt my ability to cycle completely contradicted and overruled my difficulty in walking, and the opinion of those around me aggressively reinforced this—"There wasn't anything wrong with you when you were on the bike!" When I got off my bike and struggled to walk, or when I needed to cycle in a pedestrianized area, conflict, hostility, and obstruction were the norm, and this added to my shame and confusion about my seemingly contradictory abilities.

It was twenty-five years later, after my mobility had decreased even further, that I discovered, via a chance meeting with another disabled cyclist, that many disabled people cycle and that my abilities, rather than being anomalous, were in fact quite common. Indeed, for most people with physical disabilities, cycling is easier and safer than walking or wheelchair propulsion (Inckle 2019). Cycling also aids independence, contributes to sustainability, and has mental and physical health benefits for people who may otherwise face barriers to transport, mobility, and exercise.[2] There are also a huge range of cycles that are practicable for people whose disability prevents them from riding a standard two-wheeled bicycle. These include tricycles, recumbents, and handcycles, as well as e-assisted bicycles and cycles, which may also be designed for tandem as well as solo cycling.[3] It also transpired there was a campaign group, Wheels for Wellbeing (WfW; https://wheelsforwellbeing.org.uk/), who were working to improve awareness about, and access to, cycling for disabled people.

This meeting came at a pivotal time for me. I was transitioning to becoming a full-time wheelchair user, but I was desperate to continue cycling as I loved the freedom and the access to nature that it gave me. WfW introduced me to the handcycle, which is more or less a front wheel with hand pedals that clamps onto the front of a wheelchair and converts it into a hand-peddled tricycle (see picture at the opening of this chapter). My handcycle is now my primary means of transport. I cycle to the swimming pool before work each morning, and most days I also commute to and from work on it. I also use it for the daily necessities of life (such as shopping) and sometimes simply for pleasure. Plus the handcycle often accompanies me on train journeys to conferences and holidays around the United Kingdom.

Cycling is an essential part of my life in terms of mobility and independence, enabling me to remain active and healthy while enjoying the capacities of my body. However, it is also important to me ethically and politically. As a vegan and an environmentalist, I want to cause as little harm as possible to any of the life forms that make up our precious ecosystem. I want to minimize noise and pollution, and I want to travel through the environment in a way that leaves me open to and connected with it, rather than sealed off in a destructive metal box. Living without harm is fundamental to my veganism and my environmentalism, and these are also inseparable from my cycling and my disability politics.

Cycling as Politics: Handcycling to a Vegan Fair

There is a myth about London that it is so busy and diverse that no one ever stares at anyone, no matter what they are doing or what they are wearing—even if it is a Darth Vader costume. However, this is absolutely untrue. As I wait for the Overground train to pull into the station, my fellow passengers are already ogling my handcycle and making no secret of their staring. I sigh—it would be nice just for one day to be able to go about my business without being an object of curiosity and attention— but I know that we are a long way from a woman with a handcycle being past remarkable. The train pulls in and its doors open to shed a few passengers. It's still earlyish on a Saturday morning and the platform and carriage are relatively unoccupied. I maneuver my handcycle into the space near the door to ensure I am near enough to alight easily but without obstructing anyone else.

The Overground is slow, and I enjoy watching north London trundle by as we head toward the Animal Aid Christmas Fair in Kensington. I have been going to this fair for years now, before I moved to London and since moving away. It usually falls close to my birthday and provides a double excuse for a weekend of indulgence in London. Living in London made it much easier to stock up with goodies—everything from lip balm to bamboo socks and every kind of cake known to woman.

Today, I have brought bags and Tupperware containers so I can get pies and cakes and pastries safely back across London later on. By the

KAY INCKLE

time we arrive at Kensington Olympia, the train has filled up and there is a crush of people on the platform. I can see the man with the ramp at the back of the small crowd, and he is being totally ignored as he requests they use another door so he can put the ramp down. Stations that do not have level access are much more stressful to navigate. I can never be totally confident that I will be able to get off the train—especially on the days when the person with the ramp does not show up. At least he is here today.

He finally gets the ramp to the train doors and I alight. As I cycle away I notice that my chest has tightened, and I inhale to release it. Anxiety is a frequent traveling companion when I use public transport, and it is only when I am cycling toward all the delights of the vegan fair that my feeling of joyful anticipation returns.

■　■　■

I became a vegetarian when I was fourteen because I did not want to cause harm to animals. I turned vegan when I was nineteen and could no longer pretend to myself that "dairy" products were somehow devoid of the violence and cruelty inherent in other animal-based products. I consider veganism to be the most important aspect of my identity, more important than my gender, sexuality, disability, class position, or occupation. Part of its importance is the fact that it is a choice that I have consciously made and one that shapes and interconnects all other aspects of my life.

Carol J. Adams's *The Sexual Politics of Meat* (1990/2015) was pivotal in my understanding the violence and oppression behind the so-called dairy industry, linking my burgeoning consciousness of both animal rights and feminism. I found Adams's concept of "feminized protein" (80) a particularly powerful encapsulation of the way in which gendered violence intertwines both speciesism and patriarchy. It also invoked a sense of sisterly empathy with nonhuman animals and their suffering. Moreover, understanding that exploitation, oppression, and violence against nonhuman animals (and the planet/"nature") are foundational to the systems of oppression exacted on humans (through, for example, patriarchy, slavery, and colonialism) helped me to further unpack the origins of inequality rather than accept them as the "natural order" of things in which contemporary society epitomizes progress and civilization.[4]

Nowadays it is increasingly common for vegans to draw links between the exploitation, use, and abuse of nonhuman animals, and violence and oppression against humans and the environment (Colling 2012). It is also commonplace for environmentalism to be linked with veganism, now that the climate impacts of animal "farming" are beyond dispute.[5] Likewise, cycling and veganism commonly intersect around concerns for the protection of the environment and using the least destructive forms of transport. And this is where I have hoped to find community with people who share these values. However, as a disabled person I am often viewed as anomalous to the vegan, cycling, and environmentalist communities—even when they are arguing for universal adoption of their beliefs and practices. The establishments, facilities, activities, and collectives run by and for these groups are very often inaccessible to people with disabilities,[6] and attitudes can be hostile and exclusionary.

Disabled animal and environmental rights activists have pointed to significant ableism in the values and language of these movements, along with a pervasive and sometimes overt suggestion that disabled people are undesirable, burdensome, and/or should not exist.[7] For example, Peter Singer, who is widely credited with conceptualizing "animal rights"[8] and is a hero to many vegans, is openly eugenicist in his attitude to disabled people. He has stated that "killing a disabled infant is not morally equivalent to killing a person. Very often it is not wrong at all" (Withers 2012, 114). He has also used arguments about the alleged potential for human happiness as a rationale for exterminating disabled people: "When the death of a disabled infant will lead to the birth of another infant with better prospects of a happy life, the total amount of happiness will be greater if the disabled infant is killed" (Withers 2012, 113).

How am I supposed to feel about sharing spaces (if I can actually get into them) with people who believe that I should have been killed at birth? How do I know who is hostile to my existence in a vegan environment? What is the personal cost to me of having to compromise my worth as a human being in order to access vegan spaces? The vegan world can feel hard, cold, and exclusionary much of the time. And it is not simply that vegans are unaware of these issues of inclusion; they often simply do not want to rethink them, and they have the privilege not to have to (Beswick 2019).

In this lonely void, I encountered writing from the eco-ability movement that not only challenged the ableism in the vegan and environmentalist movements, but also highlighted that understanding ableism is essential to environmental and animal rights philosophy (Nocella, Bentley, and Duncan 2012a). To me this was a revelation: not only were there other people like me, but they also had articulated how ableism and "ability privilege" (Socha, Bentley, and Schatz 2014, 4) are integral to violence against the ecosystem, nonhuman animals, and other humans.

Eco-ability begins with the recognition that all living things have different abilities that form an interdependent whole or "bio-community" (Nocella, Bentley, and Duncan 2012, xiv): trees transform carbon dioxide into oxygen; oxygen is inhaled by beings that convert oxygen into the physical energy required to fly, jump, walk, swim, or slither, who then pollinate flowers that grow into food or consume the waste of or clean other animals or bodies of water. Indeed, this diversity of ability is the basis of life on earth: "difference was, and is, the essential ingredient for human and global survival" (Nocella, Bentley, and Duncan 2012, xvii).

Ableism, however, views only certain capacities as abilities. For example, reading with the eyes is an ability, but reading with the fingers (braille) is classed a deficit or disability. Walking upright on two legs is an ability, but walking on four (or more) legs (or propelling wheels) is a deficit.[9] Ability is therefore defined from the perspective of a (so-called) able-bodied human, and all other capacities are invalidated (Inckle 2019). Only those with privileged abilities are considered part of the "moral community" (e.g., white, able-bodied, heterosexual, neurotypical, cisgender men). Humans with physicalities and abilities that deviate from this norm, including people of color, women, children, LGBTQ+ people, and disabled people, have been denied rights and subjected to enslavement, torture, eugenics, murder, colonization, exploitation, and marginalization. In much the same way, nonhuman animals and "nature" have also been defined as lacking the abilities/capacities that would exempt them from appropriation, abuse, exploitation, harm, and destruction. Ableism, then, justifies violence and oppression against a wide range of human and nonhuman animals and the ecosystem, on the basis of their lack of ability and/or capacity.[10] These ableist processes combine to legitimize genocidal and ecocidal practices. For example, Indigenous people in what is now the United States were given the status of "fauna" in order to legitimize their displacement and extermination (Colling 2012, 94), and lack of capacity has been used to justify the ownership of some beings/life forms, relegating them to the status of property—a concept integral to capitalism and the beliefs and practices that are destroying life on earth.[11]

From an eco-ability perspective, then, ableism is not simply a detriment to disabled people, it is a hierarchical and abusive system that underpins and legitimates all human, nonhuman, and environmental oppression, exploitation, and destruction. An eco-ability perspective also highlights the interdependence of all types of life and ability.

Interdependence: A Dark Winter Morning

It is at least another two hours until dawn, and I am cycling through the tree-lined avenue of the park toward the swimming pool. Since I moved from London to Liverpool, I have noticed something strange happening to the chain on my handcycle, but I can't figure out what it is. It feels and sounds as if the chain has somehow slipped out of place, but when I check the cogs and derailleur they all look fine, but I am only just becoming accustomed to the mechanics of the handcycle and I don't really know what I am looking for.

I continue to turn the handcrank, but there is a sensation of decreasing power and grip. Then, all of a sudden, the chain jams rigid and there is no movement at all. I give it a bit of a wiggle and try and turn the hand pedals, but nothing happens. Then I use full force to propel the handcrank and there is a resounding crack in response. Now I definitely have a problem.

I detach from the handcycle and peer at the machine. The derailleur has snapped clean off and is hanging by a wire. It is dark, I am alone in the middle of a deserted park, and I have no way to move my handcycle. Unlike an able-bodied cyclist, I cannot simply get up and push, carry, or walk with my cycle when there is a problem with it; when my cycle stops, I stop.

Fear begins to pummel my heart and squeeze air from my lungs. I am now incapacitated, and utterly dependent upon—or vulnerable to—those who come into the park and whether they choose to help me or prey upon me.[12]

■ ■ ■

In the able-bodied imagination (e.g., mainstream culture) disability is always associated with dependence and incapacity—being needy and unable to survive unassisted. And in capitalism and patriarchy, dependence is devalued at best and at worst vilified. Those who are seen as dependent on others, and especially on state welfare provision, are viewed as burdensome. But those who are positioned as being dependent by *choice* are particularly vilified. Historically, this has been the so-called undeserving poor: the unemployed or "underclass" who are viewed as morally deficient for "choosing" to live outside of social norms and values such as paid employment and heteropatriarchal family structures. However, the Conservative-led UK government's austerity program has expanded this category so that sick and disabled people are now also viewed as "undeserving" along with those whose wages are too low to sustain their basic needs (Ryan 2019, 11–37). Moreover, disabled people are seen not only as financially dependent but also socially and emotionally burdensome to others. This political rhetoric has increased hostility and resentment against disabled people, as evidenced in rising levels of disability hate crime in Britain (Equality and Human Rights Commission [EHRC] 2017, 112–14).

For a number of decades, feminists have critiqued the binary conceptualization of dependence and independence, and the reification of the latter. They have drawn attention to the gendered structures and inequalities (e.g., the invisible and unpaid work of women) from which the concepts emerge. To counter this, feminists have argued for "an ethic of care" that prioritizes relationships, context, and responsibility rather than abstract rights, individualism, and separation (Donovan and Adams 2007). The feminist ethic of care highlights interconnectedness and interdependence, and has been incorporated into a range of feminist praxis from research methods to animal rights discourse.

Despite identifying as a feminist for as long as I remember, I have always been uncomfortable with the feminist ethic of care in both gender and disability contexts. To me, the notion of care seems to emerge too directly from the gender binary (men are rational, women are emotional) and to recreate assumptions about women (we all have children or dependents to care for). As such, it seems to simply reverse the order of value ascribed to the gender binary and reinforce that binary rather than dismantling it altogether. In addition, the care that I read (perhaps incorrectly) in the feminist ethic fits neither my experience of gender nor disability, and I worry that disability has been co-opted to act as a poster child for a political movement that has often shown little solidarity or engagement with the rights of disabled women (Inckle 2014).

For me, then, the conceptualization of interdependence that emerged from the eco-ability critique of ableism had much more impact, not just because it critiques the binary of dependence/independence but also because it is based on an understanding of the diversity of ability not as unfortunate or burdensome but as essential to life on earth: "All ability is respected as part of a rich and diverse ecosystem" (Colling 2012, 98). It is ableism that creates the illusion of independence: those who have socially valued abilities use their power to create structures that conceal their dependence and enable them to exploit and harm others to fulfill their needs. Eco-ability challenges the myth of independence and values interdependence *and diversity* in tandem. As such, eco-ability "advocates for a new understanding of nature as diverse and interdependent, with each part, regardless of size, function or impact having a valued role to play. Life is not about *survival of the fittest* . . . where there is a winner and a loser. Rather we must recognize how the bio-community promotes a win-win situation instead of the win-lose relationship" (Nocella, Bentley, and Duncan 2012, xiv). It is only (some) human beings, those with ability privilege, who have corrupted the "natural order" from a system of mutual support and benefit to one of exploitation and inequality, and, in doing so, are destroying life on earth.

To me, eco-ability states more clearly than feminism (with its apparent revaluation rather than overturning of the gender binary) that *diversity is essential* and *interdependence is universal*—and, moreover, that it is power structures that link dependency and vulnerability, not the "nature" of those who depend. The socially structured and enforced dependency of disabled people and, for example, farmed animals, does not result from the differing abilities/capacity of those who are subjugated (dependent) and those who are dominant (depended upon). Rather, it is the power structure that enables those with "ability privilege" to define, own, and control those with devalued abilities and capacities. To know myself to be dependent is to know myself to be at risk within a system where those who cause harm are more valued and supported than those who are harmed. In this context, to be physically dependent on others is to be most vulnerable.

In an alternative world, where all beings were valued and all abilities were recognized as integral to an interdependent whole, would I be afraid when stranded alone in the dark with a broken handcycle? Or would it simply be another experience in the rich web of life that offers a connection with beings whose journey momentarily intersects with mine?

Imagining Disabled Vegan Cycling Futures

I have argued that a critical perspective on disability is not merely an afterthought or an add-on to vegan, cycling, and environmentalist movements, but rather is essential to our analysis if we are to fully understand and overcome inequality and oppression. If I could handcycle my way into a future based on the experiences and principles I have described, what might it look like? And how can I encourage more able-bodied vegan cyclists to open out their imagined future to include diverse bodies and abilities?

In my imagined future, all humans would be vegan and all humans would cycle. There would be an even wider range of cycles available than is currently the case, and cycling would be the primary means of transport for everyone, whether solo, tandem, or supported. Communities would be built around cycling, low consumption, rewilding, and communal responsibility (rather than ownership). All beings would be respected for their contribution to sustaining the community, and there would be no hierarchies based on any kind of ability privilege. Diversity of beings and diversity within species would be celebrated for the uniqueness that each contributes to the kaleidoscope of life, especially when their contribution is not comprehensible to a human perspective.

This future would be lived/cycled in the "slow lane," with care, attention, sharing, and avoidance of harm valued over speed, accumulation, power, and competition. Care and attention would bring joy to existence and open up the time to explore and celebrate our own and one another's capacities. It would mean less time in paid work and more hours focused on both the necessities of life (such as growing and producing food) and on creativity, arts, and community. Indeed, the basics of living would be reinvested with creativity and community, rather than automated for individualized consumption.

Yet it is a future that is unrecognizable to the values and practices that dominate the present and threaten life on earth. I know that my idealized future is barely within grasp. It is much more likely that we are going to be overtaken by climate (and political) catastrophe before we transition to living sustainably and without cruelty, and where all life is valued and respected.

However, in my own small way, I am trying to make this future part of my present, and to appreciate each moment that I can do so.

I bump my handcycle over the curb outside my local vegan mini-market and my shopping stirs in the rucksack suspended from the handles of my wheelchair. I turn into the park; a dog regards me curiously and then, in a burst of excitement, bounds alongside me, tail wagging and eyes glinting. Sometimes a child will try and race me on their bike or scooter, or an adult will catch up with me on the road and cycle alongside me for a companionable chat. I have learned at what speed to cycle at dawn so as not to startle birds as they forage for food; at dusk I often pause to enjoy the low swoops and raucous cries of the roosting crows. In these moments I am as at peace in my body as the crows and the trees are in theirs. All of us have the perfect form for our purpose and, like them, I am one of a spectrum of beings on a vast and complex planetary ecosystem. And yet, also like them, I am at heightened risk of the violence metered out on the bodies and beings who are devalued in the speciesist/ableist hierarchy that is the seedbed of all oppression and that may ultimately destroy all life on earth.

I am often hungry and thinking about food when I cycle: in the morning, on the way back from the swimming pool for breakfast before work; and in the evening, cycling home from work. I don't think that much about what to eat for breakfast as I have a pretty set range of things that I consume—always including milled flax seeds and my own blend of herbal tea: liquorice, peppermint, comfrey, and meadowsweet. Comfrey, which has been in culinary and medicinal use since the Middle Ages (known colloquially as "bone knit"), is now a restricted substance in the United Kingdom and can be sold for external use only.

In the evenings, especially when I do my favorite "four-park" cycle route home, I am often thinking about what I would like to have for dinner. This rumination is always heightened when I go through a multicultural part of Liverpool, with the many international foods on display: Ethiopian, Turkish, Indian, Caribbean, Thai, Lebanese. Not many of these outlets are both vegan and accessible, but they sometimes inspire me to try things out at home, and I have had some success with Ethiopian/East African cooking.

Any other times that I think about food while cycling, I am most likely to be thinking about cake! I am a little bit obsessed with cake, especially now there is so much good vegan cake available—carrot cake is my favorite.

KAY INCKLE

Notes

1. This is not always true; at their tenth birthday party, Wheels for Wellbeing (an inclusive cycle campaign group) ensured that there was vegan birthday cake available—but this was notable by how unusual it was.
2. See, for example, Arnet et al. (2016); Clayton, Parkin, and Billington (2016); Hickman (2015); Smith, Perrier, and Martin (2016); and Springer (2013), 77–86.
3. See Hickman (2015), 1–9, and Wheels for Wellbeing (2017), 1–44, for some examples of the range of cycles available. A *bicycle* is a two wheeled vehicle for one person which is peddled with the feet; it is often referred to as a bike. A *cycle* may have two or more wheels and may be peddled with the hands or feet and transport one or more persons (Inckle 2019).
4. Marilyn French's *Beyond Power: On Women, Men, and Morals* (1986) was also instrumental for me.
5. See, for example, Cowspiracy, "The Facts," http://www.cowspiracy.com/facts; and Monbiot (2017).
6. There is some limited equality legislation in Britain that requires public organizations (e.g., libraries) and large businesses (e.g., Starbucks) to have wheelchair access, but independent small businesses and organizations are exempt.
7. See Nocella (2012a, 2012b); Socha, Bentley, and Schatz (2014); Withers (2012); and Wrenn et al. (2015).
8. Animal rights movements and literature existed in the three centuries before Singer articulated his perspective and were largely populated and produced by women—see Donovan (2007).
9. Sunaura Taylor discusses this in her *Beasts of Burden* (2017) at 101–16.
10. See Colling (2012); Nocella (2012a); and Socha, Bentley, and Schatz (2014).
11. See Nocella II (2014) and Socha, Bentley, and Schatz (2014).
12. Help does come, in the form of a man on his way to work who pushes my handcycle to the swimming baths and also recommends a local cycle shop to me. I call the cycle shop; they send a member of the staff to collect my handcycle, and it is repaired the next day. I am lucky, and this is not the first time that I have been rescued in Liverpool—there is strong community spirit in this city, and it is something that I not only benefit from and appreciate but also recognize as part of the essential ingredient for an alternative future.

References

Adams, Carol J. 2015. *The Sexual Politics of Meat: A Feminist-Vegetarian Critical Theory*. London: Bloomsbury. First published 1990 by Continuum (London).

Arnet, Ursula, T. Hinrichs, V. Lay, S. Bertschy, H. Friel, and M. W. G. Brinkhof. 2016. "Determinants of Handbike Use in Persons with Spinal Cord Injury: Results of a Community Survey in Switzerland." *Disability & Rehabilitation* 38 (1): 81–86.

Beswick, Aaron. 2019. "Controversial Philosopher's Halifax Appearance Raises Ire." *Saltwire*, March 18, 2019. https://www.thechronicleherald.ca/news/local /controversial-philosophers-halifax-appearance-raises-ire-293121/.

Clayton, William, John Parkin, and Colin Billington. 2016. "Cycling and Disability: A Call for Further Research." *Journal of Transport and Health* 6:452–562.

Colling, Sarat. 2012. "Transnational Feminism and Eco-ability: Transgressing the Borders of Normalcy and Nation." In *Earth, Animal, and Disability Liberation: The Rise of the Eco-ability Movement*, edited by Anthony J. Nocella II, Judy K. C. Bentley, and Janet M. Duncan, 91–110. New York: Peter Lang.

Donovan, Josephine. 2007. "Animal Rights and Feminist Theory." In *The Feminist Care Tradition in Animal Ethics*, edited by Josephine Donovan and Carol J Adams, 58–86. New York: Columbia University Press.

Donovan, Josephine, and Carol J. Adams. 2007. "Introduction." In *The Feminist Care Tradition in Animal Ethics*, edited by Josephine Donovan and Carol J. Adams, 1–20. New York: Columbia University Press.

EHRC (Equality and Human Rights Commission). 2017. *Being Disabled in Britain: A Journey Less Equal*. London: EHRC.

French, Marilyn. 1986. *Beyond Power: On Women, Men, and Morals*. New York: Johnathan Cape.

Hickman, Kevin. 2015. "Disabled Cyclists in England: Imagery in Policy and Design." *Urban Design and Planning* 169 (3): 129–37.

Inckle, Kay. 2014. "A Lame Argument: Profoundly Disabled Embodiment as Critical Gender Politics." *Disability & Society* 29 (3): 388–401.

———. 2019. "Disabled Cyclists and the Deficit Model of Disability." *Disability Studies Quarterly* 39 (4). https://doi.org/10.18061/dsq.v39i4.6513.

Monbiot, George. 2017. "Goodbye—and Good Riddance—to Livestock Farming." *The Guardian*, October 4, 2017. https://www.theguardian.com/commentisfree/2017/oct/04/livestock-farming-artificial-meat-industry-animals.

Nocella, Anthony J. II. 2012a. "Defining Eco-ability: Social Justice and the Intersectionality of Disability, Nonhuman Animals and Ecology." In *Earth, Animal, and Disability Liberation: The Rise of the Eco-ability Movement*, edited by Anthony J. Nocella II, Judy K. C. Bentley, and Janet M. Duncan, 3–21. New York: Peter Lang.

———. 2012b. "Eco-ability Theory in Action: A Challenge to Ableism in the Environmental Movement." In *Earth, Animal, and Disability Liberation: The Rise of the Eco-ability Movement*, edited by Anthony J. Nocella II, Judy K. C. Bentley, and Janet M. Duncan, 242–48. New York: Peter Lang.

———. 2014. "Anarchist Criminology against Ableism and Racism and for Animal Liberation." In *Anarchism and Animal Liberation: Essays on Complementary Elements of Total Liberation*, edited by Anthony J. Nocella II, Richard J. White, and Erica Cudworth, 40–58. Jefferson, NC: McFarland.

Nocella, Anthony J. II, Judy K. C. Bentley, and Janet M. Duncan. 2012. "The Rise of Eco-ability." In *Earth, Animal, and Disability Liberation: The Rise of the Eco-ability Movement*, edited by Anthony J. Nocella II, Judy K. C. Bentley, and Janet M. Duncan, xiii–xxii. New York: Peter Lang.

Ryan, Frances. 2019. *Crippled: Austerity and the Demonization of Disabled People*. London: Virago.

Smith, Brett, M. J. Perrier, and J. Martin. 2016. "Disability Sport: A Partial Overview and Some Thoughts about the Future." In *Routledge International Handbook of Sport Psychology*, edited by R. Schinke, K. McGannon, and B. Smith, 296–303. London: Routledge.

Socha, Kimberly Ann, Judy K. C. Bentley, and JL Schatz. 2014. "An Introduction to Eco-ability: The Struggle for Justice, with Focus on Humans with Disabilities and Nonhuman Animals." *Journal for Critical Animal Studies* 12 (2): 1–8.

Springer, B. A. 2013. "Ride 2 Recovery's Project Hero: Using Cycling as Part of Rehabilitation." *Physical Therapy in Sport* 14: 77–86.

Taylor, Sunaura. 2017. *Beasts of Burden: Animal and Disability Liberation*. New York: New Press.

WfW (Wheels for Wellbeing). 2017. *A Guide to Inclusive Cycling*, 1st ed. London: WfW.

Withers, A. J. 2012. "Disableism within Animal Advocacy and Environmentalism." In *Earth, Animal, and Disability Liberation: The Rise of the Eco-ability Movement*, edited by Anthony J. Nocella II, Judy K. C. Bentley, and Janet M. Duncan, 111–25. New York: Peter Lang.

Wrenn, Corey Lee, Joanne Clark, Maddie Judge, Katharine A. Gilchrist, Delanie Woodlock, Katherine Dotson, Riva Spanos, and Jonathan Wrenn. 2015. "The Medicalization of Nonhuman Animal Rights: Frame Contestation and the Exploitation of Disability." *Disability & Society* 30 (9): 1307–27.

Naomi Stekelenburg, St Mary's National Park, Tasmania. *Photograph by Craig O'Hara.*

CHAPTER EIGHT

"Christ on a Bike, You're a Dumb Dog"

NAOMI STEKELENBURG

You are "human," but recent occurrences concerning your feet have called into question your certainty about what this means.

You're heading up a mountain range in northern Tasmania. There's you, your bike, the clothes on your back, and your supplies in two Ortlieb Back-Roller Classic waterproof panniers. You'll sleep tonight in a covered Warbonnet hammock suspended between two of anything that will hold your sixty-nine kilograms. The hammock is usually waterproof. When in it, you remind yourself of a caterpillar in a horizontal chrysalis.

The sun makes a tiger-stripe tan mark on your fur-less feet. The signs along the way promise that just over the range there is a town called Frankford. They tell you Frankford is a "tidy town" and you imagine a patriarchal figure named Frank—war medals, smelling of soap, feet astride, centered, doughy fleshed, flesh eating (though he'd deny the flesh bit and say instead he just likes a good "steak")—waiting in the middle of the road to greet you. Blocking the road, you might even say. "Welcome to Frankford": another sign and another promise. Language—even the language of fact—can deceive.

The sign promises you've arrived. Yet what is here? A driveway with, yes, some protection from the wind, but little else. You pull over and check your map. The heart of Frankford is still ten kilometers away and marked by what appears to be the town's only attraction, the "Blue Barn" café. Named because it is blue (there's no space for play in the Australian bush) and represented, it seems, by a mascot—a wooden carved cow. The carving is rough and without detail, the color of liver in some places.

You wonder if this is a sick joke by the sculptor. Did Frank himself have a hand in this?

You head farther up the range toward the cow and Frank. You watch your feet because looking up means facing a truth that will only dishearten. Right now, pushing your bike up this mountain, heart is what you need. And the shadows distort. Your feet are not feet but, shod as they are, hooves. And now feel again, "long and set parallel; they are made to move on ahead"; this is Alphonso Lingis quoting Bruce Chatwin in his essay, "The Steppe" (Lingis 2012, 299), a celebration of space, but also an experiment in collapsing notions of past and present, culture and nature—animal and human.

In this essay, I want to work through the problem of how people and things—and not-things, not-humans—can live together (Muecke 2008, 95). Through memories and field notes taken during my recent month-long cycling tour of Tasmania, Australia, I want to use the object of the bicycle to question the nature/culture human/animal divide, and in doing so, perform for you my sense of why I see veganism as more than a food choice but rather an imperative derived from my own embodiment. I hope this chapter will take the form of "an interesting fictocritical journey where the writer reveals what is at stake for him or her as they take the reader gently but firmly on a journey whose signposts sometimes express feelings, sometimes ways of knowing" (Muecke 2008, 16).

Allow me a pause here to resist the temptation to show you holiday slides. I need to counter the expectation, so ingrained by my "civilized" education, to unfold for you a linear narrative of my journey from novice to master; not-knowing to knowing; unsure to certain. You know how the story goes.

As if everything we write must be logical and rational.

In Australia with our laconic skepticism, we roll our eyes and say, "As if."

As if.

Fictocriticism, in its rejection of the (masculine) "institutional super-ego or the policing of the academic discipline" (Gibbs 2005, n.p.), subverts traditional forms of essay where the writer moves in an orderly file from premise to logical conclusion. Instead, it foregrounds—and indeed celebrates—performativity, interjection, pastiche, and fragment. It is a form that seeks new forms of relationship with academic authority and, as such, has been adopted by feminist writers (Hélène Cixous, Luce Irigaray,

Monique Wittig, Annie Dillard) seeking to speak what has been unspoken; to inject new voices into old forms of power and oppression; to wonder (at once) ethnographically, anthropologically, sociologically, and psychophysiologically—always asking at the fore, "What if?" In "turning fictocritical" (Muecke 2008, 16), we embrace what Michael Taussig (2006) refers to as "mastering the art of non-mastery" (viii).

To take this stance of nonmastery is vital to me as an essayist whose central concern is my relationship with nonhuman animals, a space where every turn is furnished with the language of hierarchy, dominance, and oppression. After all, as philosopher, Val Plumwood (2009) suggests, "Writers are amongst the foremost of those who can help us to think differently" (126).

You're at Frankford now and you set up your hammock in a memorial park for soldiers. The plaque on the war memorial says:

Frankford Soldiers Memorial

Erected in memory of the citizens of Frankford who served their country during war.

Lest we forget.

The land is completely stripped of trees, ironically echoing images of the destruction of the Western Front during World War I. The Australian national flag flies. But no birds or insects do (did Frank and his ilk spray them away?). Your space here in the memorial park is eerily uncontested. Then a man bursts through the childproof gate in the park. He's on his bike, too. He announces three facts: his name is Yoshi, he's a Buddhist, and he is hungry. He takes from the cooler strapped to his bike a six-pack of beer and three lumps of cow flesh. He drinks the beer while the flesh cooks. He tells me about his encounters with "wildlife" in Australia. He says he has "met" a wombat and "met" a possum. You like this idea of meeting nonhuman animals rather than seeing or "spotting" them, as native English speakers would say.

Yoshi adds that the echidna he saw would be worth 65,981 yen in Japan, and it bothers you he knows this figure so precisely.

You have seen only one echidna so far, and it was dead on the side of the road, recognizable only for its spikes. Yoshi tells you before he beds down that tomorrow, he will ride exactly 96.34 kilometers to the next town. You're irritated by his calculations. As if everything is set in stone. You leave Yoshi, the flesh-eating, bike riding Buddhist, next morning and head to the sea.

You ride across stretches of highway. The summer sun is so strong it illuminates everything. No dark corners. No gray uncertainties. The cows graze on the grass left after the sun and lack of rain have had their way. You lean your bike against the paddock fence. Those cows there? They don't know they're human capital. But you know it. Your bike slips on the fence and crashes into the long grass by the paddock. The cows look at you and you at them. That is all for some time.

As an Australian child in the '70s, you spent much of your holidays in the car on road trips. Seatbelts so hot they would brand your tender hips with their mark. You counted the cows as you sped past them on the highway, "1, 2, 3, 4, 5, 6, 7, 8, 9, 10, 11, 12, 13, 14, 15."

They tell insomniacs to count sheep to help them fall asleep. No clear advice, though, on how to wake people up.

You Google the term "Tasmania, food" and you get:

2. *Dairy Agriculture*
Tasmanian dairy cows are housed outside all year round grazing on grass and clover while enjoying some of the cleanest air in the world. The dairy industry is the largest sector of our agricultural industry in Tasmania and is a significant contributor to the Tasmanian economy.

Statistics are one thing, but riding through you see visible proof of the state's reliance on animal production and commodification, from the most explicit signs of the cows grazing in fields to the prominence of cheese tasting and "wildlife" experience brochures in the tourist sheds.

In the beginning, there was the word:

And God said, Let us make man in our image, after our likeness: and let them have dominion over the fish of the sea, and over the fowl of the air, and over the cattle, and over all the earth, and over every creeping thing that creepeth upon the earth.[1]

"Sorry," you mouth to the cows.

Let's get back to facts. As promised in the title of this collection, what I'm about to offer speaks to the connection between veganism and

The milk mothers produce for their babies is stolen and sold, making it a significant contributor to Tasmania's economy. *Photograph by Craig O'Hara.*

cycling. Why am I vegan? And why does this long-awaited cycling tour of the nature-culture land of Tasmania hold so much promise in answering that question?

You know why you cycle. You sold your white Toyota Camry five years ago to a student who'd recently moved from rural Queensland. He was full of black bean chicken and bubbly enthusiasm for his new means of momentum and the big-city life. You, on the other hand, were glad to see the end of your Toyota. You are with philosopher Peter Sloterdijk, who describes the car rather psychoanalytically as a "uterus on wheels" that both intoxicates and produces psychic regression, resulting in "primitive-aggressive competitive behaviour" (2016c, 23). Cars, in other words, are a means of controlling the threats of the world "outside." As Sloterdijk notes:

> I sometimes ask myself how so many friends in my circle happen not
> to have a driving licence. I'm like a magnet that pulls nails out of a
> rotten old ship—I have a curious ability to attract people from the
> intellectual scene who function completely as non-drivers. . . . We
> obviously play different kinds of mastery games (2016b, 43).

Here, on the highway, pushing up that hill again, you wonder what your particular mastery game is? Are you on an "inward" journey, back to the first form of mobility—the amniotic, mammalian comfort of your mother? Or is this an outward journey?

As you ride, you think of Pam, one of your colleagues at the university where you work. Whenever you see her, she tells you she's up to her ears in work. "Same," you say, dryly. There are two signs above the office sink: one says, "We work in a university so here's an idea: CLEAN UP AFTER YOURSELF." The other: "Please know not to touch my mug. It is the one with pugs on it."

The signs are written in Pam's well-trained hand. She breeds pugs. You know this because once you heard her telling everyone in the lunchroom about how pugs can no longer have intercourse without help, so you have to "give them a hand, if you know what I mean."

Picture this: there is no cycling lane on the road. So, there is you, your bike, and cars on their way to Christmas turkeys. Perhaps Frank is in one of those cars, salivating at the thought of cooked flesh. You wish the cars were uteruses on wheels because this way, if they hit you, you might bounce off them and fall gently to the ground. Instead, at the speeds they're traveling, a slight knock and you will plummet meters down into the cultivated timber forest.

A car slows behind you, holding up the traffic behind it. There is little space between you and the edge of the forest, so you take space on the road. The car can pass you but refuses. To prove a point? You look in a forward direction, determined not to feel threatened by the act of what Mick Smith (2012) calls a kind of "macho andro- and anthropo-centric displacement of emotional involvement in the world, the re-assertion of the centrality of the individual's autonomous and automotive interests above all else" (24). The car prohibits other cars passing and there is a confusing cacophony of angry horns. Is it cars themselves and the emotion they protect us from that elicit a disconnect from animals? Smith goes some way to suggesting this may be the case:

> What, then, happens emotionally in a society dependent on auto-mobility? Certainly our enclosure in the automobile's metal sheath, the speed of travel, the narrow beams of the headlights, the wall of sound from the stereo-system, the touch-button control of air flow and temperature, disrupt our possible attunements to the non-human world, they conspire to reduce the potential for any

emotional openness that might regard the animals encountered on the pavement as ethical Others, as beings in themselves (31).

Is that what is happening to you now? Have you, with your bike on this road, been denied a position in the category of the ethical Other?

■ ■ ■

The sun blurs the road ahead. You consider Plumwood's (2012) reflection on nearly being eaten by a crocodile; how this caused her to revise her thinking about human–animal relations: "The fact of being always on the 'winning side' of the predation relationship tricks us, conceals from us the real slant of things, the real measure of our animality and embodiment" (13). Though the cars are not going to eat you, you're prey all the same.

Sloterdijk (2016b) questions the sacrifice accorded by our modern human obsession with cars. Although cars "democratize" human societies in that the peasant can outspeed the lord, the cost in lives may not be sustainable (47). Over half a million animals are killed each year on Tasmania's roads (Cooper 2019). To counter this, colorful pamphlets with cartoon animals wearing bloody dents and wounds are circulated in tourist centers.

You count the corpses on the highway. You make a list. You bear witness this way:

> 5 wallabies
> 13 kangaroos
> 3 possums
> 13 snakes
> 6 marsupials (other)
> 1 black cockatoo

Of course, Sloterdijk talking about cars and me about bikes is really just a way of knowing our place in the world and—with that—our place alongside the nonhuman animals with which we share it. It's a way of asking, "What can that thing do that it couldn't do before and therefore, how has my place in the world shifted?" (Muecke 2008, 15).

Sloterdijk leans over the dinner table, his beard dripping with beetroot juice. As he speaks, he uses a celery stalk for emphasis: "Where are the means of transport that bring us into the open?" (2016b, 45).

You hold his stare—wordless, for once—and motion with your head in the direction of your bike, which is now leaning adroitly next to the concrete wall.

This essay has much to do with shifting places in the world. With slipping and changing atmospheres.

See there! My bike is already allowing me to see the world differently. Not now fixed nor solid, I'm "floating into the azaleas" (Shihab Nye 1998).

As Schlunke and Brewster (2005) say, in fictocriticism, "we try to write it differently. Of course, that means we have thought it differently" (394).

Fitting.

Wouldn't you say?

For as vegans and as cyclists we have necessarily thought about it very differently. By "it" I mean our being in the world in relation with other animals.

You're in Devonport, the third largest town in Tasmania, situated on the banks of the Mersey River. You're riding along a boardwalk. Thinking about this journey beforehand, you'd pictured yourself in the Tarkine forest, surrounded by trees. But on arrival you were informed by locals that there was "no way that bike would get through the forest."

"As if," they said. There it was again.

Now you find yourself here in this middle-class utopia of boardwalks, accessible bike paths, and nautical-themed coffee shops, surrounded not by trees but instead by humans. You stop to take a photo and see two shirtless men. Their chest hair glistens in the sun. They walk, chests pumped, forearms back, with a side-to-side swagger. They look at you like you're something to be bought (or taken)—consumed. (You resist here the habit of calling yourself "meat" in this context; to take you to "the intersection of the oppression of women and the oppression of animals and then do an immediate about-face, seizing the function of the absent referent only to forward women's issues, not animals,' and so reflecting a patriarchal structure"; Adams [2015], 90). Instead, let's keep motioning in a forward direction. You avoid eye contact, but they have both wordlessly decided to approach.

They inspect (your bike). "Nice setup," one says.

"You're like a turtle with its house on its back," says the other.

You show no response to their uninvited approach, so they try another tack—making hypothetical improvements to your bike, as though you're not there at all.

Naomi Stekelenburg, Bicheno, Tasmania. *Photograph by Craig O'Hara.*

As though you're not there at all.

"Saw ya riding without ya helmet on back there." One finally looks up at me again. "I know the local cop. He'll get his stick on ya if he sees that."

Riding a bike evokes reactions from others that aren't present in reactions to other forms of mobility. Some are captivated by my decision to be carless in a car-centered culture. "You're a braver man than I am," a friend said to me once. And simultaneously, people also want to correct my situation in some way, by offering lifts ('That's much too far to ride, I'll drive you,' they decide) or by changing my bike. They think the bike reduces me to some sort of helpless "animal." And they want to protect me from that.

Others again want to hurt me, manage me, keep me in line. As though the bike represents a division delineating between human and object—human and animal.

As I see it, though, people have missed the point (perhaps the speed and protection offered by their cars makes them miss a lot of points—drive right past them, they do). I'm not "reduced" by my cycling but in fact expanded by it. One night I rode home through a typical Queensland-style tropical storm. Probably a bad choice, but once in it I had to push on through. Clothes meant nothing. Shoes meant nothing.

All the vestiges of "civilization" and "culture" were dissolved by the rain. What mattered were my skin and my breath and my ability; my alertness, my sight. There's always been something about me that's been drawn to this sense of exposure of myself to atmospheres. I like the cold on my face and the way my body feels when homeostasis kicks in and it manages to heat itself while I ride past people bundled furiously in parkas and jackets, huddling against the cold. Me, in my T-shirt. Knowing what my body can do. Through my body, you might say, I am at once *only* body and *more than* body.

In Charlotte Wood's novel *The Natural Way of Things* (2015), a group of young women is bundled into a van and taken to the Australian outback. No explanation is given for the kidnapping, but we can suppose it has something to do with the mere fact that they are women. Through her hunting of rabbits for food, the main character of the novel, Yolanda, eventually frees herself of the confines of linguality and civilization—and her captors. She dreams of journeying "inwards, downwards, running on all fours, smelling the grass and the earth as familiar as her own body" (237). This "animal" freedom of course plays into the old dichotomy of "human/nature."[2] With this, Wood's text also plays directly into Carol J. Adams's (2015) critique of radical feminism's previously mentioned "about face" at the intersection of women's and animals' rights in simultaneously revealing the objectification of women through metaphors of the animal without questioning Yolanda's right to murder rabbits for food and fur. Nonetheless, Yolanda's roaming the landscape during hunting eventually brings her to a state of "beyond human": "It was to do with muscle sliding around bone, to do with animal speed and scent and bloody heartbeat and breath" (Wood 193). This description of Yolanda's transformed state is not about her transcendence "out of" humanity at all, but rather, about an embodiment that we have difficulty conceptualizing because of the age-old culture–nature dichotomy. To be human is to be "civilized"—lingual—and means an escape from the boundaries and constraints of the animal body.

As if it were that simple.

■   ■   ■

The complexity of Yolanda (although one that the text itself does not acknowledge explicitly—to its fault) is she is human, capable of using imaginative forces to experience other than body. She is simultaneously

NAOMI STEKELENBURG

embodied—material. One of Yolanda's captors, whose body smells "as sour as milk," exclaims to her, "Christ on a bike, you're a dumb dog." Of course, this comment is derisive, and it neatly foregrounds Yolanda's eventual nonlinguality, but it is also a nod to how the bike connects the transcendent human—the Christ-like figure—and the nonhuman animal. Yolanda accompanies me in my little narrative about cycle-touring Tasmania. Like me, Yolanda is an Australian figure with a complicated relationship with the "outback," but she also stands as a reminder of the outdated ways of exploring our relationships with nonhuman animals.

Yolanda watches your turtle-back from the shrubs with her keen eyesight. You know how this script goes: you are meant to show interest in the men's comments, to learn from their insights, and to thank them with giggly gratitude as they saunter off. But you're not feeling the Christ-like patriarchal vibe. You ignore their comments, throw your leg over your bike, and ride through them.

A busker is blowing bubbles from two giant metal wires beside the boardwalk. You look up into the sun as you ride through the sea of bubbles and it's here, you realize, that you are getting to the heart of the matter.

"No animals allowed." *Photograph by Craig O'Hara.*

Plumwood (2009) critiques any philosophy that makes us "choose between human and non-human sides" (116) because it invariably "precludes a critical cultural focus on problems of human ecological identity and relationship" (116). "Philosophy, I think, must understand humans as immersed in a medium that is both deep and shallow (although not in the same place)" (116). Western philosophy provides a firm basis for anthropocentrism and the discrimination against nonhumans that follows from it.[3]

I digress for a moment (or do I?) to (amended) field notes from the bike tour. Talk about sharing space!

> They built a road right through the rookery but put tunnels underneath it, which apparently the penguins use.
>
> Sat for two hours in the freezing cold with a galley of human strangers in expensive high-vis adventure wear, waiting for the penguins to make their way from the ocean to the rookery where they house their babies.
>
> Ranger told us to sit perfectly still and silent. Tourist in front of me constantly moved between his phone, binoculars, camera and girlfriend, as though they were all one and the same distraction.
>
> Saw some penguins and shearwaters but felt like an intruder. Wanted the penguins to get to their babies without being disturbed.
>
> This should not be a spectacle.

"On ya bike," as they say in Australia when the conversation is going nowhere.

"The bike is a great way to experience changing atmospheres," says my friend Stephen Muecke to me in an email. So, let's ride.

Sloterdijk's work on spheres (2011, 2016b), though not specifically or explicitly ecological in its context, is a possible way through the false, constructed, human–animal, nature–culture separation. In his three volumes of work that comprise his "spheres project," Sloterdijk is broadly preoccupied with spatial concepts of being in the world. His spheres project rejects the linear notions prefiguring the question "What is man?" and instead opts for a philosophical spatiality in the question "Where is man?" (Schinkel and Noordegraaf-Eelens 2011, 11). The spheres project has little to say about nonhuman animals. However, "Sloterdijk's work has a strong evocative character. It is meant to bring about new thoughts and

NAOMI STEKELENBURG

practices" (Schinkel and Noordegraaf-Eelens 2011, 8). This is not a theory designed to be relegated to the shelves of the philosophy workshop, but instead is intended to provide a force for thinking and doing anew. Because this essay deals primarily in relational concepts of human and nonhuman animals, Sloterdijk's exploration of spatial being in the world is an apt starting point for a vision to replace the defunct, anthropomorphic notion of society.

"Ah, so you're an animal person," the bartender says as you place your order: chips and salad—no egg, no mayo, no bacon. You're in a place called Coles Bay and it is Christmas, so the pubs are full of boating-obsessed holiday makers. The bartender looks puzzled as you morph his bar menu into one your ethics can tolerate. "Haha, you've taken out the best stuff," he says chuckling to himself. He rolls his eyes to the back of his head in fake ecstasy and says, "Baaaccccon." The bar mats are sticky with old beer. Funny how ideas, like beer, can stick. I explain to the bartender that animals suffer pain when we take their secretions and flesh ("secretions . . . flesh" he repeats and shuffles uncomfortably). He's trying hard to follow the story—to draw a neat line from premise to conclusion. "An animal person?" you say to him. "Not any more or less than I'm a human person." And now he's completely flummoxed, and I'm the weirdo contrarian, so he says something about the weather.

■   ■   ■

That night, you sleep in a rotunda in a national park, your hammock suspended between two of the rotunda beams. A passel of possums passes through the rotunda at about 11 p.m. One of them perches on the beam centimeters above your head, hissing and barking. You're certain Christian imaginations of the devil were derived from hearing the sounds made by the Australian brushtail possum. Of course, the possum has little interest in you, but her communication with her companions, together with the belly need to protect yourself from her intrusion into your hammock, conjures fear in you. You can't run because in twisting out of your hammock, there's the chance you'll come into contact with the body of the possum. You want, desperately, immunity from the outside.

From then, you sleep with the light on and music playing so you can't hear the possum sounds. Hardly optimal for a sound sleep. Once the possums pass through, the mozzies begin biting you through the hammock.

Then the rains come.

Morning finds you on the concrete rotunda floor, sleeping in possum poo.

An animal person. Yeah, right. As if.

Like hammocks, spheres are membranes that offer protection from the world through immunity and meaning (Borch 2011, 29) According to Sloterdijk (2011), the first spheres are bubbles, which are the smallest versions of immunity and represent the most intimate co- relationships, like that of a mother and child. The second—globes—describes macrospheres, with one center and containing the "world" (Schinkel and Noordegraaf-Eelens 2011, 14). An example of this is monotheistic religion. Last, foams represent the transition to modern society where belief in one god falters in the face of multiple truths and worlds are formed from multiple isolated bubbles that coexist and share membranes with neighbors in a chaotic foam. Foam paves the way for a conception of ourselves as being with and sharing membranes with other species, while simultaneously recognizing that we are protected and hold different meanings from the ones they may hold (Sloterdijk 2016a).

And the membranes are delicate. What happens to one bubble affects the other. There is no hierarchical distinction between bubbles (Borch 2011, 32). Each is as vital to others as to itself. According to this spatial way of seeing, how humans view and subsequently treat non-human animals is not, as it is so often represented, a "mere" issue of animal welfare. It is a deeply ontological issue that carries with it felt (though perhaps not consciously) psychosocial repercussions. Factory farming practices, speeding along highways in cars, stealing milk from mother cows—these all affect the foams. What is done to one is done to the others.

When we eat other animals, we eat ourselves.

> Met fellow bike tourer, Stephanie from Colorado USA, whose blonde plaits remind me of my past aspiration to play lead in the high school production of Rogers and Hammerstein's Oklahoma!
>
> Despite the cold, she's dressed in a light flannelette shirt and shorts. Stephanie tells me these are the only clothes she carries. She'll sleep down by the beach, she says, and pulls a lightweight sleeping bag from her pannier. It's cold down there by the water when all you're covered in is polysynthetic fibre and skin. I marvel at how un-shook by cold

she is, as I carefully unfold my protective hammock. She's the same age
as my daughters and I'm taken by a need to lie with her to cover her
from the wind. Instead, I offer her my jacket.

I mention to Stephanie I'm writing a paper on meeting animals. She tells me of three encounters with Australian animals:

1. many leeches
2. tiger snake × 1
3. dragging the bodies of two dead roos from a highway

Picture this brave young woman stopping her bike on a busy highway, risking her body to protect the bodies of others—intuitively understanding her place in the foam.

Stephanie and I ride through St. Mary's national park. Her plaits flow behind her like a superhero's cape. "Ride to the top just up here and you'll see all the world," she tells me loudly, so her voice carries over the wind. And she's right. We stand at the edge of a cliff that overlooks the Tasman Sea. Two black cockatoos fly past us, squawking. Yolanda puts down her traps; Frank—his can of insecticide.

And we float off into the atmosphere.

When I cycle-tour, these are generally my go-to food supplies:

- 20 × packs of oats, sultanas, cacao, nuts, and seeds
- 5 × Vego bars
- Rice
- Curry paste—taken out of the jar and put in a resealable bag
- Store-bought hummus
- Fresh vegetables from roadside stands and farmers' markets
- Chickpeas, canned
- Soy milk powder
- Little packets of salt and pepper I collect from cafés and restaurants

Although what I end up eating is contingent on what's available.

Notes

1. Genesis 1:26, King James Version.
2. According to Val Plumwood (1993), this requires "anti-dualist remedies" (41).
3. See Steiner (2013), Plumwood (1993), and Grosz (1994).

References

Adams, Carol J. 2015. *The Sexual Politics of Meat: A Feminist-Vegetarian Critical Theory*. New York: Bloomsbury.

Borch, Christian. 2011. "Foamy Business: On the Organizational Politics of Atmospheres." In *Medias Res: Peter Sloterdijk's Spherological Poetics of Being*, edited by Willem Schinkel and Liesbeth Noordegraaf-Eelens, 29–42. Amsterdam: Amsterdam University Press.

Cooper, Erin. 2019. "What to Do When You Come across Orphaned Baby Animals and Injured Wildlife. *ABC News*, February 18, 2019. https://www.abc.net.au /news/2019-02-17/why-does-tasmania-have-so-much-road-kill/10815210.

Gibbs, Anna. 2005. "Fictocriticism, Affect, Mimesis: Engendering Differences." *Text* 9 (1). http://www.textjournal.com.au/april05/gibbs.htm.

Grosz, Elizabeth. 1994. *Volatile Bodies: Toward a Corporeal Feminism*. Bloomington: Indiana University Press.

Lingis, Alphonso. 2012. "The Steppe." In *Emotion, Place and Culture*, edited by Mick Smith, Joyce Davidson, Laura Cameron, and Liz Bondi, 299–309. London: Routledge.

Muecke, Stephen. 2008. *Joe and the Andamans*. Sydney: Local Consumption Productions.

Plumwood, Val. 1993. *Feminism and the Mastery of Nature*. New York: Routledge.

———. 2009. "Nature in the Active Voice." *Australian Humanities Review* 46:113–29.

———. 2012. *The Eye of the Crocodile*. Canberra: ANU EPress.

Schinkel, Willem, and Liesbeth Noordegraaf-Eelens. 2011. "Peter Sloterdijk's Spherological Acrobatics: An Exercise in Introduction." In *In Medias Res: Peter Sloterdijk's Spherological Poetics of Being*, edited by Willem Schinkel and Liesbeth Noordegraaf-Eelens, 7–28. Amsterdam: Amsterdam University Press.

Schlunke, Katrina, and Anne Brewster. 2005. "We Four: Fictocriticism Again." *Continuum: Journal of Media & Culture Studies* 19 (3): 393–95.

Shihab Nye, Naomi. 1998. "The Rider." In *Fuel: Poems by Naomi Shihab Nye*, Rochester, NY: Boa Editions.

Sloterdijk, Peter. 2011. *Spheres: Plural Spherology: V. 3: Bubbles*. Translated by Wieland Hoban. Los Angeles: Semiotext(e).

———. 2016a. "We're Always Riding down Maternity Drive." In *Selected Exaggerations: Conversations and Interviews 1993–2012*, edited by Bernhard Klein (ed) and translated by Karen Margolis. Cambridge, UK: Polity Press.

———. 2016b. "Uterus on Wheels." In *Selected Exaggerations: Conversations and Interviews 1993–2012*, edited by Bernhard Klein and translated by Karen Margolis, 23–24. Cambridge, UK: Polity Press.

———. 2016c. *Foams: Spheres III; Plural Spherology*. Los Angeles: Semiotext(e).

Smith, Mick. 2012. "Road Kill: Remembering What Is Left in Our Encounters with Other Animals." In *Emotion, Place and Culture* edited by Mick Smith, Joyce Davidson, Laura Cameron, and Liz Bondi, 22–33. London: Routledge.

Steiner, Gary. 2013. *Animals and the Limits of Postmodernism*. New York: Columbia University Press.

Taussig, Michael. 2006. *Walter Benjamin's Grave*. Chicago: University of Chicago Press.

Wood, Charlotte. 2015. *The Natural Way of Things*. Sydney: Allen & Unwin.

Geertrui Cazaux and her husband Jim Feys with their tandem bike. *Photograph by the author.*

CHAPTER NINE

We Live and Ride in Tandem

GEERTRUI CAZAUX

Cycling Is in Our DNA

I live in Belgium, the heart of Europe. More specifically, in Flanders, where cyclism is—besides football—a national sport, birthplace of the Flandriens. The nickname *Flandrien* reportedly originated at the beginning of the twentieth century, when it was used to refer to Flemish track cyclists who participated in the six-day races of the 1910s and 1920s. When the Flemish cyclists traveled to the United States to compete in the velodromes of New York and Chicago, they were announced as "blokes who eat raw meat." Today, the term is used more indiscriminately to refer to a cyclist with an indestructible attack instinct and fighting spirit, who rides through all weather types, never hangs his head, and preferably also wins the race (Cycling in Flanders n.d.). It invokes images of cyclists beating against wind and rain on slippery, muddy cobblestone roads. The connotation with eating raw pieces of animal flesh luckily seems to have dwindled in modern-day uses of the term, although the nickname still seems to be reserved for male cyclists only.[1]

Flanders is home to many racing classics in the spring, the most renowned and notorious one being the Ronde van Vlaanderen (Tour of Flanders). Other racing events, like the three-week Tour de France in July, or the national or world championship, are also followed closely by cycling fans. My grandparents had a radio and television shop, and I remember hot summer afternoons in the 1970s when workers from nearby factories and shops would sneak out of their workplace and come to the TV repair atelier at the side of the shop to watch snippets of the Tour de France. This mélange of visitors heavily commentated the race, and to my young ears they all sounded like cycling experts. The names of cycling heroes—Belgian, but also foreign ones—are etched in our collective memory: Merckx, Anquetil, Zoetemelk, Hinault, and later fallen heroes such as Armstrong and Museeuw.

Although I'm not really a vivid fan of professional cycling myself and I do not follow the races closely, there is really no escaping it in the land of the Flandriens. In the first weekend of April, public life here nearly comes to a standstill when the peloton of the Tour of Flanders races through Flanders' Fields, tackling the cobblestones and small but steep hills, in a race of more than 260 kilometers. Nearly a million spectators follow the race live along the route (to put it in perspective, Flanders only has a population of 6.7 million), while many others watch the race on screen at home or in the pub.

Besides being a national and recreational sport activity, cycling is also practiced widely for functional reasons (commuting to school and work, shopping) and for leisure. With 497 inhabitants per square kilometer,[2] Flanders is a very densely populated area, and the urban sprawl has erased a clear-cut distinction between countryside and city, although that distinction is still subjectively felt by many "rural" inhabitants and "city" dwellers. Being a very small region,[3] Flanders has no "far" distances to travel as do, for example, expansive countries such as China or the United States. Middle-sized cities are generally only ten to twenty kilometers apart, and a travel destination of two hundred kilometers is literally on the other side of the country (or even beyond the border) and considered far away. This, together with relatively easy surfaces and trails (except for the small hills and cobblestones here and there), makes a lot of trips relatively easy to make by bicycle for many people.

People who do not know how to ride a bike, or even do not own a bicycle, are rather rare in Flanders. Nine out of ten people here own a bicycle, and one out of three of these uses it more than once a week for shopping. More than a quarter of the active population uses a bicycle daily to commute to work or school.[4] On sunny weekends, cyclists are abundant on the paths along the canals and in the parks: in the morning mainly with groups of *wielertoeristen* (recreational racers), in the afternoon more with families or friends doing a leisurely excursion, often coupled with a visit to a café for pancakes, waffles, or (a couple of) Belgian beers.

All of this illustrates how "biking is in our DNA," as a recent brochure from the Flemish government states (Fietsberaad 2018).

One of my earliest childhood memories is my grandfather teaching me how to ride a bicycle. As I grew up in the city, we went to practice in a nearby city park, where there was no traffic. My grandfather had attached a steel bar to the back of my bicycle with which he could guide me and hold me upright. Before I knew it, I was riding the bicycle without his helping hand. It felt magical! I longed for the moment when I would go to high school, as I would then be allowed to use my own "grownup" bicycle, which was waiting for me stored up safely in my granddad's atelier.

Cycling has always played an important part in my life, both as a child cycling to school (come rain or shine) and meeting friends to go out, attending college classes, or—at the beginning of my professional career at least—commuting to work.

It Takes Two to Tango: Using a Wheelchair and a Tandem

Over the last couple of years, my cycling has become less functional and more recreational, but at the same time also therapeutic. Because of several autoimmune diseases, I have mobility issues and chronic pain, and cannot walk long distances. Although I was diagnosed with Crohn's disease and ankylosing spondylitis more than thirty years ago and have dealt with many physical issues along the road, it has only been since the last couple of years that these diseases have profoundly affected my social and work life. I am now no longer professionally active, and pain and chronic fatigue necessitate careful planning of day-to-day and social activities. On occasions that require long periods of standing, walking, or sitting on uncomfortable chairs (my threshold for chairs has gotten very low and I now consider most chairs without cushions or backrest, with short seating surfaces, or where my feet cannot reach the floor very uncomfortable and painful), I now mostly use my wheelchair. Riding a bicycle has become a good—albeit sometimes painful—therapeutic exercise.

To make cycling more enjoyable and feasible for me, since 2008 my husband and I have been riding a tandem bicycle. To discover what riding a tandem feels like, and whether we would enjoy it, we rented one from a nearby bicycle shop to give it a try. It was a hilarious experience! As a tandem bicycle is obviously longer, the center point is differently situated compared to a standard bicycle, which makes taking curves feel completely different. Sitting in the back (as I always do), with no possibility of steering or braking, also means one has no other choice than to hand over a lot of control to the front rider. We survived the maiden tandem trip without any major difficulties, and actually quite enjoyed it! Shortly afterward, we bought a secondhand tandem. (Anecdotal side note: when we arrived at the sellers' house, they appeared to be an older couple who had known my late grandparents quite well and had bought their first TV from them some fifty years earlier.)

In those first years of riding the tandem, we improved our riding skills and synchronicity while learning that communication is key for smooth starting and stopping. Although our first tandem bike gave us much joy, we gradually discovered some comfort and technical issues that could be improved: the feel and type of the saddles, biking posture, size and position of the steering handles. To some people a bicycle is just a bicycle, but its material and shape sure make a lot of difference in determining the overall biking experience.

So, a couple of years later, after having thought these things through, we bought a new tandem: a very steady and strong foldable Multicycle, with a straight sitting position that is much more comfortable for me. When we bought a new car, we made sure that the folded tandem could fit in the back so we could take the bicycle with us on holiday.

Besides the tandem, we have several other bikes in the house. My husband, the front rider when we use the tandem, is himself a cycling fan and recreational rider, and he commutes forty kilometers round trip to work in the city of Bruges every day (during which he has unfortunately been scooped up by a car twice already, with a broken shoulder and hip as a result, but luckily no head injuries—hurray for helmets!). Along with his home-to-work bicycle, he also uses a racing bicycle for longer cycling routes on Sunday mornings, a mountain bike to explore rougher terrains, and a small foldable bike he sometimes takes along on the train. We each have a classic city bike, too, although I hardly use mine anymore.

Although many people assume that I just "ride along" on the tandem (and hardly a ride goes by without one or more persons along the road jokingly shouting something in this respect to us) and that I do not have to put in an effort, as I am sitting in the back position, I really do cycle, too, and the combined effort even makes us go faster than many recreational solo riders. But there is a core of truth in those assertions, because on our tours, and certainly near the end of a tour or while biking uphill, my husband can put in extra effort and "carry" me home, as I simply peddle along. After all, being able to rely on the extra force of my husband's legs is exactly one of the reasons why we started riding a tandem. Another bonus: sitting in the back, as I do, is a way more relaxed biking experience. I don't have to steer (I tried the front position once but realized how much power it requires to keep the tandem bicycle going straight) and I don't have to control the brakes. The latter can on occasion be quite scary and daunting, too, especially when speeding downhill at fifty-five kilometers per hour—our top speed so far. On more quiet paths and excursions, with my hands free, I can certainly look around, take photos, and check the map or my mobile to give navigation directions. Riding a tandem requires coordination and mutual trust, especially from the stoker in the pilot.

Starting off from home, our tandem excursions take us to the nearby city of Bruges and other smaller towns in the area. We bike through the scarce open spaces and scattered agricultural fields, and even scarcer nature reserves, that are left in between. For a change of scenery, we sometimes stow the tandem in our car and drive a small distance first. To the north, it takes only a half an hour with the car to bring us into the Netherlands. France is just an hour's drive away on the south. An hour by car and a similar time on the ferry takes us to Dover in the United Kingdom. We often take our foldable tandem with us on holiday, cycling along the banks of the Seine in Paris and the canals in Amsterdam, and also enjoying the glowing hills of the British countryside. On many occasions, our synchronized peddling on the tandem makes us a tourist attraction in itself.

Some years after my transition to using a tandem instead of my own "single" bicycle, I began using a wheelchair for most outdoor events and excursions that I otherwise would have done on foot. On the one hand, using a wheelchair and a tandem bike both imply giving up some control and freedom, entailing dependence on others. Although public spaces in Western countries now have many facilities for wheelchair users, there is—literally and figuratively—still a long road to go with respect to accessibility, and traveling from one place to another on wheels remains challenging. Even when stairs have been turned into slopes and the curbs on the footpaths are not too high, I often do not have the power to navigate them on my own and need help from my husband. With respect to riding the tandem, it should be fairly obvious that a smooth ride requires two people on the bike: it takes two to tandem!

On the other hand, these wheels (be it in parallel on the wheelchair or in sequence on the tandem) have lent me a new dimension of freedom. In the years prior to my using the tandem and the wheelchair, my outdoor excursions became few and far between, as the pain and fatigue made it too hard to go to concerts, museums, exhibitions, or festivals, or simply take a leisurely walk. If it were not for these wheels, I simply would no longer be attending such events or making these excursions—or if I did, it would be for a very limited time. Using the wheelchair and tandem doesn't make the pain and fatigue disappear, but they do make such excursions somewhat more manageable. As paradoxical as this might seem for some people, both devices "enable" me and have given me back some freedom.

Our recreational tandem excursions can be anything between a couple of kilometers and (or a very good day) a couple of dozen kilometers, largely depending on my condition that particular day. Sometimes, we have started off for an afternoon journey but then have had to return home without even having made it to the end of the street, because my joints and muscles let me know that they are not up for a ride that day. On other occasions, we have to take a break every couple of kilometers, or even more frequently near the end of longer trips. The pain can hinder me from dismounting the bicycle easily, but having a sturdy rider in front holding the tandem upright is definitely an advantage in those moments.

People living with a chronic disease or disability—especially invisible ones—often face a lot of prejudice. It is a widely held misconception that a chronic disease equals a stable, quasi-permanent state of impairment, disability, or degree of sickness that visibly manifests itself to the bystander ("But you don't look sick?"). The truth is that although I'm permanently facing certain physical and psychological issues because of my autoimmune diseases, my condition fluctuates, sometimes even day to day. Chronically ill people can have good days and bad days. Being chronically ill does not (necessarily) entail being bedridden all day, and it certainly isn't always visible on the outside. Facing social judgment and being questioned for participating in outdoor activities ("So you cannot work, but you can ride a bicycle?") can be upsetting and emotionally hard to deal with. People often do not realize how deep chronically ill people need to dig to do these "fun" things, or how long it takes to recuperate from such energy-draining excursions. In my experience, living with a chronic disease feels (much to my frustration) like living part time, precisely because I need so much time to rest and recuperate.

Two Vegans on Wheels

Many vegans seem to have a "veganniversary date" and can precisely recall the moment they went vegan. For my husband and me, it was a gradual process, and we cannot recall the exact date that we decisively went vegan. I am writing in the plural sense here, as we evolved from being nonvegan, through vegetarian, to going vegan jointly and simultaneously—*in tandem*.

Our shift to vegetarianism happened sometime in the mid-1990s. Some classic animal "rights" books[5] instigated a change in both our perspective on the moral status of animals and our diet. Backed by undercover footage showing the horrible use and abuse of animals in animal agriculture, during animal transport, and in slaughterhouses, and the many subsequent agricultural crises of that period (the outbreaks of swine flu, foot and mouth disease, and bovine spongiform encephalopathy or "mad cow disease," and in Belgium specifically the dioxin crisis), we gradually made the switch to not eating animals anymore.

Although we considered ourselves advocates for other animals, and I academically explored the relationships between humans and other animals from a non-speciesist angle for my criminology dissertation (Cazaux 2002), it took several more years before we finally went vegan. In 2009, we attended the first Minding Animals Conference in Newcastle, Australia (https://www.mindinganimals.com/). It was one of the first major conferences to bring together animal rights activists and (who we now call) critical animal studies scholars from around the world. We heard many inspiring presentations and lectures, but above all it was the conversations with vegans that made us question our lifestyle and brought about the mental "click" to go vegan. Being in an environment where veganism was a normalized affair was a very uplifting experience. In the months thereafter, now fifteen years ago, we gradually put that click into practice and transitioned to veganism.

Vegan or animal rights activism is always, in one way or another and sometimes very subtly, part of our bicycle excursions. We often wear T-shirts with a vegan or animal rights message when we go cycling. Our water bottles have vegan or animal rights themes. Showcasing an animal rights message amid a landscape of industrial farms sometimes feels like riding in the lions' den. Strangely, I often feel more at ease wearing my animal rights T-shirt during a cycling trip on the tandem, than I do attending a vegan festival using my wheelchair, an environment where I supposedly should be more comfortable and relaxed wearing it. The strong focus of some proponents within our movement on the health benefits of adopting a plant-based diet, combined with a consumerist and marketing approach to veganism ("selling" the vegan lifestyle) implicitly—and sometimes even explicitly—frames not just disabled bodies but also those that are deemed "unattractive" for being older or larger as unfit ambassadors of veganism. The underlying rhetoric is that disabled bodies do not "sell" well and could even scare people away from trying veganism! Only those radiating the image of "perfect" health and having a youthful appearance are apparently considered apt to sell the vegan message. Such voices within the community, who frame veganism not as a message of compassion, of justice and liberation of all, but as a consumerist message that needs to sell—together with a lot of body shaming, health shaming, and ableism—have often made me feel uncomfortable both in my relations with other activists and, as a consequence, when reaching out to nonvegans. Although I realize my feelings are partly also due to internalized ableism, I feel more relaxed when bringing the animal rights message during our cycling excursions, when my disability is less visible and I can "pass" for an active, healthy vegan.

Along with wearing T-shirts, we leave a trail of stickers with animal rights or vegan messages along our route. We try to discover new vegan-friendly places to eat out and add them to the HappyCow Guide (https://www.happycow.net/), and I also document our dining-out experiences on my blog, The Bruges Vegan (https://brugesvegan.com). Sometimes we will take homemade sandwiches and picnic along the way. We always pack energy bars and usually some fruit as backup, because in some areas, especially the more rural ones, there are hardly any vegan-friendly options along the way.

Sometimes we encounter animals in need during our cycling excursions, and we provide hands-on help: freeing a goat whose head was stuck in wire mesh, or taking birds with injuries from road accidents to the wildlife sanctuary. At the end of the summer of 2018, my husband spotted a little white fluffy dot in the distance on the middle of a mountain bike trail. As he approached, he noticed a tiny white kitten crawling to the roadside, barely alive and only weighing 350 grams. He placed the kitten in his shirt and cycled to a point where I could meet him by car and pick the kitten up to take him straight to the vet. It was touch and go for several weeks, but kitten Boris fought strong against dehydration and severe pneumonia from a lungworm infection, and was for two years a playful and happy member of our family, his life unfortunately cut short by a congenital kidney malfunction.

As Flanders is a densely populated area with a corresponding high amount of road traffic, the sight of many car victims (hedgehogs, cats, birds, badgers, rats, frogs . . .) on the asphalt is also deeply disturbing. On several occasions we have stopped to take a traffic victim from the middle of the road and place them on the roadside, so at least scavenging animals would also not be at risk of being run over. One sad example was the discovery of a dead cat in a plastic bag not far from our home, discarded on the side of a nearby cornfield. Although we had already passed this field by car, we did not notice her until we rode along on our tandem. The poor animal was already in a state of decay, but we took her home and buried her in our pasture.

It is immensely frustrating that we cannot offer hands-on help to the millions of animals who are living around us, locked up in factories, their lives brutally taken in the slaughterhouse. Although Flanders is a very densely populated and highly urbanized region, agriculture still occupies 45 percent of total land use. More than half (55 percent) of that agricultural land is used for animal feeding, signifying the dominance of animal agriculture in the area.[6] The animals themselves remain largely invisible, but animal farming determines the architecture of the rural landscape: lots of fields with crops for feed (a lot of corn), and large buildings housing thousands of animals.

The area where we live, on the outskirts of Bruges, is considered more rural, and the Flemish pig-farming industry is mainly concentrated in this area. At any given time, there are well over five million pigs locked up in Flanders[7]—around three-quarters of the human population in this part of Belgium. And yet, while driving or cycling through the countryside, I have never seen a single living pig on a farm. As five million pigs produce a lot of manure, their presence can be smelled, and sometimes their squeals are audible as they are being rounded up for transport to the slaughterhouse. Only the feeding silos and the large ventilators on the outside of sealed-up buildings give away the presence of these animals, who spend their short lives indoors. Their living experiences are in stark contrast with the cartoon-like images of happy pigs on "educational" charts, set up here and there along heavily frequented cycling routes. Euphemistically depicting the process from piglet to "bacon" or "pork chops," stressing the good welfare conditions and traditional or artisanal qualities of these local "products," these signs frame animals as products to be used by humans and sustain the speciesist indoctrination. The pigs' lives, their individual histories and their personalities, remain invisible— literally and figuratively locked away from the public eye.

The same invisibility occurs with the forty-five million chickens in Flanders. Besides some "backyard" hens and the occasional crowing rooster in rural gardens, only the smell and large buildings reveal the presence of tens of thousands of "broiler" or "laying" chickens inside each facility. The only farmed animals still visible on the Flemish countryside are its 1.25 million cows, some bred for milk production and others for "meat," although cows kept for milk production are now increasingly also held indoors year round.[8]

While living farmed animals in Flanders are mostly placed out of sight and banished to factories in the countryside, their fragmented bodies are clearly visible in the urban landscape: billboards with larger-than-life photos of roasted animal parts, restaurants depicting them to advertise their menus, butcher windows with cut-up carcasses. In a way, pigs, chickens, and cows are more visible in their death than in life, although speciesist thinking leads many people to not even make the connection between a steak and the muscles of a once-living sentient being.

Whether cycling along the factories in the countryside, or among the restaurants and billboards in the more urban areas, "seeing" so much animal suffering, exploitation, and death is quite confrontational as a vegan. There's no escaping it. It's like riding in a dystopian world. While we also ride the tandem as a leisure activity, realizing how ubiquitous the use of animals is, and how we have no chance of changing the lives of these individuals, can be very hard to cope with.

GEERTRUI CAZAUX

We Live and Ride in Tandem

At the end of the nineteenth century, suffragist Susan B. Anthony said, "Let me tell you what I think of bicycling. I think it has done more to emancipate women than anything else in the world. It gives women a feeling of freedom and self-reliance. I stand and rejoice every time I see a woman ride by on a wheel . . . the picture of free, untrammeled womanhood" (Bly 2014). I sympathize with Anthony's words and I can see how the development of bicycles may have played an important part in the emancipation of women at that time. It does, however, place a heavy onus on "independence" being the highest desirable state a person can be in, while framing persons who require care or assistance as burdensome. Western capitalist society heavily considers being dependent as degrading, as entailing a loss of dignity. But all humans and other animals are to some degree dependent on one another, constantly living interdependently.

I wonder what Anthony would have to say about me riding the tandem. I depend on another person to enjoy cycling, but at the same time this interdependence also gives me a feeling of freedom. Riding the tandem literally en-ables me to explore the surroundings, to do activism, in a way that I would not manage to achieve by myself, on foot, or with my wheelchair. It has also strengthened our bond as a couple. Riding the tandem requires mutual trust and clear communication. As vegans for animal rights, as partners, we live and ride in tandem.

When we cycle in mainly rural areas, we most often pack some homemade sandwiches. These are usually straightforward, no-fuss sandwiches with hummus, or a curry or tomato spread, or some slices of vegan cheese and tomato. We also pack some freshly cut fruit to have on the side, and always carry an apple or banana.

When our excursion will include crossing a town, I will try to figure out in advance if there are any vegan restaurants or restaurants with vegan options in the area, so we can dine out. I love to discover new places that offer vegan options, and I always document our dining-out experiences on my blog, The Bruges Vegan (https://brugesvegan.com), and on HappyCow (https://www.happycow.net/).

If we are unable to take homemade sandwiches (for example, due to a hotel stay), and there are no vegan-friendly restaurants around, we try to look for grocery stores to buy some bread and spread to fix something on the go. Tip: always make sure you have some cutlery in your bags to slice a tomato or cucumber or spoon out a pudding or yofu (vegan yoghurt!).

But in any case, we always pack energy bars as backup. And we always have our water bottles with us.

Notes

1. See, for example the overview in *Het Nieuwsblad*, "Wat is nu eigenlijk een 'flandrien'? En welke renner is daar het perfecte voorbeeld van?" November 1, 2017, https://www.nieuwsblad.be/cnt/dmf20171031_03163495.
2. Statistiek Vlaanderen, "Bevolking. Omvang en groei," December 20, 2023, https://www.vlaanderen.be/statistiek-vlaanderen/bevolking/bevolking-omvang-en-groei.
3. The size of Flanders is about 13.6 thousand km². To put it into perspective: Connecticut, one of the smallest of the United States, is just under 14.4 thousand km². Germany is about 357 thousand km², and the Netherlands are around 41.9 thousand km². Wikipedia, s.v. "Flanders," accessed April 22, 2022, https://en.wikipedia.org/wiki/Flanders.
4. Fietsberaad, "Fiets DNA 2018," 2018, https://fietsberaad.be/wp-content/uploads/FietsDNA_2018_A5_lwr.pdf.
5. Some of the first works I read in that period were Carol J. Adams, *The Sexual Politics of Meat* (1996); Carol J. Adams and Josephine Donovan (eds.), *Animals & Women: Feminist Theoretical Explorations* (1995); Robert Garner (ed.), *Animal Rights, the Changing Debate* (1996); Tom Regan, *The Case for Animal Rights* (1985); and Peter Singer, *Animal Liberation* (1994).
6. Statistiek Vlaanderen, "Landbouwareaal," December 20, 2023, https://www.vlaanderen.be/statistiek-vlaanderen/landbouw-en-visserij/landbouwareaal.
7. Statistiek Vlaanderen, "Veestapel," December 20, 2023, https://www.vlaanderen.be/statistiek-vlaanderen/landbouw-en-visserij/veestapel.
8. Statistiek Vlaanderen, "Veestapel."

References

Adams, Carol J. 1996. *The Sexual Politics of Meat. A Feminist-Vegetarian Critical Theory.* New York: Continuum.

Adams, Carol J., and Josephine Donovan, eds. 1995. *Animals & Women: Feminist Theoretical Explorations.* Durham, NC: Duke University Press.

Bly, Nellie. 2014. " 'Let Me Tell You What I Think of Bicycling:' Nellie Bly Interviews Susan B. Anthony, 1896." *The Hairpin*, April 28, 2014. Originally printed as "Champion of Her Sex: Miss Susan B. Anthony," *New York World*, February 2, 1896. https://web.archive.org/web/20180117014156/https://www.thehairpin.com/2014/04/let-me-tell-you-what-i-think-of-bicycling-nellie-bly-interviews-susan-b-anthony-1896/.

Cazaux, Geertrui. 2002. "Anthropocentrism and Speciesism regarding Animals Other Than Human Animals in Contemporary Criminology." PhD diss., Ghent University.

Cycling in Flanders. n.d. "What Is a Flandrien?" Accessed August 1, 2019. https://cyclinginflanders.cc/story/what-is-a-flandrien.

Fietsberaad. 2018. "Fiets DNA 2018." https://fietsberaad.be/wp-content/uploads/FietsDNA_2018_A5_lwr.pdf.

Garner, Robert, ed. 1996. *Animal Rights, the Changing Debate*. New York: New York University Press.

Regan, Tom. 1985. *The Case for Animal Rights*. Berkeley: University of California Press.

Singer, Peter. 1994. *Dierenbevrijding* [Animal Liberation]. Translated by Linda Knopper. Breda: De Geus.

Sheri E. Barnes. *Photograph by Logan A. Barnes.*

CHAPTER TEN

Dispelling Myths and Shattering Stereotypes as a Vegan Cyclist in Kansas

SHERI E. BARNES

"Well, you *look* healthy," said the older man, dressed in the overalls of a farmer, as he checked my Biking Across Kansas (BAK) badge verifying my status as a vegan and granting me access to the vegan chili at the baked potato bar in a tiny north central Kansas town. I smiled and thanked him, strongly desiring to radiate vibrant health and fitness.

I believe there are many ways to work toward increasing compassion in the world. Each of us who is committed to this cause must find her or his own best avenues. With the overarching life goal of contributing to the creation of a healthier, more compassionate world, cycling is one of my most important and effective assets.

Whether wearing my Team Vegan cycling jersey, flashing my vegan BAK name badge, consulting with rural Kansas towns about how to feed vegans, or just living my life as a vegan cyclist, I have many opportunities to shatter stereotypes and dispel myths about how vegans look, what we can do, and who we are.

I have participated in BAK since 1999, vegetarian the entire time, vegan for the last fourteen tours. (The 2020 and 2021 tours were canceled due to COVID-19.) I currently serve on the board of directors and have been part of the volunteer staff since 2013. During that time, I have been fortunate that my fellow BAK leaders have invited me to contribute my knowledge about surviving and thriving as a vegan while pedaling across a rural, agricultural state. I write an article each year for a pre-tour BAK newsletter. The most recent article was titled "Pushing the Pedals with

Plant-Based Fuel."[1] Each year, I encourage vegan BAKers to take responsibility for their own nourishment and pack supplemental food, like energy bars, single-serving packs of nut butter, shelf-stable plant milk, nuts, seeds, and dried fruit. I urge them to purchase food from the vendors who make the effort to serve us vegan food and to thank them graciously. I offer suggestions for supplementing with food from local grocery stores when necessary. For instance, some years, I have included a story about sharing a meal with a vegetarian cycling friend in a very small town near the Oklahoma border in 2013. We purchased a can of vegan refried beans, tortillas, and grape tomatoes from the local grocery store. We asked the deli manager to open our can, picked up some plastic utensils, sat outside on bags of potting soil, and enjoyed a fine and memorable lunch. I try to inspire resourcefulness in the BAKers who read my annual articles. With a little creativity, we can eat well, even if it is not exactly what we would eat at home.

In addition to my annual article, I connect with new vegan riders via email to reassure them and give them suggestions to prepare for BAK. Perhaps even more significantly, I communicate with the volunteers charged with feeding our traveling band of hungry cyclists as we move east each June. Sherry, our wonderful board member who is the primary early liaison between BAK and the towns on the tour, offers these towns my written suggestions for feeding vegan cyclists and provides my contact information to volunteers who have questions or need additional information. I created the document that Sherry sends them several years ago to provide recommendations to community organizers who may not know where to start when feeding people who don't consume animal products.

In this document, I point out that anyone can eat vegan food, and I try to help people realize how simple it can be. I suggest breakfast items like smoothies made with plant milk, whole-grain cereal or oatmeal, tortillas with nut butter, fruit, and nuts. Lunch options I mention include salad bars with hearty vegan toppings like beans, nuts, and dried fruit; hummus and veggie wraps on pitas or tortillas; pasta with marinara sauce and veggies; and baked potato bars with a variety of vegan toppings. At the bottom of the document, I state, "The main things to avoid are any meat; fish; animal fat; animal broth; dairy products of any kind, including butter or most margarines; eggs and honey. It is easier than most people think. Processed foods are where label reading becomes necessary. Plant-based foods in the same basic form they come in nature are always safe."

SHERI E. BARNES

I want to be sure that my fellow vegans and I have delicious food that will fuel us for long days in the saddle through whatever conditions Kansas dishes out, so, in addition to the document I created, I am always willing to communicate by email, text, and phone with those towns who need more information or details. I love helping to remove the fear associated with feeding vegans and aiding them in realizing that we are not so weird after all.

Many of our lunch and overnight towns have served us wonderful vegan options, sometimes recognizing that plant-based eating does not have to be as complicated or as exotic as they'd previously believed. In preparation for the June 2019 tour, I communicated extensively with a western Kansas caterer who was eager to learn what to feed us, telling me, "I have never fed a vegan before." When I walked into the lunch stop the day we got to Hoxie, her town, two vegan women from Seattle, who had returned for their second spin across Kansas, shouted enthusiastically across the room to me, saying, "This is the best lunch ever!" and giving me thumbs-up signs while enjoying the lavish baked potato bar, complete with cooked kidney and garbanzo beans, steamed broccoli, hummus, and fresh vegetables. On the final morning, at the Missouri border, these same women thanked me for advocating for vegans (and, by proxy, animals). One of them had told me at the beginning of this year's ride that she had purchased a Team Vegan jersey after seeing mine in 2017.

The colorful, fresh food available to vegans is often the envy of those who did not request vegan meals. That is why we wear vegan name badges. Cyclists with food allergies often request them, too, because they know their options will be better and more likely to suit their needs.

It is not uncommon for nonvegan riders to see yet another meal of pulled pork or animal-based sloppy joe and want fresh vegetables instead. The communities are asked to reserve the vegan meals for those with vegan badges, since the other riders did not request alternatives and can apparently eat anything that is offered. Some towns take more pains to enforce this rule than others. My family gets on the road later than a lot of riders, so, if lunch communities are not reserving our meals, it is not impossible that they will be gone when we arrive. That is frustrating and disheartening in the middle of a hard day on the bike, particularly with a ravenous teenage boy in my party, but it testifies to the appeal of plants as fuel to many of the riders. I have heard several of them speak of their weariness with the animal-based meals as the week presses on. They crave fresh veggies and want what we are served.

As most of us vegans experience from time to time in various settings, I encounter occasional backlash or passive aggression on BAK. One post-ride survey respondent complained a couple of years ago that BAK "caters to vegans." I assume they thought so simply because there is public acknowledgement of our presence (and food for us), and this triggers some cognitive dissonance for him or her. Even a former board member made a comment about "trying to please the vegans" during a seemingly unrelated discussion about electrolyte replacements. He sent me an apologetic text later that evening.

When we arrived at the Lions Club where lunch was being served in a small town on the first full day of riding in 2019, we discovered that the only vegan options were apples and oranges. While both are great, they are food for a SAG (support and gear) stop, not lunch. A nonvegan rider snidely said, "I don't know how you can ride without protein anyway." I calmly told him that plants have protein and that we generally do quite well, given an adequate supply of plant-based foods. Fortune was in our favor, however, because one of the longtime supporters was there with her family. She has a vegan sister and always takes good care of us. Her brother and nephew were there eating lunch and went out to her car, returning with Clif bars and trail mix to supplement the fruit provided by the Lions Club. That was enough to get us down the road.

I love being the face of veganism on BAK and felt that identity more clearly in 2019—the last year before COVID forced a two-year suspension—than ever. Following the first-timer meeting on opening night of BAK 2019, where I spoke to newcomers about meeting special dietary needs on the ride, several riders approached me to express their gratitude for my article in the March newsletter or to ask specific questions about finding vegan food throughout the week. One older man stopped me to ask, "So, I guess you feel pretty healthy as a vegan?" I told him I did, and we had a respectful conversation, in which he asked if I was vegan for ethics or health. I told him that my primary motivation is ethical, followed closely by health. He brought up his concern about "Big Pharma's" complicity with the food industry and acknowledged that much of the information we are given is confusing, if not downright misleading. I suggested some books, documentaries, and websites that might help him educate himself on issues around food, health, plant-based eating, and animal agriculture.

In May 2018, during a long training ride, my husband Kenny and I stopped in Norwich, Kansas, about twenty-eight miles from our home in the state's south central region. It just so happened that BAK would be having lunch in that same town a couple weeks later. We went into the small grocery store on Main Street for a bathroom break and water. As we were preparing to get back on our bikes, the owner of the café next door came out to the sidewalk and asked, "Do you happen to be with BAK?"

I said, "Well, we're not on BAK today, but we will be here with the ride in a couple weeks."

She asked, "Do you happen to be one of the vegans?"

"I am!" I exclaimed.

"What do you want to eat?"

I provided several simple suggestions, and, as the menu ideas began to take shape in the café owner's head, she said, "I'm a culinary arts teacher. I can do this!" She shared that the BAK lunch was a fundraiser for the culinary arts students at the two high schools where she taught in small, neighboring towns. Our lunch fees would help fund a trip to Europe for the students.

That serendipitous encounter led to a fabulous vegan lunch of veggie wraps, fruit, and chocolate chip cookies, when hundreds of cyclists gathered for lunch in the community center a couple weeks later. It was one of the best lunches we have had. I thanked her profusely, and she and the students clearly took pride in what they had produced. I felt great because my fellow vegans (and vegetarians) and I got a terrific meal, and I had the opportunity to expose a culinary arts teacher and her students to the delicious possibilities for plant-based meals. Everyone got to see that the vegans were making it across the state just as well as everyone else.

Each year brings heartwarming and/or entertaining encounters with locals along our route. One of the classics occurred many years ago in western Kansas. My son Logan and I were in the parking lot of the school where BAK had spent the night, eating some cereal and shelf-stable almond milk we had brought, along with some blueberries from the local grocery store, since that morning's breakfast of biscuits and gravy did not meet our needs. The local Chamber of Commerce president pulled up in her car, after having surveyed the morning events as BAKers got on the road to leave town. She asked why we were not eating the fundraiser breakfast. I told her we were vegan, and there was no food for us. Excitedly, she exclaimed, "Oh! We are getting so diverse! We have the Blacks, the Mexicans, the Vietnamese, and now we have the vegans! A vegan family just moved into town last month!" As I have relayed that story to my vegan friends over the years, we have joked that we are the

Vegans from planet Vega, so foreign that (political correctness aside) the Chamber president considered veganism in the same realm as an ethnicity or nationality.

In 2013, I was delighted to find a family selling vegan kebabs in the eastern Kansas town of Oswego. I bought several of them and thanked them for being there with vegan food. The mother said, "We're the token vegan family in Oswego." I smiled with a sense of familiarity at her words and said, "We're the token vegan family in Andale." There was instant understanding in our shared experience as the "oddballs" in our respective small Kansas towns.

Breakfast burritos usually don't do anything for us because they are generally filled with egg, cheese, and/or sausage. On our last morning of BAK 2019, I walked past the breakfast burrito booth in Holton High School without paying attention, but did a double take when the word *vegan* caught my eye. Reading the poster carefully, I discovered that there were vegan breakfast burritos. I always try to support the local groups who make the effort to provide vegan food, so I quickly decided to purchase burritos for my son and me.

When I asked if they still had vegan burritos, they directed me to a sweet, grandmotherly woman, who is likely in her eighties. She said, "I researched diligently to make sure I could feed you right." She had made perfectly seasoned tofu burritos. I feel confident that it was her first venture cooking with tofu, but she had taken the time to learn how to do it properly. The tofu had been pressed and was delicious. I thanked her after we had eaten and was pleased to see her smiling proudly when I told her how much we enjoyed them. I hope that interaction and her exposure to tofu as a dietary option may have opened her eyes to new possibilities. One of the things I love about sharing the vegan message on BAK is showing people on the ride and along the way that we can all eat plants and thrive—that the food can be delectable, nourishing, and sustaining for a long day of cycling.

Cycling in Kansas is beset by inaccurate stereotypes. One of those was memorably articulated by a flight attendant many years ago, as my husband and I boarded a plane in Florida for a return trip to Kansas. Kenny was wearing a Biking Across Kansas T-shirt. The flight attendant, apparently a noncyclist, pointed to his shirt and said, "Biking Across Kansas. At least that's easy. I've driven it on I-70." The implication, we knew, was that Kansas is flat. It is fairly flat on I-70; however, we don't ride

SHERI E. BARNES

on I-70 or any other interstate. Depending on the route in a given year, we may encounter the verdant, yet formidable, wind-swept Flint Hills of eastern Kansas; the long, blast-furnace-like inclines of the Gypsum Hills in southwestern Kansas; or the switchback-filled climbs of the Blue Hills in north central Kansas, just to name a few. While we don't have mountains (other than Mt. Sunflower, the highest point in Kansas, at 4,039 feet), I'll put our wind up against anyone's mountains. I am often asked if I ride "in this wind." My answer is generally that, living in Kansas, if I didn't ride wind, I wouldn't ride. Most days have some wind; many days have a great deal. In my mind it is the defining feature of cycling in Kansas. Despite the flight attendant's misperception, cycling in Kansas is rarely easy and often very challenging.

Early in 2019, I set out on a twenty-mile training ride after assessing the forecast. I knew that the wind was supposed to change directions and pick up dramatically, but I thought I had enough time to finish safely. Shortly after the halfway point, it became clear that the fickle forecast had deceived me. As I pedaled west on a wide shoulder, I realized that my anticipated cornering tailwind was not present. Not only that, but I was having to work significantly harder to make forward progress. After five miles westbound, I turned north for my final five miles home. Suddenly, it was unbelievably difficult. I was battling a ferocious northwest wind that threatened to (and at one point did) literally blow me off the road. Although the shoulder was gone, thankfully, there was not a significant drop to the gravel on the side of the road. I was able to stay upright and get out of my pedal, resisting the wind's efforts to blow me over as I stood there, gathering my thoughts and psyching myself up to finish my ride. I returned home to discover that a high wind warning had been issued.

That was not the first time I was blown off or across the road in Kansas. BAK can be particularly unnerving on our east-to-west journey, when (as is often the case in June) a powerful south wind arises as we are traversing hills. The wind becomes squirrelly in the valleys between climbs, and holding our line takes a great deal of effort. This is truly frightening on two-lane roads with oncoming semis. Days like those are grueling, no matter how much I love cycling across our state.

The wind makes so much difference. I remember finishing my first century in Burlington, Kansas, in 1999. The previous day had been around eighty miles, with a long headwind stretch on a road between Cassoday and Rosalia that was better suited to covered wagons than skinny bicycle tires. I was a new road cyclist at the time and had been thoroughly beaten up by the wind and the road when I finally arrived in El Dorado for our overnight stop. I felt discouraged and depleted, and I couldn't imagine how I was going to ride to Burlington the next day. But I got on my bike the next morning and discovered, to my unending delight, that the wind had subsided. It was a beautiful day, on well-maintained roads, with light wind that even pushed us part of the day. I was new enough that I didn't have a computer on my bike. When we arrived in Burlington, Kenny wanted to ride around a little more, and after a couple miles of easy riding, he showed me his computer. I had just ridden a hundred miles, with so much more ease than the previous day's ride, although that had been around 20 percent shorter. That was a lesson in how much difference Kansas wind can make. It is less about the number of miles than it is about the wind ferocity.

In addition to Kansas wind, animal agriculture is currently a fact of life in Kansas, although I dream of a day when this may not be true. I sometimes face an internal struggle because the quietest roads that I love to ride are often the same roads where I encounter the most evidence of farmed animals. I have a practice of looking at the cows, horses, sheep, and goats whom I ride past and saying out loud, when I am alone, "Vegan blessings to you, my friends! I am trying to help." If I am with other cyclists, I usually just send the animals silent love and blessings. Some of my more painful memories of witnessing animal suffering include riding past miles and miles of feedlots in western Kansas and past slaughterhouses in Dodge City. Besides the horrendous odor emanating from the feedlots, I am all too aware of the suffering that exists in the overcrowded conditions. Even though I am not contributing to the violence, I experience guilt and the feeling of not doing enough when I pass those nightmarish establishments.

One year on BAK, a SAG stop was set up in the gravel drive of a factory farm. I stopped, refilled my water, and silently blessed the poor pigs whom I knew were imprisoned behind the long shed walls and under the whirring ventilation fans. Again, guilt consumed me, despite the fact that I was not contributing to the problem. Similarly, seeing a cattle truck pull into a farm on a training ride a few years ago ruined an otherwise terrific ride. I saw the cows in the field, whom I had blessed countless times on previous rides, and I knew that they were soon to be carted away to their deaths, possibly in one of the slaughterhouses I had passed

SHERI E. BARNES

on BAK. When I got home, I vented online to my Wichita Animal Rights Facebook group because I knew I would find some empathy there. Most people don't understand.

On most rides, locally or across Kansas, I am passed by pickups bearing "EAT BEEF" license plates on their front bumpers. I feel sad when I notice them. Even as I give them a friendly wave for passing me safely and courteously, it hurts. I often feel like an outsider, misunderstood and considered freakish because I care about animals and believe they have a right to their own lives. I'm thankful to Kansas for the many years of terrific cycling I have experienced here, but I often feel conflicted and tortured by the inevitable sights along the road.

In 2018, I taught two classes on plant-based nourishment to people living with diabetes and prediabetes. I started my presentation with the story of meeting Dale a couple months earlier.

When getting back on my bike after a bathroom stop in the middle of a training ride, an older man rolled up and leaned his bike against a park bench. We exchanged greetings and then talked, like any two cyclists might, about bikes, bike rides, and our gratitude for the excellent cycling in south central Kansas. I asked him if he had ever ridden BAK. He said, "Well, I have never done BAK, but my brother and I rode across Kansas in four days. But I was only in my late seventies when I did that. I'll be ninety in two days." Wow!

BAK is an eight-day ride, with multiple days typically covering seventy to ninety miles, so crossing the state—presumably self-supported— in four days as a late septuagenarian was quite an accomplishment. Let alone the fact that we were meeting on our solo training rides, two days before Dale's ninetieth birthday. I told him how impressed I was. He said, "The Lord's been good to me. I don't take any medicine, and that's pretty good for my age. And, I'm kind of a health nut. My wife and I have been vegetarian since 1951."

"Awesome!" I said. "I'm vegan."

He replied, "Well, to be honest, we eat vegan all the time, except when a relative makes us mac and cheese because they know we don't eat meat. We'll eat it, but we eat vegan the rest of the time."

I shared with my classes how special it was to have encountered Dale. (What are the odds of running into a nearly ninety-year-old, nearly vegan cyclist in Kansas?) I acknowledged that he is a sample size of one, and shared information about Dan Buettner's concept of Blue Zones

(Buettner 2012), regions of the world populated by the healthiest concentrations of people in their nineties and hundreds. All the communities feature largely plant-based diets, among the characteristics found to contribute to their healthy longevity.

In both classes, older men who identified as exercisers questioned me about how it is possible to ride my bike as much as I do without eating animal products for protein. I helped them understand that plants have protein and showed them photographs in my presentation of many different types of vegan athletes, including one of myself in my Team Vegan cycling jersey and one of my son, a healthy, fit, teenage vegan distance runner, cyclist, and swimmer.

One of the men in the second class stayed after everyone had left. He had not seemed very engaged and even said to the group, as I finished, "I'm going to go out and get me a Big Mac." However, as he was walking out the door, he turned around and said to me, "Well, you have changed my way of thinking. I'm going to do things differently."

While I doubt that he has become vegan, I am grateful for the opportunity to have been able to plant some seeds. He was able to see that I am a fit, healthy vegan who rides her bike thousands of miles a year and has done so for many years, and he heard a story about a nonagenarian cyclist who is vegan except for occasional macaroni and cheese made by well-intentioned, if misinformed, family members. I believe I shattered some stereotypes and dispelled some myths that night, and that I do the same every time someone learns that I am a vegan cyclist and can see that I am not malnourished and weak.

Fitness is advocacy.

For me this means that people see that I am out there on the road, doing challenging things—facing hours and miles of fierce headwind, riding up and down hills and sweating in Kansas heat—just like everyone else. All of us vegans have been asked, "Where do you get your protein?" Cycling across Kansas without consuming animals or their secretions demonstrates that I am getting enough of what I need.

One of the many things I cherish about BAK is the diversity of riders. It is a family-friendly ride. My son's first BAK was in 2004, when I was five and a half months pregnant with him. There are many multigenerational BAK families. In addition, I love telling people that BAKers come in all ages, shapes, sizes, and abilities. It is undoubtedly going to be safer and more fun if one has trained well, but that does not mean that everyone looks like a world-class cyclist. I have been awed many times by the octogenarian cyclists who pedal across the state. Paraplegic cyclists on low handcycles and amputees with prosthetic limbs also participate. One year, a paraplegic veteran pedaled a good portion of every day on a hand-cycle that allowed him to turn the cranks with his thumbs, the only digits in which he retained function. Every half hour or so, in hot conditions, he rode into an air-conditioned trailer to lower his body temperature below the point of injury (since his body no longer did that for him).

Then there is the mettle demonstrated by cyclists who embark on the journey across Kansas carrying a lot of extra body weight. Not only do they have to push that weight into Kansas wind and up hills, but some, I am sure, have to overcome the fear of judgment from other cyclists. I respect the fact that they are getting out there, working in the same tough conditions I am and breaking stereotypes of their own.

While I see my fitness as primarily vegan advocacy, at times it has also been gender advocacy. For instance, when a man told me on a par-ticularly tough hill several years ago, "No way a chick is going to beat me up this hill," I smiled, stood up in my pedals and made sure I did. He may or may not have known that I am vegan, but he did know that a woman dug deeper and pushed harder to demonstrate that women can be powerful, too.

I don't think I am better because I am vegan or because I strive to remain fit (or because I am a woman), but I do want people to know that I am just as good. When it comes to veganism, if they see that plants make me strong, maybe it will encourage someone to take the plunge into animal-free nourishment. I was thrilled with the 2018 documentary *The Game Changers* (Psihoyos 2018), which highlights a wide array of vegan athletes. Like cycling across rural Kansas as a vegan, this documentary exposes people who may have misconceived ideas about what vegans look like and can do to the reality that vegans can be strong and healthy and adventurous.

I do other exercise, but cycling is my passion and the centerpiece of my movement menu. Just as *vegan* is an integral part of my identity, so is *cyclist*. The two are intertwined, each a critical facet of who I am, complementing and informing the other. Throughout 2020 and 2021, as all of us had our perceptions of the world turned upside down by a pandemic, and as my personal identity took multiple blows because of family crises, my passion for cycling and vegan living remained constant, serving as lifelines in times that have become increasingly difficult to navigate. I have recently learned that my son endured relentless bullying in school for being a trim, vegan endurance athlete in an agricultural, football-worshipping Kansas town. This both breaks my heart and reinforces my commitment to use my platform as a vegan cyclist and ride organizer to dispel myths and shatter stereotypes about who vegans are. I hope my advocacy will contribute to a healthier, more compassionate world, one Kansas town at a time, for the animals as well as for those of us whose ethics compel us to fuel our bodies with plants instead of with the flesh and secretions of sentient beings.

Like many vegans I know, food is an important part of my life! I love to eat nourishing, delicious food and believe in its power to fuel me down the road, both on the bike and in life.

I have tried-and-true fueling rituals that help me feel prepared to pedal and have consistently left me ready to ride again. When I am at home, breakfast is generally a smoothie, always including ground flaxseed, maca, magnesium gluconate, and turmeric. I look forward to my smoothies every day and usually incorporate dark, leafy greens; banana; frozen berries; plant milk; and assorted other flavorful additions, like cacao nibs, nuts, and spices.

Shortly before getting on the bike, I drink Vega Preworkout Energizer and swallow Energybits (spirulina). On the bike, I eat Gu or Hammer Gel or, when riding at home, steamed new potatoes. Although I wouldn't eat lunch on a training ride, I typically do on BAK because lunch in a small town is part of the experience. Thankfully, the vegan lunch options are generally suitable riding fuel, like baked potatoes or veggie wraps, unlike the heavy pulled pork frequently offered to omnivores.

At home, I prime my body for post-ride recovery with a smoothie that includes Recoverybits (chlorella). Did I mention that I love my smoothies? Often, on long rides, where I get particularly hungry, I begin dreaming of my recovery smoothie. Imagining a cool, creamy, chocolatey (with cocoa or cacao nibs), fruity delight inspires me to continue pushing through the Kansas wind.

SHERI E. BARNES

Notes

1. Sheri E. Barnes, "Biking Across Kansas e-News," May 7, 2023, http://hosted
.verticalresponse.com/914825/8c25e66b9a/.

References

Buettner, Dan. 2012. *The Blue Zones: 9 Lessons for Living Longer from the People Who've Lived the Longest*. Washington, DC: National Geographic.
Psihoyos, Louie, dir. *The Game Changers*. 2018. Laguna Niguel, CA: ReFuel Productions.

I was thirty weeks pregnant with my third child and we went on a long, long bicycle trip—eight or ten hours. My husband had the kids in the bike trailer. We were somewhere in Marin County. I was bicycling with this big belly. I recently saw that photo! It was a really nice day, and I took my time. *Photograph by Oliver Zahn.*

CHAPTER ELEVEN

Vegan Black Mama
Scholar Cyclist

A. BREEZE HARPER

Until recently—because my bike just broke and I didn't get back into it after the fourth baby was born—we were bicycling everywhere. Around 2015–2016, I started a new job at the University of California at Berkeley, and I had to put my two girls in nursery school. And I was wondering, "How is this going to work, because my husband takes the car every day?" So, I thought, "Okay, I bicycle all the time anyway, so we will attach a double-seater chariot to my bike and I will bicycle those girls to school."

I think people were surprised that I bicycled so much and that I was bicycling these girls. Some of my friends and acquaintances also learned that I am vegan. And then the questions began. "How do you do that? Where do you get the energy to be a mom of three kids"—at the time—"and bicycle?" And then I became pregnant with my fourth child, and I'm bicycling these girls, and there's this awe—"Where do you get the energy to do that?" People see that I've been nursing since 2009 and I was obviously pregnant and I am bicycling these girls in the chariot.

Their reactions got me to think, once again, about how most people in the United States are ignorant about nutrition and what's possible, and as well about the assumptions about women's strength. But equally about assumptions about what you can and cannot do when you are pregnant.

I'm not a stay-at-home mom. I'm going to do it my way. It makes people uncomfortable, whether it is bicycling while visibly pregnant, hauling these girls, or deciding to have a plant-based diet and to have home births. I communicated to those asking that I have a well-balanced diet. I have done a lot of research because of my interest in nutrition.

Yet, there is constant judgment and judging that you will never be "good enough." Or, an unrealistic fantasy exists about what the perfect mother or mothering practice is. What should be a joyous time in the lives of most pregnant people (not everyone chooses to be pregnant and sometimes it is stressful, but what should be joyous for most)—why do we have to deal with those stresses under the guise of "we are just trying to do what's best for you and the baby" when they are really just interested in controlling us because of some unresolved anxieties that they have around how certain bodies should perform and be more civilized?

I began biking when I moved to Berkeley in 2007 and I enrolled in a University of California at Davis doctoral program. I realized there was a train to UC Davis, which would be better than driving. My husband bought me a bike. I thought, "I don't know about this," feeling worried about biking in the city. I grew up in the middle of nowhere, a rural area, and then I went to school at Dartmouth College which is very rural. We bicycled a lot and I didn't worry about being hit by a car. My positive experience bicycling around Hanover, New Hampshire, for four years really helped me turn bicycling into a habit. I loved it.

Fast-forward ten years after graduating from college, and I found myself loving the new adventures that bicycling in the East Bay area as well as Davis, California, had to offer me. I enjoyed getting on a bike and figuring out the bike paths in Berkeley and being able to bicycle to the train and feeling really good because I'm not getting stuck in traffic. I could put my bike on the train, get to school, and bicycle around. It was liberating, but at the same time it also pushed me to research more into "how can I make my vegan diet better so I can thrive as someone who's bicycling a lot?"

It encouraged me to constantly make sure I was getting the nutrition I need. And I liked solving a puzzle, because at least for me there are times I want to bicycle and maybe I'm on my period and I don't feel as strong, but I still want to bike. And I thought, "I'm going to research what plant-based foods and herbs I can take so I can continue to bicycle, so I can continue to get the power and energy I need to continue biking."

I thought, "Maybe I could be anemic, but I don't need to eat meat. What can I do?" And the answer was, "Oh, stinging nettles can give me the energy I need. It's high in iron."[1] Vegan cycling gave me a problem-solving challenge: how can I figure this out in terms of nutrition?

When I was pregnant with my first child and doing that route, I was a little scared, wondering, "How is this going to work? I'm going to have

A. BREEZE HARPER

to take care of myself and feed the child in my womb." I never had a problem. But it was hard not to listen to people sometimes. Again, I decided, "I am just going to research this and see what power I need to bicycle while pregnant: bicycle to the train, bicycle at school, bicycle back." And in researching it, I was finding information to share with other people, and for my other physical activities.

One thing leads to another, another, and another. In this case, I discovered the power of stinging nettles. I knew about them before, in general for women's reproductive health, and had forgotten about it and then put it back into my diet. Also, I learned about hemp seeds as a powerful food source. I was constantly figuring out what foods I can eat that are plant based, so I could continue bicycling.

As a result, when I was pregnant with my first child, and doing my dissertation work at the University of California at Davis, I would bicycle to the train and bicycle around campus until I was about eight and a half months pregnant. The only reason I stopped is because my belly was so big, I couldn't bicycle without bumping my belly with my knees.

I encountered many assumptions that I was endangering my unborn child by bicycling. I was hyperconscious of bicycling not really being a huge part of the US's tradition, especially if you are pregnant. I experienced it in questions like, "Is it safe bicycling while visibly pregnant, while *that* pregnant?"

People masked their judgment as concern—"Should you be doing that?"—and progressed to, "You're vegan? Is *that* safe?" And then the assumptions that I was endangering my child with a plant-based diet: "You are going to do a plant-based diet while pregnant?!" That response exposes the ignorance around veganism.

My response was, "I'm fine. I practice a holistic vegan diet. I get the nutrition I need."

During my second pregnancy, my ob/gyn told me that I could not nurse my first child while pregnant with my second because I was going to give myself osteoporosis. And then when I told her I'm vegan, she said, "No, you can't do it; that's very bad." It wasn't said in a judgmental way, but those were her assumptions about what it means to be a vegan. She had also been reading statistics that Black women have higher rates of infant mortality and maternal health problems than the mainstream.

I told her, "I am doing my PhD work in cultural vegan studies. I am able to do what I need to do and able to research and understand what nutrients I need and how that translates into a plant-based diet."

This is not just about me bicycling, but it is those assumptions over-laid with assumptions about veganism, of Black women and higher infant mortality, and what it means to be pregnant.

I trained myself to learn what you need if your body is going to assimilate calcium in combination with a good vitamin D. I understood you cannot just take calcium pills even if they are vegan, because your body does not necessarily assimilate pills. You need to do things so that your body assimilates the calcium, the boron, and the magnesium for strong bones. I learned that five tablespoons of chia seeds would give me not just the calcium I need but also the boron and magnesium to assimilate the calcium. I followed a diet high in chia seeds, hemp seeds, and kale.

I gave birth to my second child, and she was born with two teeth. I had left my other practitioner and chosen a midwifery practice that supported a birth at my home. And when the baby was born, she said, "Oh my god, is there a tooth in there? Oh my god, there are two teeth in there! It looks like you were getting plenty of minerals."

When I was about seven months pregnant with my third child, we went camping for seven days, and I carried my six-year-old son back down to the campsite. My children are used to that energy and strength, and I like modeling myself against the stereotype that there is only one way to be a girl or a woman. Lots of times there are these representations of girls and women not doing things that could be perceived as physically challenging, like bicycling well into your third trimester, or hiking while pregnant with someone on your back.

By 2016, the time of my fourth pregnancy, I was also working full time. But I was confident after my previous experiences, and that's why I decided, I'm going to bicycle my girls—who were two and four at the time—to nursery school. It was challenging, especially the first trimester; I was so tired. Some people made comments, like "Maybe you have to eat red meat," "Maybe you are anemic." I *was* anemic but combining stinging nettles tea with liquid chlorophyl and a good source of vitamin C all taken together addressed this deficiency. After that, my hemoglobin stabilized.

I bicycled them until I was laid off at UC Berkeley. I wore my fitted bicycle clothes. I never tried to hide my pregnancy. I always wore fitted clothing. I would wear something that was not a maternity spandex top and my belly would be hanging out. I don't understand why women are supposed to cover their bellies or not make their pregnancy visible.

I always wear my bikini whether pregnant or not, so I wore it while visibly pregnant. We went to the beaches a lot, but I think I have only seen three women in my entire life in the USA wearing bikinis while visibly pregnant. It's something, supposedly, that "you don't do." I don't get that. I don't want my belly to be constricted. Why is that taboo? Why are so many things taboo? Whether showing your belly in a bikini, or when I am bicycling and you can see part of my belly because I am not wearing the "right" clothes. I never understood the anxieties that are created about appearances.

I hear the constant surprise in reactions like "Breeze, you are so energetic" or "Wow, look at that woman who is bicycling her kids while she has this big belly." There's always that shock that a pregnant woman can bicycle her kids. But then people also learn that I practice veganism, and I did home births, and my kids were nine pounds or bigger—my last was ten pounds—and the assumptions have to be confronted.

The women I meet living in the USA (whether they are vegan or not) but were raised outside the United States and have been pregnant and bicycling say they experienced similar judgments, being asked, "Is it safe that you are bicycling while you are this pregnant?" A professor at UC Davis from Holland said, "We all do this until we give birth. But when I came here [to the US], people were saying, 'But that's dangerous. Why are you doing that?'"

We get into the realm of others monitoring my body, and strangers dictating what they think I should be doing "for the good of the baby." This resonates with attitudes in the US where a woman doesn't know what is best for her body when she's pregnant, so the state or community has to come in and tell her what she needs to do, "for the good of her child." And then there is also the presumed incompetence of being a Black woman. And those are the things that I have to navigate: to what extent people are overtly saying these things because of that? Or is it more implicit bias, because many are taught that the worst moms are Black moms?

Those are the assumptions that I encounter and can't separate from when I am biking as a Black woman, whether visibly pregnant or not, and pulling that trailer with two children behind me.

I was able to take care of myself and document how I was successfully taking care of myself, then share it with other people who are pregnant and who are having challenges with energy, or who are missing certain minerals or other nutrition they need for pregnancy. Say I decide to bicycle too strenuously with the girls attached, up a hill. And I think, "Oh god, my legs hurt; this hurts." And I remind myself, "Don't forget to take more chia seeds tomorrow." I am always thinking in terms of nutrition.

I am able to share that information and say, "I am not just saying this because it is book knowledge. I was able to have four pregnancies, have home births, but I also was very active. It gave me energy. Until eight or eight and a half months pregnant, I bicycled everywhere."

The girls were two and four, and they think it is normal. They are used to seeing Mom being a badass. For them it's, "Why *wouldn't* Mom do that?" And they giggle and say, "Mom, wow, you are really strong! How can you do that?"

And I tell them, "A lot of things you can put your mind to, and you can do it. It's not easy, but I like to challenge myself. It's a workout."

They say, "I want to get my workout on!"

They are learning by seeing me do it, seeing me not complain.

Yes, they learn, you can do that regardless of your gender. When we do things, whether it is bicycling or hiking, I am always telling my children why we are eating the foods we eat, what that nutrition will do for certain parts of your body. This becomes a whole lesson, and bicycling was part of the lesson. They might ask, "Well, how do you do that?" And I have my green smoothie in the water holder, and it has the kale, the chia seeds, the hemp seeds. They begin making all these connections: "Mommy's strong. She can do this. Why can't she do this even though she is pregnant? She is telling us she drinks her super greens. And what's in it that helps her get the energy and strength that she needs?" It's a whole story that the girls are learning and that is important to them.

Now the older two bicycle, and it shows them the possibilities.

Our second child, Eva Luna, who became the youngest girl to summit Mount Shasta,[2] had seen me doing things like this—for instance, bicycling with them to the nursery school while pregnant. She asked herself, "Why can't I do that?" She had seen what I could do.

I haven't got back into bicycling since the baby was born the way I had been doing it before then, because it's been logistically difficult. I want to start bicycling the younger one to the bus stop, and the toddler to nursery school.

There are assumptions in the United States about a body—showing your boobs, or showing that you are pregnant outside of the domestic sphere and doing something outside beyond what is expected of you—you are hiking while this pregnant, you are bicycling while visibly pregnant, dropping your girls off at nursery school so you are going to your job—it makes me think that we are rebelling against a lot just by doing that, by being, in my case, a vegan Black mama scholar cyclist.

Notes

1. On stinging nettles see https://web.archive.org/web/20160713030318/, http://www.sistahvegan.com/2016/07/07/kids-drinking-nettles-for-optimal-nutrition-sistot-vegans/, https://web.archive.org/web/20160718202013/, http://sistahvegan.com/2016/07/14/nettles-tea-wont-dismantle-racism-but-can-help-with-racial-tension-headaches/, and https://web.archive.org/web/20141208122801/, http://sistahvegan.com/2014/07/21/vegan-secret-1-for-minimal-menstrual-pain-and-heavy-bleeding/.
2. Cydney Devine-Jones, "Berkeley Girl Who Climbed Mount Shasta: 'I Wanted to See the World from the Top,'" *Berkeleyside*, July 19, 2019, https://www.berkeleyside.org/2019/07/19/berkeley-girl-who-climbed-mount-shasta-i-wanted-to-see-the-world-from-the-top.

CHAPTER TWELVE

Start Where You Are and Keep Going

CAROL J. ADAMS

My daily ride starts in the alley behind my house in a suburb of Dallas. Alleys provide access to the garages at the back of the homes. Because our comings and goings happen more frequently in the alley, we see our neighbors behind us more regularly than those whose houses face ours on the street. My alley neighbors wave when they see me start off on my ride.

When we first moved here, back in 1987, I reached out to a feminist philosophy professor at the University of Texas at Dallas, inviting her to lunch. She asked if she could bring a feminist studies graduate student. This is before *The Sexual Politics of Meat* was completed, before it was published, before it had become a "classic" (meaning: something you need to know about but perhaps don't have to read). The graduate student knew nothing about me, and in her view I was not someone who offered social capital or theoretical weight. From the moment she arrived, she complained about the suburban neighborhood.

"It looks dead," she said, as she started eating a luscious vegetable soup I had served. "It looks like no one lives here."

"I live here," I wanted to say. "I, who prepared this delicious lunch for you."

She continued, "It's empty."

"The alleys," I wanted to say. "It's not an apartment stoop culture; it's a back-of-the-house, facing-garages type of culture," I wanted to say.

She took a bite and continued her one-note complaint, "I can hardly wait to move. Who would want to live here?"

Well, the person who fixed your lunch, for one.

"There are no pedestrians."

"People are at work," I wanted to say. "Also, it's noon and it's hot out. This is Texas after all."

The city of Dallas starts about a thousand feet from my house. The layout of our neighborhood is just like that found a thousand feet to our south. But the suburbs and their residents received all her contempt. I felt her dismissing me, too.

Frankly, I was in shock from our recent move. The Dallas suburb I found myself in was alien to me, too. I missed so much. Nothing was within walking distance, except the elementary school—no grocery stores or other amenities. We had lived in a small city of sixteen thousand. True, we had sued that city for racism in housing and acquired a few fans and many haters. But the small steel-producing city along Lake Erie had offered beautiful sunsets when I took the time to see them.

We arrived in May, and the challenge of reconciling myself to living in this suburban area was complicated by the question of "How do I live in this climate?" The heat of the Texas sun created cabin fever in the summer. It reminded us of how winter's snowstorms in the north functioned that way.

I was out of Eden. The land felt stripped of all that I loved. No hills to speak of, no view from those hills down to a lake or across the lake, to Canada. No smell of grapes or apples as you traveled by car, bike, or foot in the autumn. I was so homesick.

At that time, I had a fixed idea of how to be "in nature." I had grown out of childhood, but not my childhood ideal of what it meant to be out in nature among orchards and grape vineyards, rolling hills and lake views and swimming in ponds or lakes and riding ponies. One summer, helping my sister and brother-in-law build a cabin, my biking took me through rural roads over streams and through forests fresh with the smell of rain. Another summer, I used my bike to visit an elderly Jamaican couple trying to make a living off their scrabbly, unproductive land. I helped them apply for loans and grants while biking in the midst of vineyards bursting with Concord grapes. Biking was sensuous.

In Dallas, I felt I had lost the biking environment I knew and loved. Though torn from my roots, I actually suffered from a lack of imagination. I did not think to approach this suburb as Derek Jarman did the land around Prospect Cottage, the place he bought near the Dungeness nuclear power station in southeast England (Jarman [1994] 2009), a landscape at least one person dubbed a "post-apocalyptic wasteland" (Macdonald 2015). There he planted a beautiful garden filled with lavender, daffodils, sea kale, crocus, roses, holly bushes, houseleeks, marigold, dianthus, saxifrage, campion, wallflower, purple iris, calendula, rue, chamomile, poppy, valerian, nasturtium—and others (Jarman, passim).

I was also enduring a lengthy gestation of thirteen years as I tried to figure out how to write the book that became *The Sexual Politics of Meat*. I had left behind my advocacy job and needed to recreate myself as a writer. It was here, in this suburb of Dallas, that I was making a new life with my spouse and our two-and-a-half-year-old child. We hung our bicycles from the ceiling in the garage, and there they remained.

■   ■   ■

On my bike, I head down the alley. Sometimes I stop and chat with the neighbor who runs an appliance repair business from his backyard. We both followed Trump's candidacy and presidency with shock. The week before, I offered him a Biden yard sign. "Sure, sure," he said, "just put it in my front yard."

I turn right when the alley ends, feeding into the street. My suburb created bike/walking paths a few years ago, and now, if she were here, the graduate student would see people out walking by themselves, with partners, with dogs, with strollers. The bike/walking path is my goal. My bike lifts my body off the ground and opens my mind, offering me rhythm, movement, a changeable view. Through my biking I recalibrate what *scenic* means, what *nature* means. Not something "out there." Not something I am exiled from. But something thriving, right here.

Along with the stereotype that the suburbs are uninhabited and uninhabitable, is another—that you can't find "nature" in the suburbs. But just as Lisa Couturier (2005) discovered a world of urban animals, from snakes to vultures, in New York City, my biking introduces me to a host of animals who share this suburb with me.

In *H Is for Hawk*, Helen Macdonald (2014) talks about "a long vein of chalk-mysticism buried in English nature-culture" and finds herself susceptible to it, as she stands on a chalk hill, with the wide downland valley in view: "I know that loving landscapes like this involves a kind of history that concerns itself with purity, a sense of deep time and blood-belonging, and assumes that these solitudinous windswept landscapes are finer, better, than the landscapes below." She quotes H. J. Massingham from the 1930s: "The frequenter of downland is occupied with essentials; with structure, with forms and with textures," whereas "aloft, he breathes an air that tunes him to the grand, archaic, naked forms of things" (260–61).

I think about how the equivalent of the English chalk lovers' "upland" and "downland" is being "in nature" versus "living in the suburbs," and about the elitism of certain nature lovers, that *their* kind of nature is the best kind of nature. I think about that as I bike in my suburb.

There is so much to see, like how the trees change: the live oak trees that lose half their leaves year round (so that one friend said they should be called "half-live oaks"), the colorful crepe myrtles, the blossoming rose of Sharon, and our own jasmine blooming twice a year. The freedom of moving through air in this way offers me a sense of liberation. I miss those open rural roads, but this is where I am.

■   ■   ■

My first bike was my mother's. It was a very heavy bike, a grownup, 1950s bike. With training wheels attached to it, I biked on the sidewalk, never entirely secure as the bike shifted from one training wheel to the other. The summer after second grade, I learned to ride without training wheels. Across the street, my friend Marcia and her brother received two beautiful, kid-sized bikes. One day their father patiently walked with one child and then another, up and down the sidewalk. Talking to them, holding on, and then a push and they were on their own.

I called over and asked, "Will you teach me, Mr. Petersen?" and he agreed. I felt liberated into space in a new way. The training wheels were removed from my mother's bike, and when school started, she let me borrow it to ride to school. Mom's bike was still very heavy and cumbersome, but a new freedom accompanied my understanding of balancing on a bike. We were "walkers," and the school was about a mile away. I mounted the bike, careful to pull my dress down (no pants allowed for girls back in the '50s and '60s), and headed to school. There was a small hill that led to the high school; once one had successfully conquered that, one turned right and coasted down to the elementary school. I stood to

CAROL J. ADAMS

pedal harder up the hill, but even with my short legs pedaling away as fast as possible, I could not command the heavy bike to get to the top. I began to feel the bike slipping slowly backwards. Then I heard the chuckle of a high school student, a football player recognizing that I was in trouble. My savior gave me a huge push that got me going forward again, and the bike and I crested the hill.

I made it the rest of the way unassisted. But after school, anxious to get home because the Brownies were meeting at our house, I turned the corner onto our stone and dirt driveway too quickly and fell, skinning my knee. Rather than being the host to all the girls, I, feeling humiliated, limped into the house, where my mother cleaned the wound and applied mercurochrome.

■   ■   ■

The bike/walk path heads past the electrical-power "set aside" with its immense electrical lines and its high-tension transmission poles. Across the street is the elementary school. When I want to cross at school opening and dismissal times, I must wait for the crossing guard to escort me with the elementary kids. In the spring of 2020, I can hear the school's eight o'clock bell announcing the start of class even as the pandemic emptied the building weeks earlier.

One hundred and ten different languages are spoken in the school district, and many of them can be heard on the bike/walk trail.

I was in elementary school when I received my very first bike. It was May 1960, my ninth birthday.

It was a Huffy three-speed bike. Oh lord, it was beautiful. I had just had my tonsils out and was not permitted to go outside. From the front door, I saw my big sister—who had been deputized to go uptown and get the bike from the hardware store—stop to talk to Marcia's older brother as he prepared to deliver the afternoon newspaper on his bike. I wanted to call out to her to bring me my bike, but my throat was raw from the tonsillectomy.

Finally, she came across the street with this amazing thing, my bicycle. Yet because I could not go outside, riding it seemed impossible. I begged my mother to let me ride it inside and she agreed. The house, a towering 1870s brick structure, had a circular first floor—a large hallway led to an oval dining room, a massive kitchen, and then a right turn around through the bathroom, the sewing room, the playroom, into the living room, and then back to the hallway. I pursued this circular track until dinnertime, speeding up on the straightaway down the hall, slowing for the turns and the furniture.

■ ■ ■

Past the elementary school, the bike/walking trail requires one to cross a six-lane thoroughfare. Commuters rush to work, often speeding as the light turns red. Then the traffic is parted, and I cross. In the early months of the pandemic, for the first time, the thoroughfare emptied of cars, much less speeders, because no one was hurrying to work.

Just before another elementary school, the path along the creek begins. Egrets hang out here and rabbits, too. A squirrel holds a large green sphere in her mouth, four inches in diameter, a daunting task to lift it up. At first, I think it is an errant tennis ball, but I see that it is fruit of the bois d'arc tree.

Carol's spanking new Huffy three-speed bicycle, May 1960. *Photograph by Carol J. Adams.*

Along with the bike/walk trail, my suburb created a linear park, developed along a creek that was expanded, rebuilt, and constantly managed with chemicals to keep it clear. Now I ride past herons and more egrets, as well as turtles sunning on the human-made spillways.

Two years after I received the three-speed Huffy bike, my sisters and I were given a pony by a client of my father's, a lawyer. Soon we acquired another pony, as did many of the neighborhood girls. Everything the Lone Ranger did on a horse (except killing people), we did. We ran up to our trusted steeds from behind, placed our hands on their rumps, and propelled ourselves into the saddle. We rode under the perfectly positioned limbs of a maple tree and swung off, teaching the ponies to stop when they felt us spring away. We galloped down country lanes and stood up on their backs. We galloped down country lanes and switched horses. We played hide and go seek on the horses and ponies through woods. We raced down cornfields.

Pre–Title IX—the act that prevents discrimination in education, including sports—we invented our own athletic competitions. Tomboys, the lot of us.

■   ■   ■

Along the Duck Creek linear path, I zip past the ducks, egrets, herons, turtles, squirrels, loose dogs, leashed dogs.
The great blue heron by the side of the creek.
The great blue heron in the middle of the creek.
The great blue heron flying along the creek.
The great blue heron in the tree.
The great blue heron on the side of the creek—alert, near a baby heron.
I don't feel as closed in knowing I share this space with that grand bird.
One day at dusk, I saw the great blue heron standing on our front lawn. I like to imagine the heron was returning the visit.

■   ■   ■

In 1965, my sister was heading to Vassar, and my parents urged me to let her take my bike to help her get around the campus. They pointed out I wasn't using it. I had the ponies and I was practicing to be a cheerleader.

Carol standing on top of Jimmy. *Photograph from the author's collection.*

The bike was loaded in the car and my parents and sister left for the six-hour trip to Poughkeepsie. Did I watch the bike's departure with more regret than I felt for my sister's leaving?

At the end of her first year, my sister returned home. "Where is my bike?" I challenged.

"We thought it better for it to just stay at Vassar for the summer," a parent said reassuringly.

I didn't remember agreeing to this, but by then I had succeeded in becoming a cheerleader, and there were lots of summer practices to prepare for football season.

■   ■   ■

Now it's egrets, sentinel in the midst of the pond. Some days the water is a pure blue, and sometimes it is a muddy mess. Still, the egret knows something is underneath and, with a dart of the beak, succeeds. The heron is watching nearby.

My sister graduated from Vassar in 1969, and after the ceremony, we loaded up the car. A painting lay across the space below the back window, and suitcases and boxes were stuffed into the trunk. I stopped and looked around.

"Where is my bike going to go?" I asked innocently.

"Carol, there is something we have been meaning to tell you," one of my parents said. Someone seems to suppress a snicker.

"Your bike was stolen in the fall of Nancy's freshman year."

The fall of Nancy's freshmen year.

My beloved Huffy, stolen? I felt hurt, a double injury, the loss and then the lie. Why had they not told me this three and a half years ago?

"It's just as well," someone said (another suppressed snicker), "there's no place for it in the car."

Later, my sister said she wanted to tell me the whole sad story—how she searched the campus for weeks after realizing it had been stolen—but my parents had told her not to. There was a suggestion they were afraid of my anger. Why were my parents so fearful of my anger when I was fourteen? And then fifteen? And then sixteen? True, when I was younger, I was known for having tantrums. I would jump up and down, feeling I could make the old house shake with my fury. When I engaged in this behavior, my mother called me Rumpelstiltskin. But that had been more than a decade earlier, when I was five or six. Yet, something about my anger supposedly postponed the revelation of the bike's theft.

The result of this deception was that I felt both betrayed and distrustful. Over many years, as I interacted with my family, the suspicion continued. I wondered, "What else aren't they telling me?"

A few years ago, my brother-in-law, a retired therapist, asked me, "What was there about your anger that made your parents afraid to tell you about the bike?"

"That's right," I laughed, "blame the victim."

Yet my anger was also a part of the engine that kept me working at writing *The Sexual Politics of Meat* for more than a decade. And one of the most important insights I had in writing the book was that no one would want to read an angry screed. I realized the job of the book wasn't to ask my readers to handle *my* anger about the injustices I was describing, but to allow my readers to discover their *own* anger. I had to adjust the tone and approach to accord with that insight.

■ ■ ■

The trail has a few inclines, but nothing challenging. It's about 7¼ miles round trip, but I do laps along my favorite part, a 0.9-mile stretch of the trail, to make it longer.

I feel that my veganism is so deep it is in the marrow bone. In my fifties, I helped provide caregiving for three elderly relatives. I wrote about these experiences in *Never Too Late to Go Vegan* (Adams, Breitman, and Messina 2014), *Even Vegans Die* (Adams, Breitman, and Messina 2017), and an essay in *Critical Inquiry*. In that essay, I wrote,

> I am aware that my veganism moved to a deeper place during the most intense caregiving years. When there was so much I could not control, my veganism provided a reminder of some of the areas where I still had control and of the person I was beyond my full-time responsibility for an elderly person. When I felt isolated by my caregiving duties, veganism provided a sense of connection to others. (Adams 2017, 788)

Being a vegan cyclist happened in my sixties, and I find my veganism deepening again. It is related to how I experience and embrace the dailiness of veganism and biking.

Some things are done over and over again as daily practices because that is how we make meaning in our lives. For me these are journal writing, preparing vegan food, and biking.

When I began keeping a daily journal twenty-five years ago, I recopied a quotation from Morton Kelsey's *Adventure Inward* (1980) into each journal: "Journal keeping is a living process, like exercise. One does the same thing over and over to *develop* and maintain a skill. Healthy living in body and soul and mind requires the constant repetition of certain practices" (13).

Veganism is a living process, too. When nonvegans declare, "It's too hard to become a vegan," I think they actually mean, "I don't know how to develop the skills of being a vegan." But the way one develops skills in *anything* is to start where one is, make one change (for instance, eating vegan when going out to eat) or many changes (eating vegan when at home), and in doing so, practice being a vegan. Recognize that veganism, too, is a living process. The idea to "start where you are and keep going" is from Pema Chodron, an American Tibetan Buddhist. It sounds obvious—start where you are. After all, where else could we start? But folded within it is "Don't be held back by regrets, guilt, judgment." Don't be frozen in place by what was left undone in the past.

Yet, so many people want something dramatic to start them. They can't get started eating vegan full time—*that* is too much of an event—and so don't start where they are, just changing what they eat that day. And it doesn't have to be a vegan gourmet meal; a humble Dragon Bowl of rice, veggies, tofu, and a sauce could serve appetites just fine. Or a homemade marinara sauce. By postponing until a dramatic entry can occur, they miss the joys of the daily practice: a humble bike ride, a humble vegan meal.

I only returned to biking after my caregiving years were over. How shaky I was when I began bicycling again after decades of not bicycling. But I started where I was, and I kept going.

I have told the story of the origins of my veganism before. It involves my return home to the small upstate New York town where I had grown up at the end of my first year at Yale Divinity School. As I was unpacking, I heard a furious knocking at the door. An agitated neighbor greeted me as I opened the door. "Someone has just shot your horse!" he exclaimed.

That evening, still distraught over Jimmy's death, I bit into a hamburger and stopped in mid-bite. I was thinking about one dead animal yet eating another dead animal. What was the difference between this dead cow and the dead pony who I would be burying the next day? I concluded I was a hypocrite and I needed to be a vegetarian. Becoming a vegetarian in turn catalyzed my awareness of linkages between meat eating and patriarchal culture, and between feminism and vegetarianism.

Learning about the experience of animals in the maw of animal agriculture often prompts grief. Vegans become anguished thinking about how many animals' deaths they caused before they became vegans. But start where you are—you are no longer complicit in that way—and keep going. Nonvegans often seem afraid of opening to that grief. Perhaps they fear that an awakened empathy for the suffering of the animals might incapacitate them. Nonvegans may also think being aware of the death of animals is a dead end in terms of enjoying food, and so suppress those feelings. But start where you are and trust that you can, in fact, handle this grief, and you may discover that there is so much more to veganism than these feelings. One discovers the delight of plant foods combined in new ways from new recipes and new meals to enjoy when eating out. You also learn that the grief becomes a part of your consciousness, but it does not kill you. You can live with the grief because it is a sign of connection and compassion.

While I started developing my ideas for a book on meat eating and patriarchy in 1975, a friend went with me to the Bicycle Exchange on Bow Street, near Harvard Square, and helped me pick out a silver Motobecane bike; another birthday present fifteen years after my first bike, from my parents. Until I moved back to rural Western New York the following year, we shared rides along the Charles River.

■　■　■

One day, as I biked in my suburb, a duck surge nearly wiped me out as they turned around from the path they were on, scared by something, and suddenly barreled toward my wheels. When they—and my heart— settled down, I marveled that while I anticipated so many ways of having an accident—cars, dogs, people—ducks darting into my wheels had not been one of them.

The rural roads I biked on after leaving Cambridge were in Chautauqua County, New York, where I grew up. Biking among grape vineyards, forests, creeks, apple orchards, and the sights of Lake Erie after living in East Coast cities was thrilling. Few cars traveled on the roads I chose.

In the summer of 1977—back when riding helmetless seemed okay—I was working with my mother to address housing and other issues for migrant and poor people in the county. One day, I rode out to visit two of my favorite people, Zak and Clover, the elderly Jamaican couple who had first moved to the South, and then, as part, of the Great Migration, came to Chautauqua County. As I mentioned, the unfriendly soil of their land was thwarting their efforts to farm. I was on my way to get their signature for a loan. I often arrived to find them both chopping at the land with hoes, and I can still remember how Zac would lean against his hoe and talk about his and Clover's life. But that day, I never made it to their farm.

Passing a farm on my way to theirs, I saw two dogs tear down the driveway and head straight toward me. "These dogs are going to run

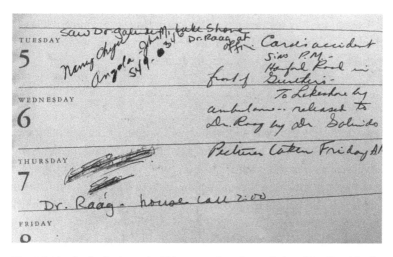

My mother's calendar for the week of July 1977, noting when and where "Carol's accident" happened, and what happened afterward. My mother's calendars are a part of my archival collection. For my use of her calendars as a source of information about my life, see Adams (2019). *Photograph by Carol J. Adams.*

straight into me," I thought, and I sped up to try to streak past them. That's the last I remember.

A neighbor saw them plow into the front wheels of the bike, which flipped me over the handlebars and onto the road.

I came to with a policeman leaning over me.

"Are you Judge Adams's daughter?" he asked me.

How does he know? I wondered, as I felt the macadam road underneath me, and then, why is *that* the first question he is asking me?

"Yes," I said.

I had already come back to consciousness twice and begun answering his questions, and then passed out. Of course, he was trying to figure out whom to contact. I had suffered a concussion.

I got a helmet and began biking mainly to and from my work in the small city. I had become a domesticated bike rider.

■   ■   ■

When I bike on the shared path of humans and cyclists, I am on the lookout for humans with dogs. To everyone, I announce my presence, "Hello! Coming to your left! Good morning!" Almost everyone says, "Thank you." I watch the dog walkers to see if they are casually gripping the leash, inattentive to the dog's attention to me. Sometimes one is heading toward my wheels before the dog walker pulls them back.

■　■　■

Biking, ironically, allowed me to enter car culture. I used the insurance settlement from the dog attack to buy my first car. During the day I was an advocate, traveling to county and state meetings, starting a hotline for battered women, opening a soup kitchen, and creating other resources in our county. I also helped to coordinate a suit against the city of Dunkirk for racism in housing. I learned the owner of the local radio station—a Rush Limbaugh type before Rush Limbaugh—was helping to foment the opposition group working against integrated housing. He gave them free range on his three-times-a-week hour-long talk show, where they spewed racist beliefs. I argued with him on the air one day about airing these racists without offering other perspectives. I also began to research how to challenge his Federal Communications Commission license.

One afternoon, I was biking home, within the city, but on a long stretch of road that wasn't frequented much by car traffic. Before I knew it, the owner of the radio station came along and forced me off the road, smiled at me, and then continued on his way.

■　■　■

The stereotype of a suburb is failing both in terms of nature and politics. Suburbs are spaces designed more than half a century ago to serve the purposes of white supremacy. Now this space is vibrantly multiracial. And there are ways of living in the present that allow us to repurpose these spaces. It's not surprising to see "Black Lives Matter" chalked on the sidewalk along my path.

■　■　■

Midpoint in my ride, where I turn around and retrace my route, I can see a monk parrot colony across the street. Their nests are five feet long and sit on steel high above the ground at the electrical substation. The parrots are continually repairing and adding to their nests, staggered on different levels of the horizontal bars. Once in a while, bright green shapes dart past me toward the water.

Is this monk parrot substation colony another midpoint? With these parrots colonizing the substation, is this a moment of change where something is going to turn? It's not just that the monk parrots are another example of how suburban spaces do not represent an absence of something but are spaces that are full of life and energy if you are open minded and willing to see it. Are their colonizing efforts also announcing something about the future, a future in which nature retakes the world?

Midpoints are often reckoning points.

By the time we join the novelist John Coetzee on his cycling route between Austin and Bastrop, Texas, he is at his midpoint, and he is hot. Very hot. The sun is baking both the road and him. He grabs Texas's ethos by its essence: "It is eccentric not to drive a car in the United States, doubly so in Texas. It is eccentric not to eat meat in the United States, doubly so in Texas" (Coetzee 1995, 44). All of this is memorialized in his essay "Meat Country." His thoughts seem prompted by a woman in Austin who couldn't comprehend his vegetarianism. When he informed her of it, she replied, "We're having ribs first and then chicken. You don't eat chicken? There won't be anything else."

East Richardson electrical substation with monk parrot nests. *Photograph by Carol J. Adams.*

Close-up of a monk parrot nest. *Photograph by Carol J. Adams.*

Monk parrots near nest. *Photograph by Carol J. Adams.*

Coetzee's exchange with an unthinking meat eater reminds us that many social occasions prompt "event anxiety" for vegans and vegetarians. We are often most anxious when we have to attend an event and we wonder, is all they are going to give us is dead cow or chicken (see Adams [2001] 2022)? The event anxiety Coetzee describes in "Meat Culture" was in 1995, and—as I point out in an interview in *Historical Geography*—Austin, of all places, should have had more enlightened people (see Wise 2020).

I like to think Coetzee's long rides outside of Austin freed him from the lack of imagination of a host who would say, "There won't be anything else." What a catalyst for the birth in Coetzee's fertile imagination of someone like Elizabeth Costello, who speaks her mind on meat eating. Biking is good for the imagination. I wonder if Elizabeth Costello was born on that hot Texas ride.

Coetzee evokes the event anxiety common to vegans and vegetarians: is all we are going to be offered parts of a dead chicken?

It's Coetzee's "Meat Culture" that got me thinking about what I think about when I am cycling. On a ride, writers can work out problems in their writing, chew over an idea or an interaction, while rhythmically peddling. A beloved book on writing explains:

> Horseback riding; knitting; shuffling and dealing cards; walking; whittling; you see they *have* a common denominator—of three figures, one might say. All these occupations are rhythmical, monotonous, and wordless. (Brande [1934] 1981, 160)

Let me interrupt the author here to add that cycling and preparing vegan food (all that chopping!) are also excellent rhythmic activities.

> [E]very author, in some way which he has come on by luck or long search, puts himself into a very light state of hypnosis. The attention is held, but *just* held; there is no serious demand on it (Brande [1934] 1981, 160).

Like many cyclists, Coetzee thinks about food as he cycles, as do I. His thoughts summon peppers and rice; mine, butternut squash steaks, rosemary-infused white bean spread, turmeric latte, farro salad, ratatouille cassoulet, banana bread, and a lemongrass-and-ginger-infused summer vegetable soup. I run my mind through more possibilities to prepare: a Greek salad with tofu feta; blackened tofu with cheesy grits;[1]

tofu satay with peanut sauce and cucumber salad; a pizza with arugula, olives, mushrooms, Miyoko's mozzarella, fresh basil, and garlic; or crispy tofu with cashews and blistered snap peas? Today, I decide, I will learn to make smoked tofu.

Vegan food preparation is a living process. We do the same thing each day because it matters, and yet, each day, it is also different—a different bike ride, a different meal preparation.

■   ■   ■

The linear community along Duck Creek includes walkers, walkers with strollers, cyclists, runners, dog walkers, skateboarders, kids on scooters.

We become familiar with each other. We are Chaucer's Canterbury pilgrims, though we rarely tell each other stories. But just the other day, a man hailed me. "How far do you ride each day?" he asked me. "I see you every day and I was curious."

"It's strange," I tell him. "I just figured it out yesterday. About ten miles."

"That's good." he says. He runs. He's seventy-two so he has a few years on me. Pandemic-style, we are a good six feet apart.

The pandemic has heightened our sense of community—we are surviving, we are here, we are outside, we are trying not to be defeated.

I am a beneficiary of the tragedy of the pandemic in one small way. I am able to bike more safely than before on the streets of Dallas County. Car travel stopped so thoroughly that auto insurance was slashed in half for a quarter of 2020. I now know the freedom of traveling down the empty streets of my neighborhood and assuming that no one is going to hit me.

■   ■   ■

People at a picnic table eat their fast food, attempting to create a feeling of normalcy. I think of making lobster mushroom fettuccini, banana bread, pumpkin muffins, sweet potato muffins, bowtie whole wheat pasta with pesto and vegan parmesan, a smoked tofu sandwich, sesame noodles with sriracha tofu, gazpacho, quinoa salad, cauliflower curry, cheddar spinach scones.[2]

Like a cloudy day, the sense of the vileness and evilness of animal agriculture hangs over me when I see the fast food on the picnic table. I want to discuss the relationship between animal agriculture and pandemics, how often diseases begin in animals and jump to humans. I want to yell, "Aren't you thinking?"

* * *

After arriving in Dallas, my dread of biking built up over the years, helped along by the demands of caring for young children. Inertia sided with not biking because I would have to lift the bike down and then back up from the garage ceiling. Then fear took its place alongside inertia. Where is it safe to ride in Dallas? I didn't want to die that way. We felt that the Dallas drivers sped up rather than slowing down when they saw a pedestrian in their path, or a cyclist trying to cross a street. Coetzee's Texas car culture may be doubly deadly. After a brief period when we rode with our kids in a park, my bike became further inaccessible when it was dismantled for storing. Then the deaths of bicyclists being reported in the metropolitan section of the *Dallas Morning News* seemed to increase. Many of these cyclists were called "experienced." A cyclist friend pointed out that experienced cyclists had greater odds of being hit because they were on the road more frequently.

Instead, I walked, and stayed indoors practicing yoga, and rowing, and then came caregiving.

* * *

The turtles are sunbathing, except for the turtle trying to cross the path to find a place to lay her eggs. A few purple flowers that fell from a blossoming tree have stuck to her shell; she is a one-turtle parade.

The heron is still fishing in the pond to my left as I go up the wee hill this path offers. I think about how Republicans have blood on their hands for this pandemic. Quarantined in Texas, as I cycle I sometimes FaceTime with my new granddaughter when she wakes up and my son calls. I pull over and she gets to see her helmeted Nana, and I tell her of the paddling of ducks on water, a make-way-for-ducklings moment as they head single file in the middle of the stream. The ducks and their babies are off and away, and then my son and his baby, too.

Thirty years after our move to Dallas, I was being interviewed with my co-authors of our new book, *Even Vegans Die* (Adams, Breitman, and Messina 2017), and we were each asked, "What would you like to do now?" I heard the question as, "What joy do you want to bring into your life right now?" Since even vegans die, what have I been postponing? Spontaneously I said, "I want to go biking."

I thought mournfully of my dismantled 1975 Motobecane bike frame. Having graduated from child raising and then caregiving, I had found myself at the age of Medicare coverage and disconnected from something that had been an intricate part of my childhood and young adulthood: my athleticism.

"I know just what you should get," the interviewer said. And she sent me a picture of her Specialized bicycle. I went to the store, showed the photograph, and ordered the same bike. Trying it out, I felt so nervous, slightly fearful, and a little wobbly, but excited. Would I remember how to bike? It came to me that one does not forget how to ride a bicycle. Start where you are and keep going.

It's ironic—I got back to biking after finishing a vegan guide to death and dying. And with the creation of bike and walking paths, I realized I didn't have to compete with cars.

And then my sister, who forty years ago walked around the Vassar campus for days looking for my Huffy, insisted on buying the bike for my birthday. Some debts, she felt, needed to be paid. I had never viewed it that way.

Through biking, I have reawakened the memory of being a cyclist on a country road, in love with the world—the blue sky, the clouds, the trees, the smells.

When people tell me, "Well, I tried to be a vegan, and it didn't work," I usually say, "Well, maybe you tried the wrong way. Try again in a different way." I think, "Imagine telling a Buddhist priest, 'I tried to meditate, and it didn't work, so I gave up.'" Of course, there's going to be failure in these attempts to change our lives. Mistakes, wrong turns, challenges, falls. They are all part of the path of change. Start where you are and keep going. The goal is to learn from the failure, not to reject the change one aspires to achieve.

■   ■   ■

Someone is doing push-ups near the creek. Another person is practicing tai chi by one of the ponds. There is the birdseed man with his big bag of seeds for the ducks. Oh, how they love him, and then I see people with bread for the ducks and I want to say, "Please, please, ducks aren't supposed to have bread," and I think about the people at Rocky Mountain National Forest standing in front of a sign that says "Please don't feed the wildlife" feeding the wildlife.

"Gotta feed the turtles," shouts one woman to me, proudly displaying a bag with two slices of whole wheat bread. I'm past her before I think about how turtles aren't supposed to be fed bread, either.

As I bike past the birdseed man, I notice that the geese, newly arrived, are feeding along near the ducks.

I call out, "The geese and ducks are happy." And he shouts back, "The geese!" He is so pleased.

The baby heron sits in full display on top of the retaining wall by the creek, wings outstretched.

Vegan cycling. I get to stretch my wings.

There goes the great blue heron. And the egrets, who were cleaning themselves, startle and take off, slowly flapping their long white wings. We're all traveling together along the space as it winds along the creek.

A friend in Dallas learned I was biking again and told me about how he rebuilt Raleigh bikes from the 1970s. Would I like him to rebuild one for me? Would I? It's so beautiful.

Carol on bike with wings spread. *Photograph by Benjamin Buchanan. Used with permission.*

I feel the spirit of my Huffy reincarnated for the twenty-first century. It is probably more bike than I need, this suburban biker, but so what?

And now I am the one keeping a secret from a sister. I suspect she imagines my rides are on my beautiful Specialized bike she gave me. I have shared that bike with the woman who lives behind us in the alley, and she shares her pool with me. During the summer I have what I call, laughingly, my own mini-triathlon—an early-morning walk with the rescued dogs who live with us, a bike ride, and a half-mile swim. But still, my sister and I have different ideas about my bike, and does this mean I am repeating the pattern of the 1960s?

■ ■ ■

When I walk dogs in the morning—and lots of other times—I listen to audio books. When I listened to Haruki Murakami's *What I Talk about When I Talk about Running,* it made me think of the 2014 collection *Running, Eating, Thinking: A Vegan Anthology,* edited by my friend, Martin Rowe, himself a runner. And it confirmed for me the joy of bringing a commitment to athleticism back in my life. My vegan body wants to move.

I have stamina. What is natural childbirth but an athletic accomplishment? When writing, I push myself mentally and in certain physical ways, staying up late, getting up early. I decide to add another lap to this part of the ride. A man carrying a turtle back to the creek. "Look what I found! This turtle so far from the creek," and I want to say, "She was going to bury her eggs."

■ ■ ■

Soon I am back at our alley. Sometimes, when I bike down this alley with the crepe myrtles and the rose of Sharon in blossom, or the mulberry trees laden with fruit, when the honeysuckle or trumpet vines crown the fences that border the alley, and the live oak trees arc over the alley, I look straight ahead, focusing my view on them, and the driveways leading to the garages disappear, and I tell myself I am on a country road in Western New York, or that *this is almost like being on a country road in Western New York.* And then I'm at my driveway, my garage. I disembark and remove my helmet.

My daily ride starts in the alley behind my house in a suburb of Dallas.

I start where I am, mounting my bike in the alley, then head to the bike path, and I keep going.

Notes

1. The cheesy taste in the grits is from nutritional yeast and creates a wonderfully tasty dish. The recipe can be found here: https://www.rabbitandwolves.com/vegan-blackened-tofu-cheesy-grits/.
2. For the scone recipe, which uses both vegan cheddar cheese and nutritional yeast, see https://caroljadams.com/carol-adams-blog/cheddar-spinach-scones or Adams (2022), 211–2.

References

Adams, Carol J. 2017. "Towards a Philosophy of Care through Care." *Critical Inquiry* 43 (4): 765–89.

———. 2019. "Finding Myself in My Mother's Calendars." *New York Times*. August 17, 2019.

———. (2001) 2022. *Living among Meat Eaters: The Vegetarian and Vegan's Survival Guide*. New York: Bloomsbury Revelations.

Adams, Carol J., Patti Breitman, and Virginia Messina. 2014. "Veganism and Caregiving." In *Never Too Late to Go Vegan: The Over-50 Guide to Adopting and Thriving on a Plant-Based Diet*, edited by Carol J. Adams, Patti Breitman, and Virginia Messina, 183–204. New York: The Experiment.

———. 2017. *Even Vegans Die: A Compassionate Guide to Living Your Values and Protecting Your Legacy*. New York: Lantern Books.

Brande, Dorothea. (1934) 1981. *Becoming a Writer*. New York: Harcourt, Brace & Company, 1934. Reprint, New York: TarcherPerigee.

Coetzee, John. 1995. "Meat Culture." *Granta: The Magazine of New Writing*, December 5, 1995. https://granta.com/meat-country/.

Couturier, Lisa. 2005. *The Hopes of Snakes & Other Tales from the Urban Landscape*. Boston: Beacon Press.

Jarman, Derek. (1994) 2009. *Modern Nature*. Minneapolis: University of Minnesota Press.

Kelsey, Morton. 1980. *Adventure Inward*. Minneapolis: Augsburg Press.

Macdonald, Helen. 2014. *H Is for Hawk*. New York: Grove Press.

Macdonald, Kriss. 2015. "Derek Jarman's Garden" https://wildabouthere.com/derek-jarmans-garden/.

Rowe, Martin, ed. 2014. *Running, Eating, Thinking: A Vegan Anthology*. New York: Lantern Books.

Wise, Michael. 2019. "Vegan Fermentation in Place: An Interview with Carol J. Adams." *Historical Geography* 47: 113–40

CONTRIBUTORS

Carol J. Adams is a feminist scholar and activist whose written work explores the cultural construction of overlapping and interconnected oppressions, as well as the ethics of care. Her books include *The Sexual Politics of Meat* (Continuum 1990); *Burger* (Bloomsbury Academic 2018); *Protest Kitchen: Fight Injustice, Save the Planet, and Fuel Your Resistance One Meal at a* Time (Red Wheel 2018); the new and updated *Pornography of Meat* (Bloomsbury Academic 2020); and many others.

Sheri E. Barnes, MA, MEd, RYT-200, is an avid cyclist and board member of Biking Across Kansas. Sheri has been vegan since 2008 and vegetarian since 1982. She works full time as an academic advisor for the Human Performance Studies Department at Wichita State University, advising athletic training, exercise science, and physical education majors and teaching an online Mind & Movement class. She holds a vegan nutrition diploma and certifications in health coaching, life coaching, and academic life coaching and is a certified yoga teacher, working to create new avenues for serving families affected by mental health and substance use disorders through resilience coaching and yoga.

Marc Bekoff, PhD, is professor emeritus of ecology and evolutionary biology at the University of Colorado, Boulder. He has won many awards for his scientific research including the Exemplar Award from the Animal Behavior Society and a Guggenheim Fellowship. In 1986 Marc became the first American to win his age class at the Tour du Haut Var bicycle race (also called the Master's/age-graded Tour de France). Marc has published numerous essays (popular, scientific, and book chapters) and thirty-three books, and writes regularly for *Psychology Today*. Some of his most recent books include *The Animals' Agenda: Freedom, Compassion, and Coexistence in the Human Age* (with Jessica Pierce; Beacon Press 2017); *Canine Confidential: Why Dogs Do What They Do* (University of Chicago Press 2017); *Unleashing Your Dog: A Field Guide to Giving Your Canine Companion the Best Life Possible* (with Jessica Pierce; New World Library 2019); *A Dog's World: Imagining the*

Lives of Dog in a World without Humans (with Jessica Pierce; Princeton University Press 2021); *Dogs Demystified: An A-to-Z Guide to All Things Canine* (New World Library 2023); *The Emotional Lives of Animals* (New World Library 2007, 2024); and *Jane Goodall at 90* (edited with Koen Margodt; Salt Water Media 2024).

Sune Borkfelt, PhD, has cycled to work as a lecturer and literary animal studies researcher at Aarhus University, Denmark, for more than a decade. He is author of *Reading Slaughter: Abattoir Fictions, Space, and Empathy in Late Modernity* (Palgrave 2022), as well as co-editor (with Matthias Stephan) of *Literary Animal Studies and the Climate Crisis* (Palgrave 2022) and *Interrogating Boundaries of the Nonhuman: Literature, Climate Change, and Environmental Crises* (Lexington Books 2022). His research on topics such as nonhuman otherness, the naming of nonhuman animals, postcolonial animals, vegan literary studies, and the ethics of animal product marketing has appeared in a variety of journals and edited collections.

Matthew Calarco, PhD, is professor of philosophy at California State University, Fullerton, where he teaches courses in Continental philosophy, animal philosophy, and environmental philosophy. His research focuses on the intersection of animal issues, environmentalism, and social justice movements. He is the author of *Beyond the Anthropological Difference* (Cambridge University Press 2020), *Animal Studies: The Key Concepts* (Routledge 2020), and most recently, *The Boundaries of Human Nature: The Philosophical Animal from Plato to Haraway* (Columbia University Press 2021) and *The Three Ethologies* (University of Chicago Press 2024).

Geertrui Cazaux, PhD, has been an advocate for other animals since the mid-nineties. She has a doctorate in criminology focused on anthropocentrism and speciesism. She later worked in youth care and as a policy advisor for the Flemish government. Now retired because of chronic diseases, she enjoys gardening, quilting, caring for other animals at her microsanctuary, and riding a tandem bike together with her husband. She is the editor of *Mensen en Andere Dieren* (Garant 2001) and co-editor with Kiki Baaijens of *Een Ander Soort Zuster* (Pumbo 2020). She writes about veganism and animal rights at the websites Graswortels, Brugesvegan, and Crip HumAnimal (about the interconnections between ableism and speciesism).

A. Breeze Harper, PhD, created and edited the groundbreaking anthology *Sistah Vegan: Black Women Vegans Speak on Food, Identity, Health, and Society*. (Lantern Press 2020). Her book *Scars: A Black Lesbian Experience in Rural White New England* (Brill Press 2014) interrogates how systems of oppression and power affected the life of the only Black teenager living in an all-white and working-class rural New England town. In the fall of 2024, her novel *Potato Chips and Wine* will be published, which follows sixteen-year-old Pearl, a Black teen lesbian and vegan in the mid-1990s who rejects her Catholic upbringing and find guidance in the writings of her heroine, Audre Lorde. She is the co-founder of an innovative inclusion, diversity, and equity consulting firm called Critical Diversity Solutions that merges critical theory and methods, human-centered storytelling, and action planning and metrics.

Kay Inckle, PhD, is a recovering academic, vegan, handcyclist, writer, swimmer, and Pilates instructor. She lives in Liverpool, England, with her two young feline companions, Lovely and Precious. She has published her research about disabled cyclists in journals including *Disability Studies Quarterly*, *Methodological Innovations*, and *Scandinavian Journal of Disability Research*.

Janet O'Shea, PhD, dance history and theory, UC Riverside, is author of *Risk, Failure, Play: What Dance Reveals about Martial Arts Training* (Oxford University Press 2019) and *At Home in the World: Bharata Natyam on the Global Stage* (Wesleyan University Press 2007), and is the co-editor of the second edition of the *Routledge Dance Studies Reader* (Routledge 2010). She has given a TEDxUCLA Talk on competitive play and is currently writing a book on emotion, corporeality, and activism titled *Bodies on the Line: Physicality, Sentiment, and Social Justice*. Her essays have been published in five languages and seven countries. She is a professor in the Department of World Arts and Cultures/Dance at UCLA.

Lawson Pruett, or "Frogi" in the messenger community, is an Atlanta native and a long-time bike messenger and staple in the cycling community, organizing races, helping find work for other couriers, and supporting the local community however he can. When not whipping in and out of traffic, he can usually be found listening to or playing music, doing yoga to counteract all his poor decisions made at a younger age, and raising his daughter Rio with his partner Zoe.

Amy Rundio, PhD, is an assistant professor of sport management at High Point University. Her research focuses on how sport participation can change lives, particularly through extraordinary experiences. She's ridden her bike across the United States twice to raise money for multiple sclerosis with Bike the US for MS, and when she's not on her bike, she's usually thinking about her next big ride.

Naomi Stekelenburg, PhD, is a science communicator at CSIRO, Australia's national science agency, where she specializes in the role of digital health, especially AI, in the transformation of the healthcare system. Before working at CSIRO, she was a researcher advocate at Queensland University of Technology, where she conducted research into the experiences of vegans and taught communication, creative writing, and sociology. She works within and outside the academy to advocate for the rights of nonhuman animals.

Michael D. Wise is an environmental historian and cultural geographer at the University of North Texas. He is the author of *Producing Predators: Wolves, Work, and Conquest in the Northern Rockies* (University of Nebraska Press 2016); the co-editor of *The Routledge History of American Foodways* (Routledge 2016) and *Native Foods* (University of Arkansas Press 2023); and also has written many articles and essays on the historical dimensions of food and animal–human relationships in modern North America. His career as an amateur bike racer reaches back to the last century.

INDEX

Page numbers in *italics* refer to figures.

A

ableism: ableist gaze, 102, 104; in cycling, 31, 99–113; and privilege, 23, 30–31, 106–8; in vegan advocacy, 23, 30–31, 99–113, 142

academia: animal-human divide in, 50–51; and bike commuting, 51–52, 61, 164

activism, cycling. *See* cycling advocacy

activism, reflexive, 32

activism, vegan. *See* vegan advocacy

Adams, Carol J.: essays by, 3–14, 171–93; images, *178, 191; The Sexual Politics of Meat*, 86, 105, 172, 173, 179–80, 182

ADHD, 54

advertising and car culture, 7–8

advocacy. *See* cycling advocacy; vegan advocacy

African diets, 34n12

aging, 157–59

agriculture: and colonialism, 23–24; Indigenous, 23–24; and subsidies, 6, 19, 23, 24, 26–29. *See also* meat industry

Ahmed, Sara, 18–19

altermobilities, 89n3

anger, 179–80

animal-human boundary: dissolution of and animality, 118–31; dissolution of and *bikolage*, 13; in humanities, 50–51

animality: of bicycles, 52–53; and body as assemblage, 11; and body maintenance, 53–54; and cycling, 11–12, 49–63, 117–31; and eating, 11–12, 50; and labor, 60–62; and veganism, 50, 62–63, 121, 124; and vestibular and proprioceptive senses, 56, 62

animals: absence of, 95–96; animal rights and women's rights, 126; and colonialism, 24; and hunting, 23, 24; pro-animal disposition, 87; roadkill, x, 87–88, 97, 119, 123, 143; separation from while driving, 122–23; in suburbs and urban areas, 173; wild *vs.* domesticated, 93–94

animals, encounters with while cycling:

affinity with, ix–xi, 92–97, 119, 131, 176–77, 182, 184–85, 189, 190–91; aiding animals, ix, 58, 60, *60*, 143; discomfort with, 99, 128, 129–30, 182–84; and meat industry, 8, 66, 69–70, 73–75, 93, 120, 143–44, 156–57; roadkill, x, 87–88, 97, 119, 123, 143. *See also specific animals*

Anthony, Susan B., 145

anthropocentrism, 81, 83–88

arrival, histories of, 19

athletics: childbirth as athletic activity, 192; and gender, 177; visibility of vegan athletes, 158, 159

autism, 56

automobility, 81. *See also* driving and car culture; hyperautomobility

B

Barnes, Sheri E., *148*, 149–60

Bekoff, Marc, vii–xi, *x*

Belgium: cycling culture in, 135–37; dairy and meat industry in, 143–44; wheelchair access in, 139–40

bike lanes, 9, 20, 28, 29, 42, 44

bike messengers, 41–47

bikes. *See* cycles and bikes

Bike the US for MS, 65–73, 76

Biking Across Kansas, 149–60

bikolage, 10–13

birds: absence or decline of, 95–96, 119; aiding, 143; encounters with, ix, x, 92, 112, 123, 176–77, *178, 179, 191*; feeding of, 190–91; pheasants, 94

Black Mirror, 60–61

Blue Ridge Parkway, 68

Blue Zones, 157–58

body: animality of, 11–12, 49–63, 117–31; as assemblage, 11; and joy in movement, 192; maintenance of, 53–54

body shaming, 142

Borkfelt, Sune, *90*, 91–98

bricolage, 10

The Bruges Vegan, 142, 145

brushtail possum, 129–30
bubbles, 130
Buettner, Dan, 157
built environment and infrastructure: bike lanes, 9, 20, 28, 29, 42, 44; and gentrification, 29–30; as hostile to cyclists and vegans, 5–7, 8; interstate highway system, 6, 25–26, 27–28. *See also* roads

C
CAFOs (concentrated animal feeding operations), 6
Calarco, Matthew, *78*, 79–88
calcium, 166
capitalism: and dependence, 107, 108–9, 145; and driving culture, 43–44; and highway system, 25; and labor, 60–62; and time, 27; and wild animals, 94
captive riders, 30
carbon use, 6, 86
care, ethic of, 109
caregiving, 180
cars: costs of, 28; increase in ownership and usage, 81. *See also* drivers, encounters with; driving and car culture
cats, 87, 143
cattle: and colonialism, 24; diseases, 141; and industrialization of meat industry, 6; interacting with, ix, x–xi, 93, 94, 120; and meat industry encounters while cycling, 69–70, 93, 144, 156
Cazaux, Geertrui, *134*, 135–46
chia seeds, 166, 168
chickens, ix, 50, 54, 69, 144
children: commuting by bicycle with, 163, 166, 167, 168, 169; cycling by, 55–56, 82–83, 92, 102, 137, 174–76; infantilization of cyclists and vegans, 7; learning to cycle, 102, 137, 174–76; as less than fully human, 107
China, driving in, 34n11
Chodron, Pema, 181
Cipollini, Mario, 58
civilization, dissolution of, 126
class: and access to quality food, 26; creative class, 29; and dependence, 109; poor and working class as less than fully human, 30, 84; privilege in cycling

advocacy, 23, 29–30, 31, 33; privilege in vegan advocacy, 23, 30–31, 33
Coetzee, J. M., 91, 97, 185–87
colonialism: decoloniality and advocacy, 33; and meat, 23–24
comfrey, 112
communication and tandem cycling, 138, 139
community: bike messengers as, 46–47; and cooking, 70–71; and disabled people as outside vegan/cycling communities, 101, 106–8, 110, 142; interacting with, 83; of long cycling events, 66–68, 70–73; of racing events, 49–50, 58; and sociability, 183–84; in suburbs, 171–72, 183–84, 188
commuting by bicycle: and academia, 51–52, 61, 164; by children, 174–75; with children, 163, 166, 167, 168, 169; in Flanders, 136, 138; and time, 28; and weather, 61
concentrated animal feeding operations (CAFOs), 6
consumerism: and driving culture, 43–44; and selling of veganism, 142
contempt, culture of, 31
cooking: and recipes, 14n8, 193n1, 193n2; and sense of community, 70–71
core riders, 29–30
core vegans, 30–31
Couturier, Lisa, 173
COVID-19 pandemic, 159, 175, 176, 188, 189
creative class, 29
Critical Mass, 21
culture: and anthropocentrism, 81, 83–88; of contempt, 31; cyclists and vegans as inconveniencing, 17–23; of imagination and change, 31–33; meat and American culture, 23–25, 91, 185, 187. *See also* driving and car culture
cyborg, 12
cycles and bikes: and Adams, 10, *11*, 174–76, *176*, 182, 190, 191; adaptations for disabled people, 103, 111; as assemblages or *bikolage*, 10, *11*; bicycle as term, 113n2; body as part of, 14n7; and Borkfelt, *90*; and Calarco, *78*; costs of, 52; cycle as term, 113n2; destruction or loss of, 42, 52, 177–79,

190; development of, 10; handcycles, *100*, 101–2, 103, 108, 159; and Inckle, *100*, 101–2, 103, 108; maintenance of, 52–53, 108; and O'Shea, *16*; ownership in Flanders, 136; and Pruett, *40*; and Rundio, *64*; tandem bikes, 137–39; and Wise, 51, 52–53, *55*
cycling: and animality, 11–12, 49–63, 117–31; as disrupting hyperautomobility, 81–82, 86–88; as inconveniencing dominant culture, 17–23; as inner journey, 94–95; lack of support for vegans, 71, 74–75; language and metaphors, 14n7, 58; learning to, 102, 137, 174–76; and noticing, ix–x, 91–98; as practice, 79–88, 180; and pregnancy, 158, 163–69; restarting, 181, 190; use of resources, 20–23. *See also* commuting by bicycle; racing; safety; thoughts and thinking during rides
cycling advocacy: and disabled people, 31, 99–113; historical ties to vegetarianism, 95; and imagination, 31–33; privilege within, 23, 29–30, 31
cyclists: bike messengers, 41–47; children as, 55–56, 82–83, 92, 102, 137, 174–76; feminization of, 7, 20; as inconveniencing dominant culture, 17–23; infantilization of, 7; injuries and deaths, 17, 46, 138, 189; vegan advocacy by, ix–xi, 72–73, 142, 143–44, 152, 158; violence against, 20–21, 29, 42, 44. *See also* drivers, encounters with; vegan cyclists

D

dairy industry: in Belgium, 144; and cruelty, 85, 105; in Tasmania, 120–21; in US, 6, 26, 27
Darwin, Charles, 57
deaths of cyclists, 46, 189
Debord, Guy, 80
de Certeau, Michel, 10
deer, 94
Deleuze, Gilles, 80, 87, 88
Denmark: cycling acceptance in, 91; cycling fatalities, 28; meat industry in, 92, 93; veganism as challenge in, 92, 97, 98
dependence, 108–9, 110–11, 145
derogation, do-gooder, 22

desubjectification, 85–86
disabled people: access in Belgium, 139–40; access in UK, 113n6; bike and cycle adaptations, 103, 111; and Biking Across Kansas, 159; challenges in cycling advocacy movement, 31, 99–113; challenges in vegan advocacy movement, 23, 30–31, 99–113, 142; co-option of, 109; and eco-ability movement, 99–113; judgment of, 103, 140–41; as less than fully human, 30, 84, 101, 107; and shame, 102–3, 142; staring at/ableist gaze, 102, 104; and tandem cycling, 137–45; and trauma, 101, 102; violence against, 109, 112
diversity and interdependence, 110–11
do-gooder derogation, 22
dogs, 177, 182–83, 184
doping, 58–59
drivers, encounters with: buzzing or aggressive driving, 7, 20–21, 42, 44, 122–23, 184, 189; cyclists as inconveniencing, 17–18, 20–21; injuries and deaths from, 17, 46, 138, 189; and sexual harassment, 20; and violence, 20–21, 42, 44
driving and car culture: car costs, 28; car ownership, 81; and fast food, 6; and hyperautomobility, 81–82, 86–88; inconvenience of cyclists to, 17–23; and masculinity, 7–8, 122; as regressive and aggressive, 121, 123; safety and sterility of, 43–44; in Texas, 91, 185; US usage, 23, 81. *See also* roadkill
"drop the hammer" metaphor, 14n7
ducks, 94, 177, 182, 189, 190–91

E

eco-ability, 99–113
economic leakage, 26
egrets, 176, 177, 179, 191
elitism and virtue signaling, 22
embrocation, 54
environment: cycling and veganism as using fewer resources, 20–23; cycling's links with environmentalism and veganism, 105; and meat industry, 6, 20, 105
ethic of care, 109

eugenics, 106

Even Vegans Die (Adams, et al.), 189–90

extraordinary experiences, long rides as, 65–76

F

fast food, 6, 25, 26

feed conversion ratio, 20

femininity: and feminization of cyclists, 7, 20; and feminization of vegans, 7; feminized protein, 105; and shaving of legs, 53

Feys, Jim, *134*, 137, 138–39, 140, 141, 143

fictocriticism, 118–19, 124

Flanders: cycling culture in, 135–37; dairy and meat industry in, 143–44; wheelchair access in, 139–40

Flandriens, 135

foams, 130

food: cost of, 26, 27, 30; fast food, 6, 25, 26; food deserts, 71; highly processed foods, 27, 150; inequities in access to quality, 26, 27; recipes, 14n8, 193n1, 193n2; thinking about during rides, 112, 160, 187–88

food, finding on road: availability of vegan food as increased, 44, 97; availability of vegan food as poor, 97, 98, 129; complexity of, 44–45; logistics and organization of on long events, 66–68, 70–71, 76, 149–60; resources on, 142, 145; tips for, 47, 76, 88, 98, 112, 131, 145–46, 150, 160

Food Empowerment Project, 35n23

Foucault, Michel, 80, 85

Freund, Peter, 81

G

The Game Changers (2018), 159

geese, x, 191

gender: advocacy while cycling, 159; and athletics, 177; and feminization, 7, 20; and feminized protein, 105; and privilege in cycling advocacy, 29–30, 31, 33; and privilege in vegan advocacy, 23, 30–31, 33; and shaving of legs, 53. *See also* masculinity; women

gentrification, 29–30

globes, 130

grief: and roadkill, x, 87–88, 143; and veganism, 181–82

H

Hamilton, Tyler, 58–59

"hammer" metaphor, 14n7

handcycles, *100*, 101–2, 103, 108, 159

hands, 57

HappyCow Guide, 142, 145

Harcourt, Bernard, 81

Harper, A. Breeze, *162*, 163–69

health shaming, 142

hemp seeds, 165

herons, 177, 179, 189, 191

heteronormativity, 8

highway system, 6, 25–26, 27–28

H is for Hawk (Macdonald), 173–74

histories of arrival, 19

home births, 167, 168

horses: care and maintenance of, 52, 58–59; encounters with, x, 59, 93, 156; in essayists' lives, 52, 177, *178*, 181, 182; racers as, 58–59; as transportation, 23, 25

humanities, animal-human divide in, 50–51

humanity or personhood: hierarchies of, 84; vegan cyclists as less than fully human, 7; women, people of color, and disabled people as less than fully human, 30, 84, 101, 107, 124–27. *See also* animal-human boundary

Hummer, 7–8

hunting, 23, 24

hybridity, 12

hyperautomobility, 81–82, 86–88. *See also* driving and car culture

I

identity: and car culture, 82; and decompartmentalization, 10–11; and desubjectification, 85–86; effects of vegan cycling on, 8, 10–11, 50; and meat eating, 85; national identity, 24–25; and relation to the world, 83, 86–87; self-identification and self-silencing by vegans, 22, 33n8; vegan and cycling identity as intertwined in Barnes, 152, 159; vegan identity as central for Inckle, 105

imagination and advocacy, 31–33
immaturity, 7–8
immigrants, 21, 30, 84
Inckle, Kay, 99–113, *100*
inconvenience, politics of, 17–23
independence, 102–3, 108–11, 145
Indigenous peoples, 23–24, 107
industrialization, 5–7, 8
infantilization of cyclists and vegans, 7–8
infrastructure. *See* built environment and
    infrastructure
Ingold, Tim, 57
insects: decline of, 95–96, 119;
    mosquitoes, 129–30
interdependence, 110–11, 145
interstate highway system, 6, 25–26,
    27–28
invisible cyclist, 34n22
Irigaray, Luce, 80, 118
iron, 164

J
Jarman, Derek, 172–73
journal keeping, 180
justice, social, 29–30, 31, 33, 142

K
killjoy behavior, 33n5
Koeppel, Dan, 34n22

L
labor and animality, 60–62
land use and meat industry, 20
language and metaphors, 13, 14n7, 58
Latour, Bruno, 12
Laufmaschine, 10
legs, shaving, 53–54
Lepore, Jill, 10
LGBTQ+ people, 8, 20, 30, 107
Lugo, Adonia, 22, 29, 31

M
Macdonald, Helen, 173–74
Martin, George, 81
Marx, Karl, 61–62
masculinity: and car culture, 7–8, 122;
    and dominance over women, 124–25,
    127; and feminization of cyclists, 7, 20;
    hegemonic, 7; and meat eating, 7–8,

86; and racing, 135; and shaving legs,
    53; and strength, viii; and "taking the
    lane," 29. *See also* gender
mass motorization, 81. *See also* driving
    and car culture; hyperautomobility
McDonald's, 6
meat: and American culture, 23–25, 91, 185,
    187; and car culture, 6, 8; displays of meat
    eating, 21; as eating ourselves, 130; and
    identity, 85; and masculinity, 7–8, 86
"Meat Country" (Coetzee), 91, 97, 185–87
meat industry: in Belgium, 143–44; in
    Denmark, 92, 93; encounters while
    cycling, 8, 66, 69–70, 73–75, 93, 120,
    143–44, 156–57; feed conversion ratio,
    20; and grief, 181; infrastructure of, 5–7,
    8; and insect decline, 96; invisibility of
    animals in, 144; and Kansas, 156–57, 160;
    rise of, 5–6; subsidies for, 6, 19, 23, 24,
    26–29; in Tasmania, 120–21; and trans-
    portation, 5–6, 25; and wild animals, 94
Mendoza, Louis, 34n20
mental health, cycling for, 54, 62
metaphor: cycling metaphors, 14n7, 58;
    movement as metaphor, 13
methodology, 4–5
Minding Animals Conference, 141
monk parrots, 184–85, *186*
mosquitoes, 129–30
mothering, judgment of, 163–64, 167. *See
    also* pregnancy
Motobecane, 182, 190
movement, metaphorical *vs.* actual, 13
Multicycle, 138

N
nationalism, 24–25
The Natural Way of Things (Wood), 126–27
nettles, 164, 165, 166
noticing and cycling, ix–x, 91–98

O
obesity, 159
O'Shea, Janet, *16*, 17–35
Ozersky, Josh, 6

P
Pantani, Marco, 58
paratopic practices, 32

parking, bike, 20, 42, 44

permaculture, 34n14

philosophy: and animality of cycling, 117–31; cycling and veganism as practices of, 79–88; movement as metaphor in, 13; remove of from everyday life, 79–80; trends in modern scholarship, 79

pigs, *x*, 6, 24, 75, 93, 141, 156

Plumwood, Val, 119, 123, 128

police, 29, 42

pollution, 20, 26–27

possums, 123, 129–30

posthumanities, 51

power: and ableism, 110; anthropocentrism, 81, 83–88; hyperautomobility, 81–82, 86–88; philosophical approaches to, 80–81; and privilege within cycling and vegan advocacy, 23, 29–31

prairie dogs, x

prefiguration, 35n25

pregnancy, 158, 163–69

privilege: and ableism, 23, 30–31, 106–8; within cycling advocacy, 23, 29–30, 31, 33; loss of privilege by vegan cyclists, 6–7, 19; within vegan advocacy, 23, 30–31, 33, 45

proprioceptive sense, 56, 62

Protest Kitchen (Adams and Messina), 14n8

Pruett, Lawson "Frogi," *40*, 41–47

public transportation, 19, 26, 27–28, 103, 105

R

rabbits, 126, 176

race: and access to quality food, 26; and infant mortality and maternal complications, 165; and people of color as less than fully human, 30, 84, 107; and privilege in cycling and vegan advocacy, 23, 29–31, 33; and safety of cyclists of color, 21, 29; and scrutiny of Black mothers, 167; and segregation, 25–26; and suburbanization, 184; and whiteness of built environment, 8

racing: and animality, 50, 53–54, 57–58, 62–63; and Calarco, 83; and community, 49–50, 58; culture in Belgium, 135–36; and masculinity,

135; and mental health, 54; and Wise, 49–50, 51, 53–54, 57–58

railroads, 6, 25

ranchers, 24–25

recipes, 14n8, 193n1, 193n2

reflexive activism, 32

rest stops, 66–68, 76

roadkill, x, 87–88, 97, 119, 123, 143

roads: choosing to avoid meat industry, 75; development of, 5–6, 28; hills and flats, assumptions about, 154–55; interstate highway system, 6, 25–26, 28. *See also* transportation

Rosen, Jody, 10

Rundio, Amy, *64*, 65–76

S

safety: and bike messengers, 41–43, 44, 46–47; and "breaking" the rules, 41–42; and COVID-19 pandemic, 176, 188; and cyclists of color, 21, 29; and driving culture, 43–44; fatality statistics, 28; and fear, 183, 189; and pregnancy, 165, 167; and risk analysis in decision to drive, 28–29; and women cyclists, 20, 29

scenery, 68, 131, 172, 173–74, 182, 192

segregation, 25–26

self-alienation, 54

self-silencing, 22

The Sexual Politics of Meat (Adams): influence of, 86, 105; writing of, 172, 173, 179–80, 182

shame: body and health shaming, 142; and disabled people, 102–3, 142

shaving, 53–54

Singer, Peter, 106

slaughterhouses, 6. *See also* meat industry

slavery, 23, 30

sleeping on rides, 117, 129, 130–31

Sloterdijk, Peter, 121, 123, 128–29, 130

Smith, Mick, 122

snakes, 93, 96, 123, 131

social justice, 29–30, 31, 33

social media, 3, 21

Socrates, 80, 88

soul, 80, 82, 83, 88, 180

spatiality: cycling as connecting spaces

through movement, 10; and spheres, 128–29, 130
Specialized bicycles, 190, 191
speciesism, 83–84. *See also* anthropocentrism
spheres, 128–29, 130
squirrels, 176, 177
Stanescu, Vasile, 33n8
Stekelenburg, Naomi, *116*, 117–32, *125*
stereotypes, countering during Biking Across Kansas, 149–60
stockyards, 6. *See also* meat industry
subjectivity, 82, 85–86
subsidies, 6, 19, 23, 24, 25–29
suburbs and suburbanization, 25–26, 27, 171–73, 184
Süprmärkt, 35n23

T

"taking the lane," 29, 41–42
tandem cycling, 135–46
Tasmania, dairy industry in, 120–21
Taussig, Michael, 119
terrorism, 21
Texas culture, 91, 185, 187
thoughts and thinking during rides: fluidity of, viii, 5; about food, 112, 160, 187–88; and inner journey, 94–95; and scholarship, 62, 95, 187
Thrive Baltimore, 35n23
time poverty, 27, 28
Title IX, 177
Tour de France, 135
Tour of Flanders, 136
transformations: and extraordinary experiences, 73; *vs.* thinking about change, 88
transportation: and altermobilities, 89n3; and industrialization, 5–7, 8; and meat industry, 5–6, 25; policy and hyperautomobility, 81–82; public transportation, 19, 26, 27–28, 103, 105; subsidies, 6, 19, 23, 25–29. *See also* roads
trauma, 101, 102
travel, as seated, 57
turtles, ix, 58, 60, *60*, 177, 189, 191, 192
Twine, Richard, 7, 19
Tyson, 69

U

United Kingdom: cycling fatalities in, 28; disability laws in, 113n6; violence against disabled people, 109
United States: cycling fatalities in, 28; meat consumption as central to, 23–25, 91; and ranchers, 24–25. *See also* driving and car culture
utopia, 32

V

vegan advocacy: by cyclists, ix–xi, 45–46, 72–73, 142, 143–44, 152, 158; desire to engage in, 188–89; and disabled people, 23, 30–31, 99–113, 142; and imagination, 31–33; privilege within, 23, 30–31, 33, 45
Vegan Cyclist, 13n1
vegan cyclists: essay overviews and methodology, 4–5, 8–10; reactions to, vii–viii, 3–4, 6–8; as scholarly focus, 3–4. *See also* cycling; cycling advocacy; cyclists
veganism: and animality, 50, 62–63, 121, 124; and anxiety about social situations, 74, 186; consumerism and selling of, 142; as disrupting anthropocentrism, 81, 83–88; essayists' shifts to, 65–76, 85, 181; hostility to, 21–22, 91, 92, 106, 152, 160; as inconveniencing dominant culture, 17–23; infantilization of vegans, 7–8; lack of support for at cycling events, 71, 74–75; and masculinity, 7; and noticing, 91–98; as outside dominant community, 91, 92; as practice, 79–88, 180–81; and pregnancy, 165–66; resources on, 14n8, 142, 145; and resource usage, 20–23; and self-silencing, 22; starting advice, 180–82; as tandem experience, 141–46; and time poverty, 27; in traditional diets, 30–31; vegan term, 31. *See also* food, finding on road
Vegetarian Cycling Club (UK), 95
vestibular sense, 56, 62
violence: against cyclists, 20–21, 29, 42, 44; against cyclists of color, 29; against disabled people, 109, 112; of land possession and colonialism, 23–24; of meat eating, 105–6; against vegans, 21; and women cyclists, 29
virtue, display of, 22

W

weather and climate: adjusting to, 130–31, 172; and commuting, 61; and embrocation, 54

"What, Then, Constitutes the Alienation of Labor?" (Marx), 61

wheelchairs, 113n6, 139–40. *See also* handcycles

Wheels for Wellbeing, 103, 113n1

willfulness, 18

wind, 155–56

Wise, Augie, *55*, 55–57

Wise, Michael D., 3–14, 49–63, *55*

women: cycling as emancipating, 145; cyclists and safety, 20, 29; as less than fully human, 30, 84, 107, 124–27; and unsolicited help and advice, 125; women's rights, 126

Wood, Charlotte, 126–27

worms, 99